MIND THE GAP

COPING WITH STRESS IN THE MODERN WORLD

By Mary E. McNaughton-Cassill
University of Texas, San Antonio

cognella
San Diego, CA

Bassim Hamadeh, CEO and Publisher
Christopher Foster, General Vice President
Michael Simpson, Vice President of Acquisitions
Jessica Knott, Managing Editor
Kevin Fahey, Marketing Manager
Jess Busch, Senior Graphic Designer
Marissa Applegate, Acquisitions Editor

First published in the United States of America in 2013 by Cognella, Inc.

Trademark Notice: Product or corporate names may be trademarks or registered trademarks, and are used only for identification and explanation without intent to infringe.

File licensed by www.depositphotos.com

Printed in the United States of America

ISBN: 978-1-60927-814-4 (pbk)/ 978-1-60927-829-8 (br)

www.cognella.com 800.200.3908

CONTENTS

DEDICATION

I would like to dedicate this book to the people in my family who read and discussed this book with me and have always helped me to Mind my Own Gap: My parents, Anne McNaughton, and Jim and Mary McNaughton, my sister Caren Edwards, my sister-in-law Sarah Wallace, my daughters Carolyn and Julia Cassill, and my Husband Aaron Cassill.

I would also like to thank the former students who were kind enough to review early versions of the book for me: Sandra Pahl, Casey Straud, Tyler Klein, Agustin Maggio, and Glenn Malone. Thanks too, to the friends who have been so willing to discuss stress and coping with me over the years: Nancy Arthur, Dororthy Flannagan, Judy George, Kirsten Gardner, Karen Greenwood, Cecilia Taylor, Sharon Myers, Jane Lyssy, Kim Keelan, Terrie Stover, Nancy Wahlig, and Connie Williams. Finally, as a first time author I couldn't have done this without the help of my editor, Jessica Knott.

CHAPTER 1

THE STRESS OF MODERN LIFE: ARE WE JUST WIMPS?

KEY POINTS

- ✦ Stress has always been a part of the human experience.
- ✦ Your body responds to all sources of stress the same way.
- ✦ Understanding stress is the first step to managing it.

WHAT IS STRESS ANYWAY?

Somewhat surprisingly, the use of the word stress to apply to human responses is a relatively new concept. Although there is some debate as to whether researcher Walter Cannon or Hans Selye first borrowed the term from physics, and when that might have occurred, it is clear that they were both correct in their assumption that adverse events could have a negative impact on health and well-being. Cannon is known for postulating that physical or emotional stress could disrupt the body's homeostasis, or state of rest and balance (Cannon, 1932). Selye went on to argue that the body's response to stress is similar no matter what the cause is, and that in some situations this response may eventually result in illness (1978). He referred to this process as the general adaptation syndrome and argued that under stress the body first goes on alert, then moves into a resistance phase. However, if the stress persists too long, exhaustion occurs.

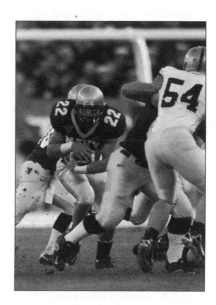

The physical response is often referred to as the fight-or-flight response. This complex physiological pattern is adaptive. It allows for rapid responses to threat (as in fighting to protect yourself, or fleeing to safety) by increasing heart rate, breathing, metabolic rate, and vigilance and by dampening pain. The stories you have heard about people saving their child from a fire or carrying their buddy off the battlefield are due in large part to the fact that during a fight-or-flight response, we literally get stronger and more focused and feel less pain, temporarily. Athletes often try to mobilize these changes to maximize their performance under pressure. However, there is also a huge body of research in animals and humans suggesting that when stress is chronic, these responses can have an adverse effect on health by straining the cardiovascular system and disrupting immune responses, which normally function to protect the body from invaders such as bacteria, viruses, cancer, and tumor cells (Ader, 2006).

THE NERVOUS SYSTEM

So what is actually happening during a fight-or-flight response? To understand, we have to talk about the brain and the body. The following is a brief summary of how the nervous system works, but of course there are many books devoted exclusively to detailing these processes. If you find you are fascinated by this topic, you may wish to track down a book such as *The Complete Mind: How It Develops, How It Works, and How to Keep It Sharp*, by Michael S. Sweeney (2009), or any of the many other reviews and textbooks of the topic out there. Students in my classes joke that they will never be able to read all the books I recommend, but somehow I just can't help myself!

To get back to the brain, the nervous system is actually made up of three components. The brain and the spinal cord form the central nervous system, while all of the connections from the brain and the spinal cord to and from the rest of the body are called the peripheral nervous system. The peripheral nervous system is itself divided into the somatic, or skeletal, nervous system, which controls voluntary movements such as clenching your hand, and the autonomic system, responsible for the control of less-conscious functions, such as the ways your glands work. The autonomic system, in turn, is comprised of a parasympathetic component and a sympathetic component. The parasympathetic system regulates the resting, or homeostatic, functions of the body, including resting respiration, heart rate, and digestion. The sympathetic system, on the other hand,

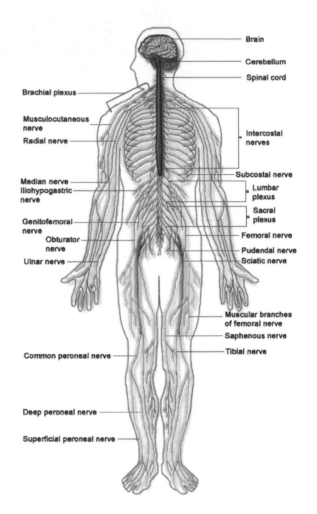

Figure 1. The nervous system.

mobilizes metabolic resources to enable the body to respond to stress. These messages are carried by nerves, or bundles of cells, called neurons. These cells run throughout the body, travel up and down the spinal cord, and enter the brain itself as cranial nerves.

The brain itself is actually a mass of specialized cells, packed into a bony version of a football helmet. It is surrounded by three membranes. The outermost one, called the dura, looks almost like saran wrap, but is actually a tough protective layer on the outside of the brain. The middle layer, called the arachnoid membrane, resembles a spiderweb, and the last one, the pia, closely adheres to the bumps and crannies of the brain. The space between the arachnoid layer and the pia is filled with a clear liquid called cerebrospinal fluid (CSF). This fluid flows through hollow chambers called the ventricles and circulates around the spinal cord. In addition to providing a cushion, it also transports nutrients and waste throughout the central nervous system. If the drainage of CSF is blocked, hydrocephalus occurs, and can result in permanent brain damage.

IS IT ELECTRICAL OR CHEMICAL?

Cells called neurons are found in the brain, spinal cord, and the peripheral nervous system. Neurons carry and receive information. Although they vary in shape and size, they tend to have a long fiber, called an axon, which conveys information away from the cell body, and other branchy projections, called dendrites, which receive information. Although the neurons in your brain are microscopically small, there are actually neurons that stretch, uninterrupted, from the base of your spine out to your big toe. In the case of many of our pro basketball players, that would be a really long neuron!

Within neurons, messages are conveyed electronically through a rapid—but complex—exchange of ions,

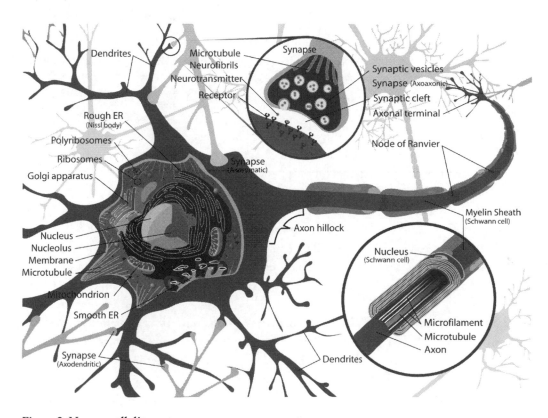

Figure 2. Neuron cell diagram.

or charged particles, across the membrane of the neuron. This is called an action potential or depolarization. When this signal reaches the end of the axon, it triggers the release of chemicals called neurotransmitters. Since neurons don't actually touch each other, these chemicals travel across the synapses, the gaps between them, to bind to the dendrite on the other side. This signal can then cause the second neuron to fire, or can inhibit firing. Since neurons are actually arranged in complex networks, an individual neuron is typically receiving input from a number of other neurons. If the sum of the signals is excitatory, it fires. If the sum is inhibitory, it does not. Amazingly, all of this happens in milliseconds, which is why neurons can respond to the environment in a rapid, continuous manner.

What these signals mean in functional, biological terms, is another thing altogether. The actual arrangement of neurons is based both on genetic and experiential factors. During development, the cells that eventually become the nervous system gradually migrate to form the brain and the spinal cord. Within the brain they differentiate into structures that control everything from breathing and heart rate to memory. They are assisted in this process by cells called glial cells, which continue to exist in the fully developed brain and spinal cord, to provide structure, as well as the transportation of nutrients and waste. Specialized glial cells also wrap around neurons to provide a form of insulation called myelin. Myelin enables neurons to transmit signals efficiently and recover rapidly so they can respond again as soon as possible. Without this ability, neuronal communication is seriously compromised. For example, multiple sclerosis (MS) is an autoimmune disease characterized by the degradation of myelin. Over time, people with MS gradually lose control of their bodies, and eventually develop cognitive difficulties as well.

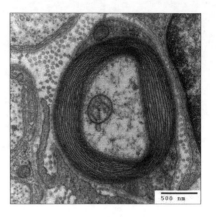

Transmission electron micrograph of a myelinated axon. The myelin layer (concentric) surrounds the axon of a neuron, showing cytoplasmic organs inside. *Generated and deposited into the public domain by the Electron Microscopy Facility at Trinity College.*

Messages between neurons are conveyed by specialized chemicals called neurotransmitters. These compounds are produced in the axons of neurons and released from their very tips into gaps called the synapses. These chemicals then travel across this synaptic gap to bind with specialized receptors on the other side of the gap. Perhaps the easiest way to think about this is by putting it in terms of a lock and a key. Each transmitter has a specific shape or configuration, and can only fit into—and activate—certain types of protein structures, called receptors. Think of it as a key sliding into a lock. If it isn't the right key, it may not go in or it may not turn. On the other hand, some master keys can fit into and activate more than one lock. This means that the same transmitter can have different effects on different parts of the brain or body.

The impact of a transmitter depends both on what type of transmitter it is and on how it interacts with the dendrite on the other side. We are not sure how many transmitters there are in the brain, but we have identified more than 100. To further complicate the picture, many transmitters have more than one type of receptor, further multiplying the possible signals they can carry. For example, there are seven known types of receptors for serotonin, a transmitter found in numerous places in the brain and also throughout the gut. Since serotonin is involved in a variety of functions, including the regulation of mood, sleep, and eating, its actions depend both on where it is located and which receptors it is activating. The drugs Prozac and Lexapro, commonly taken for depression, actually increase serotonin activity in the brain by slowing the rate at which serotonin is cleared from the synapse. In fact, most of the drugs that act on the brain do so by affecting the actions of neurotransmitters. Sometimes they increase or decrease their release from the axon, at other times they mimic or block their effects at the receptor. Some even interfere with the rate at which enzymes break down loose transmitters in the synapse, or the speed at which neurons recycle transmitters that are left over in the synapse (a process called reuptake).

If all of this is confusing, imagine transmitters as passengers on a subway system. When they leave the first train (the neuron) and enter the station (the synapse), a number of things can happen. Some cross the gap and board the next train by binding to the receptor on the other side of the synapse. Others linger in the gap and miss the train. They can wait around to cross and bind later, or get back on the first train (reuptake), or occasionally, they get mugged (broken down by enzymes in the gap). Disruption of any of these processes alters neuronal function. Certain diseases also play havoc with the action at a synapse. For example, in the case of Parkinson's disease, the parts of the brain that usually produce dopamine (a transmitter involved in motor control, among other things) stop making the transmitter. The result is a major disruption in the patient's ability to stop, start, and control their own movements.

The Terrain of the Brain

Throughout this discussion, I have been talking about the brain in terms of structures that control different functions. Although I can, and have, spent 15 full weeks of a class talking about the brain and how it works, I will try to keep this discussion under control! The brain itself can be described in a number of different ways because it is three dimensional. If you look down on it from above, you will see that the surface looks like a crumpled up tissue with lots of bulges and crevices. This is the outer part of the cerebral cortex, made of white myelinated neurons, so it is often called the white matter. In contrast, the layer below, called the gray matter, is made up of unmyelinated dendrites and cell bodies. Overall, this crumpled up mass of cortical tissue would be about the size of a pillow case if it were spread out flat, instead of being folded into our skulls. The complexity of human thought, language, and abstract reasoning occurs in this cortical area, which is more dense and convoluted than the cortex of any other animal, including our primate ancestors (Sweeney, 2009).

The top of the cortex over your forehead is called the frontal lobe. The back part of this area contains neurons that specialize in controlling motor movements. The anterior, or forward, part of the structure is involved in planning, goal setting, organizing behavior, and personality. The areas on the sides of the cortex above your ears are called the temporal lobes. Those on the right side are involved in visual memory and those on the left in language, including the production and understanding of speech. Behind the frontal lobe are the parietal lobes (on top of your head) that specialize in receiving and coordinating sensory input from the body. The occipital lobes, where the light signals relayed by your eyes are unscrambled, identified, and interpreted, are found in the back of the brain. If this area is damaged, you may be functionally blind, even if your eyes themselves are intact. Seen from above, the brain can also be viewed as two halves, or hemispheres. The left side of the brain actually controls the right side of the body and vice versa, and the left side is generally the more verbal side of the brain, with the right side being more visuospatial.

Below the forebrain, there are a number of other key brain structures that help us respond to the world. These include the thalamus and the hypothalamus, which are easy to confuse, but have

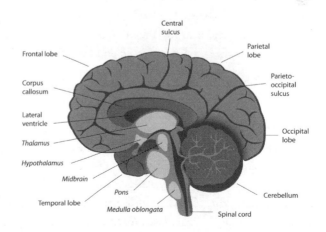

Figure 3. Median section of the brain.

very different purposes. The thalamus serves as a relay station for visual and auditory information and seems to work with the cortex to help us focus attention. The hypothalamus, on the other hand, is said to be the homeostatic regulator of the body. It plays a central role in controlling behaviors such as eating, drinking, weight, temperature regulation, sexual behavior, and stress responses. Signals from the hypothalamus are often amplified by the pituitary gland, which releases hormones into the bloodstream. These, in turn, trigger the release of hormones at other glands in the body, including the adrenal glands, the ovaries, and the testes. In contrast to neurotransmitters, hormones travel through the circulatory system rather than synapses. Consequently, their actions are slower and longer lasting. It can be confusing though, since some chemicals can serve as both neurotransmitters and hormones in different contexts. For example a substance called epinephrine, or more commonly adrenalin, can serve as both a hormone and a transmitter in different parts of the body.

The basal ganglia are involved in the sequencing of behavior and in some aspects of memory and emotional expression. Parkinson's disease, mentioned earlier as a motor disease, results from deterioration of the basal ganglia. The basal forebrain is involved in arousal and attention. Two other key structures are the hippocampus, crucial to the formation of long-term memories, and the amygdala, which is believed to play a major role in the regulation of emotion. Taken together, the hypothalamus, hippocampus, amygdala, and several other structures are called the limbic system and are seen as critical for emotion. Unlike the complex outer shell of the cortex, many of the components of the limbic system are structurally and functionally very similar across animals ranging from rats, to cats, to chimps.

The midbrain and the hindbrain are located under the cortex. The midbrain is made up of a series of neuronal pathways involved in sensory processes, arousal, and sleep. The hindbrain also contains the medulla, which controls breathing, heart rate, vomiting, salivation, coughing, and sneezing, and the pons, which connects the two halves of the back of the brain and parts of the reticular formation. At the base of the brain, the cerebellum—often described as a small cauliflower—is involved in balance and motor coordination as well as rhythm and timing that can affect movement, speech, and possibly learning and some thought processes.

How Stress Stresses Your Body

I'm sure that some of you are thinking that reading all this information is stressful itself, which it can be, but it is also crucial to our understanding of how we perceive and respond to stress. So when you are stressed, what actually happens? The first step is the detection of a threat, which can be a sensory signal like the sight or sound of a tiger running toward you, or it can be a thought, like the idea that there might be a tiger behind that rock over there. These signals and thoughts, which start as neuronal electrical and chemical pulses, are relayed through your brain and linked to memories and verbal and visual interpretations. Your cortex further processes and integrates the material, and decides whether the tiger is actually behind a fence at the zoo, in which case you don't need to respond, or has escaped its cage, necessitating a fight-or-flight response on your part. If danger is detected, your cortex and limbic system trigger a fight-or-flight response. First, the hypothalamus releases triggering hormones, which in turn cause the release of hormones from the pituitary gland, which then activate stress responses in the body (Sapolsky, 2004).

One such pathway involves the release of a hormone called adrenocorticotropic hormone (ACTH) that in turn stimulates the adrenal glands, a set of small structures located just above the kidneys to release cortisol, a steroid hormone that increases metabolic activity so your body will have more fuel (glucose) to fuel its stress response. At the same time, the neurons that make up the sympathetic nervous system and run down the spinal cord trigger the release of adrenalin from your adrenal medulla, resulting in increases in breathing and heart rate and the dilation of blood vessels. In response to signals from the pituitary, the thyroid gland secretes thyroxin, which also increases metabolism, respiration, heart rate, and blood pressure.

During a fight-or-flight response, you actually become less aware of pain, probably because of the release of chemicals called endorphins, which act as natural opiates in the body. Your eyes dilate and your attention becomes very focused, and your skin may become cold and clammy because your body is rerouting blood to large muscles to increase their strength. Your body puts digestion on hold, as it is not crucial for your immediate survival.

The sympathetic nervous system also inhibits the function of your immune system when activated. Although this seems illogical at first, it actually reflects a complicated triage plan. The immune system is made up of billions of white cells circulating through your blood, lymph glands, and body, which are specialized to detect and destroy invaders like bacteria, viruses, and tumor cells. When your immune system is activated, it uses up a lot of energy producing cells to recognize and neutralize invaders. It also increases your pain sensitivity so you will protect yourself, raises your body temperature to create an inhospitable environment for the invader, and makes you sleepy to conserve energy. If you are running from a tiger, none of these functions is particularly helpful, and they all use up energy. So, during fight-or-flight, your body prioritizes needs and uses all available energy to combat the threat. If you escape the tiger, you can take the time to hole up somewhere to rest and heal any injuries you sustained. As part of this process, the same cortisol increases your metabolic processes and reroutes the cells of the immune system into the bone marrow. That way, if you get cut running away, your precious immunity won't be lost as you lose blood. In an aside, cortisol has also been shown to impact the formation of memories during stressful events, which may account in part for the fact that our memories of extremely stressful events may be very focused or very vivid.

While remembering the details of a dangerous event may help us to avoid a similar situation in the future, it may also contribute to the development of a disorder called posttraumatic stress disorder (PTSD). Essentially, some people who experience unusually stressful events such as combat, natural disasters, the violent death of loved ones, car accidents with fatalities, or rape or torture are later plagued by flashbacks, trouble with concentration and attention, nightmares, and feelings of unreality. Brain studies suggest that the stress hormone cortisol can cause damage to neurons in the hippocampus, which may contribute to disruptions in memory and other PTSD symptoms.

The problem however, is that while the fight-or-flight response is extremely helpful when you are faced with an immediate threat for which a physical response is appropriate, many of the stressors we face in the modern world are more chronic than acute, meaning that they last for days, hours, or years rather than minutes. There may be no way to eliminate the stress physically, no matter how tempting it feels to run away or hit your boss! Over time, the mechanisms of the sympathetic response put pressure on our cardiovascular system. They contribute to high blood pressure, high cholesterol, damage to blood vessels

A U.S. Army soldier, left, returns fire while Afghan National Army soldiers and detainees seek cover during a firefight with enemy forces in Shekhabad Valley, Wardak province, Afghanistan, August 9, 2010. The U.S. soldiers are assigned to the 173rd Airborne Brigade Combat Team.

and arteries, and can result in heart disease. The dilation and constriction of blood vessels are implicated in migraine headaches and possibly even strokes. The decrease in immune function means we are at increased risk for illness, including colds and viruses, and may be less able to combat ongoing disease processes such as cancer. Our skin, the gastrointestinal system, and the musculoskeletal system may become dysregulated, resulting in rashes, acne, constipation, diarrhea, nausea, and joint and headache pain.

Researcher Bruce McEwen (2002) has called this allostasis, this process of trying to respond to changing circumstances with appropriate levels of activation because different threats require different levels of responses. If, however, the demands on the system are too high or last too long, they create an allostatic load, which then results in adverse physical and mental health outcomes. Perhaps not surprisingly, some of us seem to be more prone to these effects than others. Some people, called hot reactors, seem to show increased sympathetic reactivity when under stress in general. There is also some evidence that extreme stress experienced in childhood may predispose people to anxiety, depression, and other mental health issues much later in life. Men in particular show strong fight-or-flight responses, which may in part contribute to their increased rates of heart disease.

IS STRESS THE SAME FOR EVERYBODY?

In addition to trying to figure out how we respond physically to stress, many researchers have struggled to determine how and why we find certain things stressful, how to measure and compare stress across people, and how to assess the psychological impact of stress and to foster effective coping. Traditionally, measures of stress have asked people to indicate whether they have experienced a particular life event in a given period of time (Dohrenwend and Dohrenwend, 1974). These experiences—often called life events, or stressors—are then evaluated, either on the basis of the individual's own perception of the stress (Sarason, Johnson, & Siegel, 1978) or in relation to some sort of external set of judgments regarding its probable disruption of their life (Holmes and Rahe, 1967; Brown & Harris, 1989). Factors that are often taken into account include the desirability of the change, the amount of control the individual had over the choice, and how much it disrupts the particular situation. For example, if a person loses their job, it may be related differently if they have savings or another job lined up than if they are facing homelessness.

Sometimes the meaning of an event varies greatly across people as well. Compare, for example, the stress of a married woman finding out she is pregnant after years of trying, to that of a young, unmarried girl who does not want a baby. Clearly trying to assign objective ratings to stressful events can be very difficult. Unfortunately, standardized measures of stress often miss or obscure individual differences, while purely subjective surveys may be skewed if people over- or underreport their responses to stress.

Nevertheless, such traditional measures have amply demonstrated links between stress and both physical health difficulties (Dohrenwend & Dohrenwend, 1984) and poor mental health (Grant, Yager, Sweetwood, & Olshen, 1982; Brown & Harris, 1989). Psychologists Holmes and Rahe (1967) found links between stressful life events and illness among enlisted military men serving on navy vessels. Other researchers have found reliable links between reported stress levels, reduced immune function and susceptibility to illnesses such as colds, viruses (including cold sores), and even mononucleosis. Furthermore, people whose spouses died are at increased risk for serious illness themselves, for at least a year after the death (Keicolt-Glaser, McGuire, Robles, & Glaser, 2002).

In an attempt to clarify some of the theoretical confusion surrounding stress and stressors, Steven Hobfoll (1989) developed the Conservation of Resources model of stress, which suggests that people seek to attain and protect a variety of resources, and that the loss—or even the anticipated loss—of these resources constitutes stress. These resources include objects or material goods and belongings, conditions such as marriage, seniority, etc., personal characteristics or skills, and energies such as time, money, and knowledge. Threats are those things that represent the potential or actual loss of such assets. So, stress occurs when resources are lost. Plus, the fewer resources one has, the more stressful the loss since you then have fewer resources with which to cope.

According to Hobfoll, these resources have instrumental value in that they can meet needs and help respond to specific threats, but they also have symbolic value as they help to define who we are. A home provides shelter and can be a sign of prestige. Marriage promotes child rearing, but also defines a person within his or her culture. In some cultures, not being married can lead to extremely low standing in the community, especially for women. This conceptualization of stress is important in that it allows for the evaluation of both actual and perceived losses as some stressor, such as an impending job layoff due to downsizing of a company, which may have a negative impact on individuals long before they actually occur, even if the anticipated loss never materializes. In addition, these broad definitions of resources enable the model to account for the stressful nature of threats to psychological resources such as power or self-esteem, as well as more easily measurable losses of objects and characteristics such as money and good health.

Une noce chez le photographe (1879). Oil on canvas by Pascal Dagnan-Bouveret (1852–1929).

The Conservation of Resources model of stress also accounts for the robust finding that negative events (such as divorce) impact health far more than positive ones (such as marriage), even though both may require significant changes in our lifestyles. Transitions, then, are stressful when they represent loss, but not gain. Moving to a new city for a great new job where you quickly make friends is different from moving because your family moves, resulting in the loss of your support and resources without a compensating gain. Sometimes the distinction is made between distress or responses to negative life events and eustress, or responses to events which may require adaptation, but are also considered positive because they result in fulfillment or satisfaction.

Other approaches to quantifying stress have focused on the impact of smaller stressful events on well-being. These stressors, often called hassles, are not huge, negative events but rather smaller, annoying happenings such as traffic, dealing with rude people, losing things, and breaking things (Kanner, Coyne, Schaefer & Lazarus, 1981). There is some evidence that such experiences can have a cumulative negative effect on health and well-being. Interestingly, we seem to focus less on the small positive events, called uplifts, that occur in our daily lives. Much like eustress, they do not seem to generate happiness for us as reliably as negative events cause distress, leading some researchers to postulate that we are predisposed to focus on the negative, since identifying and avoiding threats is crucial for survival.

At the university where I teach, all students are given the opportunity each semester to rate their classes and make comments on the content of the course and the way it was taught. A common topic of conversation among my colleagues and me is why it is so easy to discount the good comments we get and to focus—and ruminate—on the couple of students who complain about a course. Sometimes the comments are contradictory:

For example, in a class of 125 students, I always get one or two students who say I talk too fast, several who say I cover things too slowly, and many who like the pace, but it is hard to discount those who are criticizing us for something we care about doing, even when we understand the psychology behind it.

CRISIS, CONTROL, AND COPING

This brings us to the topics of control and coping, two of the most complicated issues in all of psychology. Control, or the ability to change a situation, is a huge component of whether or not something is stressful. By definition, if we can easily change a situation, we don't see it as particularly stressful. If you are hungry and have a drawer full of snacks in your office, that hunger is not particularly disturbing. However, if you are hungry and just realized that you left your wallet at home and have no money, or that your city has been destroyed by a flood and there is no food available, the meaning of that hunger changes drastically. The ability to manage a stressful situation by changing the events is often called problem-focused coping. Of course, you have to have enough control and the resources needed to make the change. If you are the boss, you can change your schedule in ways that your employees cannot. If you are an uneducated woman with several children, you may have more trouble leaving an abusive relationship than someone who has a high-paying job and no children to worry about. Unfortunately, many stressful events are not easily amenable to change. Losing your home or a loved one or watching someone suffer from an incurable illness may not be something you can easily or fully fix. In such cases, people actually have to fall back on managing their *responses* to the event, rather than the event itself. In the early coping literature, this was referred to as emotion-focused coping and was often seen as less effective.

However, it turns out that coping is not so easily classified. According to key researchers in the field, Susan Folkman and Richard Lazarus (Lazarus & Folkman, 1984), coping requires adaptation in an effortful, conscious way. Although others have argued that it is difficult to define when coping is conscious (for example, is someone who chooses to drink to deal with emotional pain actually conscious of what they are doing?), the real key seems to be the match between the type of stressor the person is facing and the coping strategy they select. When faced with immutable stressors, managing your response may be your only option. Accounts of people who have experienced extraordinarily stressful situations, such as incarceration in a prison camp, reveal it is helpful to hang on to some sense of control, even if that is seen simply as being able to control what you think about, no matter what your captors do to you. It also turns out that there are different approaches to control. While some people tend to have a high need to control the things around them themselves, called internal control, others tend to believe that their lives are subject to external control. These external controls can be framed in terms of fate or chance or of a powerful other, which can refer to a higher being, or to other people (for instance, an authority figure or physician). When attempting to cope, people feel most comfortable when their coping actions are consistent with their control preference. For example, highly internal individuals prefer to be fully informed before making a decision. When ill, they want to be told about all of their options and may want to seek out further information and to participate in all care decisions. External folks, on the other hand, may be overwhelmed by too much information, and prefer to let someone else make decisions about their medical care.

However, understanding how your brain and body respond to stressors and how stress, coping, and control interact is only the beginning of learning how to manage stress. Although the physiological mechanisms of stress have not changed greatly over time, the world we live in has. The result is that our expectations, perceptions, and experiences of stress have changed significantly.

WHAT DO YOU THINK?

1. What sorts of events are most stressful for you?
2. What are your first clues that indicate you are stressed? Are they physical, emotional, cognitive, or behavioral?
3. How does the stress in your life compare to that of your grandparents?

REFERENCES

Ader, R. (2006). *Psychoneuroimmunology*. San Diego: Academic Press.

Brown G. W., & Harris, T. O. eds. (1989). *Life Events and Illness*. New York: Guilford Press.

Cannon, W. B. (1932). *The Wisdom of the Body*. New York: W. W. Norton.

Dohrenwend, B. S., & Dohrenwend, B. P., eds. (1974). *Stressful Life Events*. New York: Wiley.

Grant, I., Yager, J., Sweetwood, H. L., & Olshen, R. (1982) Life events and symptoms: Fourier analysis of time series from a three-year prospective inquiry. *Arch Gen Psychiatry*, 39(5): 598–605.

Hobfoll, S. E. (1989). Conservation of resources: A new attempt at conceptualizing stress. *American Psychologist*, vol. 44(3), 513–524.

Holmes, T. H., & Rahe, R. H. (1967). The Social Readjustment Rating Scale. *J. Psychosom. Res, 11*, 213–218.

Kanner, A. D., Coyne, J. C., Scharfer, C., & Lazarus, R. S. (1981). Comparison of two modes of stress measurement: Daily hassles and uplifts versus major life events. *Journal of Behavioral Medicine*, 4(1), 1–39.

Kiecolt-Glaser, J. K., McGuire, L., Robles, T. F., & Glaser, R. (2002). Psychoneuroimmunology and psychosomatic medicine: back to the future. *Psychosom Med.*, 64(1): 15–28.

Lazarus, R. S., & Folkman, S. (1984). *Stress, Appraisal and Coping*. New York: Springer.

McEwen, B. (2002). *The End of Stress As We Know It*. Washington D.C. Joseph Henry Press/The Dana Press, 1st edition.

Sapolsky, R. (2004). *Why Zebras Don't Get Ulcers*. New York: Holt.

Sarason, I. G., Johnson, J. H., & Siegel, J. M. (1978). Assessing the impact of life changes: Development of the life experiences survey. *Journal of Consulting and Clinical Psychology*, 46, 932–946.

Selye, H. (1978). *The Stress of Life*. New York: McGraw Hill.

Sweeney, M. S. (2009). *The Complete Mind: How It Develops, How It Works, and How to Keep It Sharp*. New York: National Geographic.

CHAPTER 2

TECHNOLOGY: WHO IS IN CHARGE, ANYWAY?

KEY POINTS

- ✦ Technology has made our lives easier, but not simpler.
- ✦ Technology has changed our entire view of the world.
- ✦ We live longer, but feel more stress than ever before.

THE GOOD OLD DAYS?

Most people in the Western world expect to live longer, physically easier lives than our grandparents. In 1900, the average life expectancy in the United States was 49.2 years (Shrestha, 2006) while today we live an average of 77.8 years (Kung, Hoyert, Xu, & Murphy, 2008). In the same period of time, infant mortality rates, which ranged from 10 to 30% in the United States, have now dropped to less than 1% (CDC Report). In real terms, that means that 100 years ago 14 out of every 100 babies died before reaching a year. To see this in human terms, all you have to do is walk the paths of any small-town cemetery. One of my great grandmothers, who lived in far northern Maine, is buried next to a small headstone that simply says, "Baby." When I asked my great aunt why they hadn't named the baby, she told me that it was born "poorly," so they didn't want to get too attached. It is hard to imagine modern-day American parents taking such a resigned approach to their infant's health and well-being.

Of course, the fact that we can keep most infants alive now isn't without financial and psychological costs. It has been estimated by the March of Dimes (2009) that the average baby born before 37 weeks' gestational age costs about $49,000 in the first year of life, in contrast to the average of $4,551 for a full-term, healthy child. According to the National Institutes of Health, total expenditure for premature births equals $26 million a year. Although we could quibble about whether families, hospitals, or governments should cover these costs, the bottom line is that saving infants' lives is not

Tombstone sculpture of a baby sleeping on a pillow, marking the final resting place of a young child who died in 1909.

cheap. On the other end of the life span, it has been estimated that people over 65 years old spend four times as much on health care as people of other age groups (Rand Corporation, 2005).

Although few of us would argue that caring for the very old or the very young is a useless endeavor, we may need to think more explicitly about the quality-of-life issues our efforts engender. Premature infants are at far higher risk than full-term babies for disabilities ranging from cerebral palsy to attention deficit and learning disorders. While most people over 65 are still independent, functioning members of society, the loss of health, independence, and mental abilities worries many people as they age and poses complex dilemmas for families trying to care for their loved ones. The question of how long to sustain life, when to discontinue life support, and how best to maximize people's potential were not issues when we lacked the medical knowledge and technology necessary to reverse most disease processes.

In terms of lifestyle, it is almost impossible to realize how much technology has changed our day-to-day lives. In my stress management classes, I ask my students to gather information on the lives of their parents or great grandparents, depending on how far back they can obtain information. The goal is for them to identify where these family members lived, where they came from, what they did for a living, how they met their spouses, how many children they had, how many of those children survived to adulthood, what sorts of communities they lived in, their hobbies or interests, what sorts of physical or mental health challenges the family faced and how long people lived. Among my 17- and 18-year-old students, this often entails calling or emailing family members to ask questions, but students almost uniformly report that they end up fascinated by the exercise.

Once they have this information, I ask them to do a comparison of the lifestyle and stressors their ancestors faced with their own situation and stress. Most typically, we find that their relatives lived more physical lives than we do. Many worked in agriculture or labor fields that required strength and stamina. Even those who worked in less physical jobs or who were from more affluent families were still affected by the lack of technological gadgets and amenities we now consider essential. Although electricity and indoor plumbing were becoming widely available in towns and urban areas during the 1930s, rural areas often lacked such luxuries until after World War II or later. Today, 70 percent of American homes have air conditioning and 97 percent have color televisions (Samuelson, 1997). Clearly, the things we take for granted—and in fact have come to see as necessities of life—were unimaginable luxuries in the recent past.

SHOULDN'T WE FEEL LESS STRESSED?

Advances in food production and availability and the prevalence of household appliances such as vacuum cleaners and washing machines have greatly changed the ways we care for ourselves and our homes (Schor, 1992; Samuelson, 1997). By the 1990s, Americans expected to have washing machines, dryers, and refrigerators, as well as dishwashers and microwave ovens in their homes. Today, frozen, convenience, and fast foods are ubiquitous, and people who sew their own clothes are the exception, not the rule. Ready-to-wear clothing and standardized clothing sizes did not come into their own until the late 1940s and early 1950s. Clearly, in the past, the daily effort to dress and feed a family, clean a house, and travel was physically difficult and extremely time consuming.

Ironically, however, automating household tasks didn't actually result in increased levels of free time. Research suggests that Americans simply increased their standards of cleanliness. Instead of thoroughly cleaning the house once a year (spring cleaning), many people vacuum several times a week. Microwaves and refrigerators have increased our food preparation options, which in turn increase our expectations regarding the quality and diversity of food we are willing to eat. While people used to have one front room or parlor

Washing clothes in the 1930s was a laborious task (top). Although improved technology brings time- and labor-saving efficiencies, (left) studies have shown that the average time a woman devotes weekly to housework has remained constant. What are some of the reasons behind this trend?

that they maintained for company use, we now feel we should coordinate the color schemes and decor of our entire homes and try to maintain them at Martha Stewart levels, to boot.

On the hygiene front, we no longer take a bath once a week or less and wear the same clothes for days at a time. Most Americans shower at least once a day, and tend to wash clothes after one wearing. According to Juliet Schor, the author of *The Overworked American*, an American mother with two kids who used to have to manage two baths a week, is now responsible for 14 baths in the same period of time. In fact, research suggests that the number of hours spent on housework remained virtually constant for full-time housewives from the 1920s to the 1990s, despite major changes in how that work was accomplished.

We have also increased the volume of things in our home and spend a great deal more time organizing and managing the things we have accumulated. Witness the proliferation of books, stores, television shows, and services designed to help you organize your house. Chances are your grand or great grandparents grew up in the Great Depression of the 1930s, when they learned to save everything for future use. In today's world, the greater challenge is letting go of things to avoid being swamped by clutter. Anyone who has bought an older house with limited closet space has faced this struggle. Not surprisingly, during the mid-1970s, self-storage units for home use started popping up throughout the suburbs.

Although there are those who suggest that the need to acquire things is simply proof of modern greed, it is actually a much more complex phenomenon. It's not that people in the past didn't hope to acquire things—in fact, tours of mansions and castles in Europe suggest that people did indeed like to own fine furniture, art, decorations, and clothing. The difference was that the production of such items was so costly that only the very wealthy could afford them. In the meantime, the poor and middle classes were struggling to eke out the basics of their existence.

As technology progressed, this pattern changed. Mass-produced clothes, furniture, even houses (the Sears Catalog offered modular houses for sale from 1908 to the 1940s) became popular and were accessible to people of modest means. Advances in transportation allowed people to distribute products on a large scale and eventually to reduce the costs of both necessary items (dishes, shoes, fabric, etc.) and luxury goods, including toys, electronic devices, and comfort items. For people who grew up during the Great Depression, the fact that you can buy clothes at Wal-Mart for less than it would cost you to purchase the material and make them is indeed a change in perspective.

As we will discuss in the chapter on media, these advances in technology, production, and availability of consumer goods have gone hand in hand with advances in mass advertising, which in turn drives up interest in acquiring items. It is not an accident that we want to purchase the things we see advertised on television and in stores. Marketers have spent countless dollars and hours figuring out what appeals to humans of different ages and backgrounds. They manipulate the color and designs on the label, the music on the commercials, the time of day the ads run, and how things are displayed on the shelf in order to tempt us. In fact, no population has ever been exposed to such sophisticated advertising.

To Choose or Not to Choose?

Having lots of choices, however, isn't always a good thing. Making choices takes time and energy and can be stressful in itself. If there are only two types of cereal on a shelf, deciding which one to eat is not nearly as difficult as it is if there were five or ten—or as in most modern supermarkets—over 100 different cereals to explore. And that does not take into account your decision about what sort of milk to put on it, what to eat with it, or even which store you choose to shop in. In today's consumer world, shopping could literally become

your job. Whether you are purchasing a pen to write with, jeans to wear, or a car, there is a seemingly endless array of brands, styles, and prices, all of which are constantly changing. Barry Schwartz, author of *The Paradox of Choice* (2003), counted 230 types of soup, 175 kinds of salad dressing, 116 skin creams, and 90 cold remedies—in one store. Now that is a lot of choice!

To make it all even more complicated, each such decision is accompanied by the realization that you might not be making the best possible choice, which in turn causes anxiety. As is inevitable, if some of your choices don't work out, that can cause stress and frustration. It is even the case that if you perceive a decision as reversible, it changes your satisfaction with your choice. Apparently, if we must choose, we put a lot of thought into the selection, and afterward we spend time reassuring ourselves that we made the right choice. However, if we felt like the decision was not binding when we make it, we are less likely to put energy into it and paradoxically may end up less happy in the end. Clearly, more may not always be better when it comes to buying and managing consumer goods.

Changes in the ways in which we communicate have been arguably even more radical than the changes in our homes. A hundred years ago, televisions, computers, and iPods would have seemed like science fiction. At the turn of the century, telephones were just coming into their own, and many of us still remember fighting with other family members about who got to talk on the family's dial phone. Today, even elementary school kids carry cell phones, and teenagers express their independence by standing outside the house to talk, or texting, when they want privacy. Few of us who discussed a date on the family phone while the rest of the family sat around the kitchen table listening, will ever forget the anguish. Not long ago, I tried to explain to my teenage daughters that when I was in college there were different rates for long distance phone calls at different times of day, so you had to sit up late, or wait for the weekend, to call home. Answering texts while they listened to me, they nodded in total noncomprehension!

Of course, technology has also created a new arena of frustration as we try to keep up with an ever changing array of gadgets, many of which are not intuitively easy to use. Cognitive psychologist Donald Norman (1993) writes about the frustrations posed by stove buttons which don't correspond to the burners, confusing doors and elevators, and remote control, stereo, and phone systems that take hours to understand. He attributes these functional flaws to the fact that the majority of design decisions are currently made to meet product manufacture and distribution needs rather than the needs of the people who actually use the appliances. Naturally, some of us are better at interfacing with technology than others. When I lecture on intelligence in my classes I often quip that technological intelligence should become a recognized capacity, in the same way we talk about verbal, mathematical, or interpersonal abilities.

INFORMATION OVERLOAD

Technology has also completely changed the way we acquire and disseminate information. In a world in which we have access to multiple sources of information on a 24-hour basis, it is hard to imagine that President Franklin D. Roosevelt's fireside radio addresses were a radical change in communication, or that during World War II people did not hear from friends and family members for months or even years because of the unreliability of letter delivery. Today, soldiers in Baghdad and Afghanistan can text their families and submariners can send emails home. We can watch 24-hour news and entertainment programming on TV, TiVo what we missed, and rent or download movies to our computers and iPods to fill the gap. The volume of information we expect (and often manage) to process is exhilarating and exhausting at the same time.

In my Stress Management class, I also ask students to record how much time they typically spend awake, by themselves, with no electronic input. The majority report less than an hour of quiet, solitary time in a 24-hour period. We wake up to clock radios, kick on our TVs and radios while we get ready for work or school, clip on our many electronic devices before we head out the door, listen to music in our cars, and multitask all day at work swinging between phones, pagers, computers, etc. Compare this to your forebears, who often spent large portions of their days walking to and from work and doing jobs which involved a great deal of physical labor at work and at home. While such effort wasn't always good for their health either, it did leave people a great deal of time for thought, contemplation, and even meditation. There is even evidence now that our brains work better when they have unstructured time to process information (how many times have you realized that you solved a problem when you weren't specifically working on it?) and that trying to do too many things at once actually slows down cognitive processing and increases our error rates.

Research repeatedly suggests that in trying to do more than one thing at a time, we actually become less efficient. Essentially, our brain, like the supercomputer it is, allocates attention and energy to tasks on a priority basis. Jumping from task to task actually takes longer than it would to complete one thing at a time sequentially (Rubenstein, Meyer, & Evans, 2001). This happens because each time we switch our attention, the executive control portions, found in the part of the brain called the prefrontal cortex, have to shift goals, refocus attention, and activate the use of new rules and responses. Laboratory studies show that as the tasks we are working on get more complex or confusing, we have more and more trouble switching between them efficiently. Think, for example, of a typical scenario in which you are working on a paper for school, a memo for work, or paying your bills while listening periodically to the television or radio, slipping in and out of your email or text messaging, and answering questions from the real people around you. As your brain repeatedly shifts from topic to topic, you have to reorient, remember what you were doing, and then figure out what to do next—all of which takes time and also makes it more likely that information will get scrambled or lost, leading to mistakes.

Of course, those errors can be fatal if you are driving a car and talking on the phone, flying a plane that is having engine trouble, monitoring life support systems, or engaged in any other task in which one small error can have huge consequences. On a less dramatic note, feelings of frustration, anger, forgetfulness, and the sense that the harder you work, the less you get done can all accompany attempts to multitask. Dr. David Meyer conducted a study which showed that the memory lapses commonly reported by women in their forties and fifties (forgetting names, numbers, objects, and what they were doing) are due less to hormonal changes or age than to stress, depression, and trying to do too much. When asked to perform memory tasks in laboratories under controlled conditions, they actually did well.

Now some of you might be thinking that people have been walking and chewing bubble gum for quite a while. It is in fact true that we can walk while swallowing, chewing, or looking around us for hazards, but the key is that these tasks are largely automatic and simple, from a brain point of view. For many of us, the basics of driving are much the same, but if you have ever found yourself hanging up the phone, turning off the radio, or yelling at the kids to be quiet because the traffic was getting bad, you were actually acknowledging that as the task became more demanding, your brain would function better if you eliminated nonessential input.

The problem in the modern world, however, is that the complexity, ubiquity, and form of the information we are attempting to monitor has increased exponentially. Those of us who still remember typewriters, carbon copies, and phone booths have a frame of reference for these changes. However, younger individuals often have a hard time conceptualizing those bad old days. I was telling my teenage daughters the story of a friend and I getting a flat tire while borrowing her sister's VW bug that promptly broke down. We sat on a bank beside the freeway for several hours before someone stopped to help us. My daughters looked at me in amazement when I told them that we hadn't used our cell phones to call for help because they hadn't been invented yet! On the other hand, I am astonished by their ability to hold their phones in their laps while texting, without even looking at the keypad.

The paradox is that these technological changes do make many aspects of our lives easier. I never want to go back to retyping the pages of a manuscript because of errors, looking up information in card catalogs, or not being able to coordinate schedules and activities using cell phones on the move. However, most of us have not spent a lot of time thinking specifically about the other ways these technologies impact our lives. Is being at the beck and call of our families, friends, and employers, at all times of the day and night, really an unmitigated advantage? Why is it so hard to ignore a ringing phone even if you are driving, eating, or carrying on a real-time conversation? For many of us, ignoring the buzzing, beeping, and ringing of our electronic world actually provokes anxiety or guilt, as we worry about whether we are missing something good or bad by not answering.

Not all of the information is pushed or imposed on us by others, either. Cognitive scientists such as David Kirsch (2000) at the University of California, San Diego also talk about the fact that we often pull information to us, whether we are online looking up facts for work, movie schedules, or the weather. Rapid access to such information is actually a very new phenomenon. Throughout much of the history of the world people struggled to get information. Early communication efforts that relied on the spoken, and later the written word were limited to the speed at which human couriers could travel. With the advent of the printing press, mass production of newspapers, fliers, and books proliferated, but supplies were still limited and many people were still illiterate. Teletypes and telephones made it possible to transmit information more quickly, as did radio and television. During the Civil War, battles continued after peace had been declared because the news had not been received yet. By World War II reporters were using telephones and radios to report and by Vietnam we had television. Now, soldiers in the Middle East text and transmit pictures and email from the battlefront, in addition to the myriad reports being filed by the news media. On the home front, everyday citizens report news, post pictures and film, and share material with mainstream media via email, blogs, websites, and sites such as YouTube and Facebook. Clearly, our problem is not the lack of information anymore, but rather an overload coupled with confusion about how best to resolve conflicting information and whom to trust.

Growing up in the 1960s, my sister and I wrote plenty of school papers using our 27-volume *World Book Encyclopedia* as our major source of information. Now we know that the information and perspectives presented in the encyclopedia were controversial or even wrong, but there were far fewer venues for exploring that possibility so we assumed it was all fact. Today, my kids hop on the Internet and get thousands of hits per topic, but struggle to know which are valid, up to date, or even accurate. A few years ago, my daughter was asked to write a paper for her World Civilization class on Akbar the Great, a Mogul ruler of India in the 1500s. In trying to figure out how many wives and sons he had, we generated hundreds of links; estimates ranged from Akbar's having two to 5000 wives. If the higher numbers are accurate, he must have had an information overload problem of his own! The point is, of course, that we live in a time where there is too much information, not too little. The result is that to function effectively, we actually have to learn how to sift through material and to screen out information, instead of trying to gather every available source. The fact that we are multitasking while doing so doesn't help either!

In the book *Data Smog*, author David Shenk (1998) argues that filtering complex, overwhelming information requires a different set of skills and conscious efforts at limiting input. Indeed, some large companies, including Intel, US Cellular, and Deloitte & Touche have been experimenting for several years with no-email days, as a means of freeing up work time and promoting other forms of communication among workers. Productivity studies suggest that many middle-management folks spend as much as half their day now on their computers, dealing with email.

According to a Nielsen study (2005), the average teen between the ages of 13 and 15 sends 1,742 text messages a month, and that does not take into account their use of online communication sites. It is also becoming apparent that as new means of communication become common, we tend not to discontinue the previous ones. Consequently, we find ourselves opening mail at home and at work, checking numerous voice mail and text messages, answering email, and trying to figure out where to fit Twittering into the equation. Many of us continue to keep up this mad pace of communication even while ostensibly on vacation in an effort to avoid the horrendous backlog of messages and mail that would otherwise await us.

THE ONLY THING SEPARATING WORK AND HOME IS YOUR COMMUTE

Of course, part of the problem is that these new means of communication have also eroded the division between work and home. In his book, *Elsewhere, U.S.A. (2010)*, sociologist Dalton Conley argues that many Americans have become obsessed with constant motion and productivity and only feel they are doing what they are supposed to do when they are in transit between tasks. He attributes this frenzy to a combination of economic changes, including huge increases in dual-earner families, rapidly changing job demands, and advances in technology which have increased our information flow, accessibility, and the speed at which we expect things to get done. Certainly, Americans do report feeling significant levels of guilt and stress about trying to balance the demands of their work and home lives.

Travel is another area of huge change. Few of us would want to go back to the horse-and-buggy days, but it is hard to emphasize how much life changed with the automobile. Strange as it seems to people in the modern world, the use of cars did not become widespread until after World War II. The rise of the interstate freeway system, in conjunction with the boom in home ownership fueled by the GI Bill, resulted in longer and longer commutes with concomitant increases in lost time and stress.

The average American commutes 50 minutes a day, but even longer commutes are not unusual. While such choices can enable people to afford nicer homes, the costs in terms of time and money are significant—and stressful. When I ask college students to list the things in their daily lives that they find stressful, driving and parking are always near the top of the list. Not only does driving on crowded roads, worrying about the costs of gas, and fighting to find a parking spot make commuting stressful, but it has also reduced the amount of exercise we get on a routine basis. How many of us who drive our kids to and from school remember walking or riding our bikes when we were their age? Although we often justify this by arguing that the world is more dangerous now than it was then, FBI statistics don't support that. However, juggling dual careers, complex athletic and after-school schedules, and tight deadlines can promote the use of cars. In fact, many of us joke about living in our cars, and actually do spend significant amounts of time eating, socializing, and even sleeping in them. One notable morning, I dropped my daughter off at school at 6:00 a.m. to go to a tennis tournament, pulled into a McDonald's to grab some breakfast, and woke up an hour later, asleep in the driver's seat. Clearly, my car really is my home away from home!

Of course, there are benefits to car ownership as well. Automobiles enable us to travel relatively cheaply and to transport the things we are buying. When I was a graduate student, I had to learn to carry a bag of groceries while riding my bike because I didn't have a car. Ironically, many of us savor the chance to spend time driving by ourselves, thinking, or listening to music or the radio. In fact, it has been suggested that one of the reasons Americans resist carpooling is the need to preserve some time in our days when we don't have to be socially "on." In addition, the road trip is a time-honored American tradition. However, driving on vacation seldom resembles the day-to-day chaos many of us face on the way to and from work.

Vehicles themselves are status symbols. Certainly, the commercials showing the latest cars in all their glory on beaches, mountain tops, and country roads do their best to convince us. Research by psychologist Bob Fuhrman (2010) on car stereotypes suggests that people do have strong beliefs about the personalities of people based on their cars. For example, they expect minivan drivers to be kinder and more caring than other drivers. Of course, cars reflect the stages of our lives as well. New neighborhoods with young families are often filled with minivans and Suburbans, while older neighborhoods populated by families with teenagers tend to have a plethora of old, dysfunctional vehicles stacked up in the driveway, while singles apartment complexes sport status symbol cars. Given that cars are an immutable part of modern life, the question is not so much how we can go back to a car-less life, but rather how we can come to understand the stress and benefits they provide and learn to make conscious choices about that balance.

In the meantime, air travel has totally changed our views of time and distance. Trips that once took months by ship take hours by plane. The phenomenon of jet lag, characterized by fatigue and difficulty functioning after changing time zones faster than the body can adjust, was impossible when travel was limited to the speed of horses and sailing with the wind. Air travel also means that people find themselves shuttling between cities or situations with little time to adjust to changing circumstances. This is particularly salient when people are being whisked from stressful situations with no time to adjust. For example, during World War II, it typically took soldiers days or weeks to get home from the battlefield and they usually traveled with their fellow soldiers. By the war in Vietnam, they often flew home by themselves on commercial airlines and reported feeling incredibly disoriented when they suddenly found themselves back in civilian life.

As a native Californian living in Texas, I have had ample opportunity to compare the relative advantages of car and plane travel. The drive from San Antonio to San Diego takes approximately 20 hours and covers a great deal of empty desert. The flight takes about four hours in terms of air time, but of course ends up taking almost double that by the time you travel from home, check in for the flight, deal with security, negotiate plane changes, and leave the airport. When driving, I inevitably wonder how people walked those vast expanses with little food and water, when we find it hard enough flitting from one McDonald's to another. However, the two-day drive does provide ample time to shift gears and process the experiences bookmarking the trip. Flying, on the other hand, takes less time, but also seems to leave me tired and strung out. Somehow the combination of dealing with airport logistics, close, uncomfortable quarters, enforced contact with lots of strangers, and uncontrollable factors such as plane arrivals and seat availability, takes a great deal of mental/emotional energy. Clearly, the spread of travel by car and train, while physically less demanding than previous modes of transportation, has created new sorts of stress in itself.

Technological advances in travel and communication have also changed the workplace. While some individuals spend days or weeks on planes covering large sales areas or attending meetings, other people now spend part or all of their workdays at home. The flexibility offered by such options can be beneficial, allowing companies to provide services in hard-to-reach areas and permitting families to juggle child care and dual careers. But the vagaries of travel become wearing over time, chronic sleep deprivation can become a persistent problem, and home and family life can become problematic.

Working from home, while appealing to many commuters, presents its own stresses. Structuring time, separating home and work life, and staying connected with colleagues can all become difficult. In addition, phone calls, voice messages, text messages, BlackBerrys, emails, Twitter, etc., all mean that we are on call 24 hours a day while paradoxically reducing our overall productivity. One survey (Leggat, 2007) suggested that 80 percent of business workers in the United States spend 90 minutes or more on email a day and that such electronic demands on our time are growing. Author David Levy argues that part of the problem with incessant email is that it is hard to put boundaries on it or to organize it, which is stressful to a species that has evolved to manage unpredictability by striving for control.

Clearly, the pace of technological change in the last century has altered everything from our life expectancy to how we maintain our homes, spend our work days, travel from place to place, and communicate with others. While most of us have trouble imagining life without our prescription medications, vacuums, computers, cars, and cell phones, we may not have spent much time thinking about how they have come to dictate our lifestyle choices, and created new types of stress. In much the same way that medical breakthroughs in infertility and neonatal treatment and the treatment of injuries and age-related diseases or military weaponry were developed and put into use well before we fully appreciated the many practical and ethical issues they would raise, we have not yet fully realized or come to terms with the impact of technology on our personal health and well-being. Taking control of how we want to let technology shape our lives is a key component of managing modern-day stress.

What Do You Think?

1. Does technology make your life harder or easier?
2. Which aspects of modern technology are most frustrating to you?
3. List five practical things you could do to control the impact of technology on your daily life.

References

CDC, http://www.cdc.gov/mmwr/preview/mmwrhtml/mm4838a2.htm

Conley, Dalton. (2010). *Elsewhere, U.S.A.: How We Got from the Company Man, Family Dinners and the Affluent Society to the Home Office, BlackBerry Moms and Economic Anxiety.* New York: Pantheon Books. Paperback Edition: Vintage Books.

Fuhrman, R.W., & Willis, J.T. (May, 2010). *Revisiting the traits commonly associated with vehicle stereotypes.* Paper presented at the annual meeting of the Midwestern Psychological Association, Chicago.

Kirsh, D. (2000). A few thoughts on cognitive overload. *Intellectica* 2000/1, 30, 19–51.

Kung, H. C., Hoyert, D. L., Xu, J., & Murphy, S. L. (2008). Deaths: Final data for 2005. *National Vital Statistics Report,* 56 (10), 1–120.

Leggat, H. (2007). Email overtakes telephone in workplace. BizReport.com

March of Dimes (2009). http://www.oregonlive.com/news/index.ssf/2009/10/march_of_dimes_report_nearly_1.html

NielsenWire (2005). *U.S. Teen Mobile Report: Calling Yesterday, Texting Today, Using Apps Tomorrow.* http://blog.nielsen.com/nielsenwire/online_mobile/u-s-teen-mobile-report-calling-yesterday-texting-today-using-apps-tomorrow

Norman, D. (1993). *Turn Signals Are the Facial Expression of Automobiles.* Cambridge MA: Basic Books.

Rand Health (2005). http://www.rand.org/pubs/corporate_pubs/2005/RAND_CP484.1.pdf

Richtel, M. (2008). Lost in E-Mail, tech firms face self-made beast. *New York Times,* June 14, 2008.

Rubinstein, J. S., Meyer, D. E., & Evans, J. E. (2001). Executive control of cognitive processes in task switching. *Journal of Experimental Psychology: Human Perception and Performance,* 27(4), 763–797.

Samuelson, R. (1997). *The Good Life and Its Discontents: The American Dream in the Age of Entitlement.* New York: Vintage.

Schor, J. (1992). *The Overworked American: The Unexpected Decline of Leisure.* New York: Basic Books.

Schwartz, B. (2003). *The Paradox of Choice: Why More Is Less.* New York: Ecco.

Shenk, D. (1998). *Data Smog: Surviving the Information Glut.* San Francisco: HarperSanFrancisco.

Shrestha, L. B. (2006). *Life Expectancy in the United States.* http://aging.senate.gov/crs/aging1.pdf

CHAPTER 3

THE MEDIA: IS IT ANY WONDER WE FEEL STRESSED?

KEY POINTS

+ Information has always been power, but the problem in the modern world is not too little input, but too much.
+ Not only do we have access to 24-hour news coverage, but it is disproportionately sensational and negative.
+ The standards for lifestyle, beauty, and material success espoused by the media are largely out of reach for most of us.

CAN WE TALK?

If the ancient stories are to be believed, humans have long been obsessed with finding ways to share information. Whether using drumbeats, smoke signals, or messengers on foot or horseback, people have sought to find ways to start and end wars, convey information about dangers and disasters, promote trade, and facilitate social interactions. Of course, throughout much of history such communication was slow and difficult. Certainly, with the advent of the printing press the ability to share information blossomed exponentially (Moran, 2001). In 1440, Johannes Gutenberg, the creator of the first movable type printing press, pro-

John White Alexander: The Printing Press [showing Johannes Gutenberg] (from the cycle "The Evolution of the Book"). Library of Congress (Jefferson Building), Washington, D.C.

duced a set of one-sheet documents sold by the Catholic Church, thought to be the first instance of a mass printing. By the 1600s, early versions of newspapers were appearing in Europe and America. By the end of the U.S. Revolution in 1783, there were 43 newspapers being published; naturally, freedom of the press was recognized as one of our inalienable rights. By the 1800s, newspapers were so prevalent and cheap enough because of advertising, that just about anybody who could learn to read could gain access to their contents.

By modern standards, the quality of reporting in these publications was often poor and erratic. It wasn't until the American Civil War that the style and quality of news reporting actually improved. Thanks to the invention of the telegraph, it became possible to send dispatches from the battlefield. In addition, people began to take still photographs. Although they could not yet be printed on paper, illustrators used the pictures to create line drawings that in turn were duplicated and distributed. By the 1900s, newspapers were big business and engaged in intense competition for readers and advertisers. During this era, publishers often used newspapers to promote their own agendas, but the concept of fair and responsible reporting was also evolving.

By the middle of the 20th century, however, radio, and later television, changed the transmission of news forever. The first regular radio news show debuted in 1938, and the CBS TV news went on the air in 1948. Radio broadcasts by reporters such as Edward R. Murrow became routine during World War II. Newsreel footage was shown in theaters, although such sources were still less vivid than live, real-time television images and were also heavily censored. A singular exception was the first live broadcast of disaster, the explosion of the airship *Hindenburg* over Lakehurst, New Jersey, in 1937 (Mooney, 1975; Deighton & Schwartzman, 1979). By chance, a radio announcer was describing the *Hindenburg* landing. When the ship burst into flames, he was able to provide a graphic description of the disaster to his listeners.

The strength of real time coverage of events can also be illustrated by the H. G. Wells *War of the Worlds* broadcast (Koch, 1970) that caused widespread panic until people realized that it was a fictional story. By the Vietnam War, television networks had established bureaus in hot spots such as Saigon and began to bring news of the war into people's homes. It has been argued that this live, often violent and disturbing coverage fostered opposition to the war in ways that were not possible in earlier conflicts. For example, Americans who were appalled by coverage of civilian casualties in Vietnam did not have access to such images in World War II. Imagine for a minute how Americans, largely convinced that they were fighting a just war, would have felt had they been exposed to live coverage of the Allied bombings of cities like Dresden, where approximately 35,000 civilian residents and refugees died.

WHEN IT COMES TO NEWS MORE MAY NOT BE BETTER

During the Vietnam War, people became accustomed to television coverage of both military and civilian suffering, but by the first Gulf War, major conflicts were being covered in real time, both on the major networks and on all news channels such as CNN. When Ted Turner announced that he was launching a 24-hour all-news show, many critics predicted its early demise. Over 25 years later, CNN is still alive and strong and has a host of competitors. Now, instead of having trouble getting information, we are immersed in a sea of live 24-hour coverage, which has become increasingly sensational as competition for media viewers has increased. Numerous studies indicate that the advent of this live coverage, in conjunction with increasingly competitive economic forces, greatly increased the availability, sensationalism, and ubiquitous nature of news coverage of such negative or disturbing events. Seeing this type of coverage as the news unfolds, including the actual deaths of victims, from your living room, lends an urgency and personal involvement to events that in the past were reserved for participants in the crisis.

In 1991, for the first time in history, viewers worldwide watched the start of a war, live, on their television screens. Despite this early coverage, both the Iraqis and the U.S. military instigated limitations on reporter

This photo from February 9, 2011 shows over one million people gathered in Tahrir Square, Cairo, Egypt, demanding the removal of the regime.

access to the war, which did limit the scope of viewer exposure. During the second Iraq war, reporters were officially embedded with the military, living and traveling with troops. Although this raised concerns about their impartiality regarding the people who were protecting them, the advent of camera phones, text messaging, and the Internet also ensured that both reporters and military personnel routinely relayed information back home. Pictures of atrocities and heroism as well as personal messages and ongoing blogs changed our experience of war once again. As wave after wave of protests have swept the Middle East, viewers are again experiencing the events through live media coverage as well as Facebook blogs and Twitter feeds. Clearly, access to up-to-date information has changed beyond all recognition.

Of course, news media coverage is not limited to wars. Viewing both positive live events such as celebrity weddings, inaugurations, and sports competitions, and negative ones such as disasters and crimes from our living rooms enables us to feel more personally involved. This is particularly evident in regard to high-profile events such as the marriage and eventual funeral of Princess Diana, the Oklahoma City Bombing, the Columbine School shootings, and, of course, 9/11 and Hurricane Katrina. The death of Princess Diana resulted in public outpourings of emotion and increased distress about her death in those women who were exposed to high levels of coverage of the event (Pillow & McNaughton-Cassill, 2001). A number of studies have shown that watching television coverage of the attack in Oklahoma resulted in significant levels of stress in both adults and adolescents who were not actually there. The scope of these tragedies pales however, in comparison to the wholesale destruction, loss of life, and disruption of the economic and transportation functions of an entire nation, watched nonstop on live television on September 11, 2001. The news media response to these attacks was rapid and extensive and resulted in depression, anxiety, and stress in individuals far removed from the events. See Gomery (2008) for a comprehensive review of the history of broadcasting.

A study of posttraumatic stress disorder (PTSD) in relation to the attacks suggested that rates of PTSD were significantly higher in New York than anywhere else in the country, but that nationally the number of hours of television coverage viewed was associated with stress (Silver, Holman, McIntosh, & Gil-Rivas, 2002). Studies of trauma in general support the argument that subjective responses to events are predictive of the development of PTSD whether or not you actually experience the event. Consequently, firemen, police officers, and medical personnel can develop stress in response to things they see in the course of their jobs, and psychologists can experience significant stress after working with people who have been traumatized or abused.

So what this means is that if you watch television in today's hyper-saturated, 24-hour, sensational news world, you are at risk for getting stressed about events that are happening far away from you, over which you have little or no control. And this is a very new phenomenon in the world. As we know, life has always been difficult and fraught with natural and man-made disasters. However, until this century, people knew little about what was going on in the world outside their community, and what they did hear was delayed or transmitted second- or third-hand. Now, we are surrounded by live pictures and coverage of negative events whenever and wherever they happen. If there isn't a shooting in our city, the local news can always lead with coverage of a disaster somewhere else. The end result of this constant barrage of coverage is that people tend to feel as though most of the things going on in the world are negative and that the situation is getting worse. In short, it is not that we live in a worse time, but rather that we certainly **know more** about the things that are occurring. Again, compare this to the Civil War, where news took months and World War II where news took days or weeks to arrive, and was censored.

Furthermore, newspaper articles, and drawings don't have the same visceral impact as actual pictures, sounds, and live commentary because television and the Internet are so vivid and catch our attention so strongly. It is also the case that the more frequently and prominently a story is covered, the more likely it is to influence us.

THE WORLD IS GETTING MORE DANGEROUS, ISN'T IT?

Communications researchers have studied the content of newspaper and television news programming and concluded that coverage of sensational stories such as homicides, accidents, and disasters, has been steadily increasing as networks attempt to attract viewers and generate income. As a result, such negative events are disproportionately represented, which can lead people to overestimate the risk of such things happening again. Work on risk assessment suggests that this is due in part to the ways in which our brains process information and make judgments. When faced with a threat—or even the threat of a threat—we immediately respond with a rapid, automatic assessment of the event that is not conscious or deliberate, but instead relies on images, pattern recognition, and emotions. For example, if a dog is running toward you growling and baring his teeth, you are likely to run or protect yourself with very little actual thought; you just respond. However, if you suddenly realize that it is your dog, and he is just excited to see you, you will respond differently. This judgment takes awareness and conscious effort and knowledge of rules or facts that pertain to the current situation. While this decision-making process works very well for the sorts of visible, immediate threats faced by humans throughout our early evolution, it is more problematic when we are faced by modern, technological threats.

According to research by Paul Slovic and his colleagues (Slovic, Peters, Finucane, & MacGregor, 2005), there is also a complex pattern of nine factors that we assess when looking at perceived risk. These include whether the event is voluntary or involuntary, chronic or catastrophic (acute), common or rare, immediate or delayed, controllable or not, and how fatal we think it will be, how familiar it is, and whether we believe we have been exposed to danger. When risk researchers ask people to assess the risk of particular events, they tend to rate those that are rare, catastrophic, unfamiliar, and uncontrollable as very risky, even when these may in fact pose little actual threat to most people. On the other hand, if a person is familiar with the risk and sees it as temporary or under their control, they will downplay it. This, of course, is why so many people fear airline accidents, despite the fact that they are statistically at much greater risk of being hurt in a car accident. Similarly, we worry about AIDS, which kills far fewer people than heart disease, and about nuclear accidents that are man-made over natural disasters such as tornadoes and hurricanes. The less familiar and predictable an event is, the more we worry.

An aerial view of the damage caused by Hurricane Sandy to the Seaside Heights Pier on the New Jersey coast (October, 29, 2012).

Applying this breakdown of risk assessment, it becomes easy to see how news media that thrives on showing us immediate, sensational, fatal events plays into our sense that we live in a dangerous, threatening world. This, in turn, generates feelings of dread and as news spreads through the media and by word of mouth, the sense of risk is amplified further. Because learning to respond to actual risks with rapid, automatic, emotion-driven responses has survival value, it can be hard to override these responses, even in the face of logical, analytical information to the contrary.

Even though more people in the United States die in hurricanes than earthquakes in an average year, people tend to fear earthquakes more because they are perceived as being catastrophic, uncontrollable, and unpredictable. Hurricanes, on the other hand, happen every year, and leave us with the feeling, at least, that we can predict and escape them. In fact, in particularly prone states such as Texas and Louisiana, a common problem is getting people to evacuate when a hurricane is approaching. Soon after moving to Texas, I was struck by the number of salesclerks in stores who looked at my California license and asked in all seriousness how I could have lived in a place that was going to fall into the ocean from earthquakes? Of course, Hurricanes Katrina, Rita, Ike, and Sandy proved that these events are actually common and can be more deadly than earthquakes.

Following the same logic, it is easy to see why parents worry about strangers abducting their children when they are more likely to be hurt while riding their bikes or swimming; why we worry about terrorist attacks instead of changing our lifestyles to decrease our heart attack risk, and by the threat of crime, rather than the threat of smoking.

VIOLENCE AND THE MEDIA

In addition, there is a major ongoing debate on how the violent images we see in the media impact us. Just as we have a hard time driving by an accident without looking, we are attracted to sensational media. This attraction to violent entertainment is not new, but rather something that has been documented since the days of the so-called blood sports, or fights to the death popular with the Greeks and Romans. Two books, *Life: The Movie* by Neal Gabler (2000) and *Why We Watch* by Jeffrey Goldstein (1998) provide entertaining discussions of our ongoing fascination with violence and drama in the media. For example, at the end of the 19th century, crime books with titles like *Vice or Victim* and *Blood Feast* were called dime novels or penny dreadfuls. During the 1920s and 1930s, movies such as *Scarface* and *I Am a Fugitive from a Chain Gang* were also quite graphic.

The question, of course, is whether such viewing actually makes us more violent. This has been argued by the lawyers and families of children who mimic harmful actions they have observed in the media. Others suggest that such exposure actually causes us to become hardened to the suffering of others, a condition sometimes called compassion fatigue (Moeller, 1999). Certainly, most of us on occasion have closed our eyes or changed the channel when faced with either real or fictional depictions of violence in books or on the screen. That does not mean, however, that at other times we won't be drawn into the action in horror movies like *Silence of the Lambs*. Watching news shows for clues as to how people were victimized in order to protect ourselves may prove useful in some instances. The problem is that so much of the coverage available to us involves negative, sensational issues over which we have little control can skew our worldview.

IS SEEING BELIEVING?

The entertainment media also provides us with an unprecedented flow of stories and narratives, which are typically far more exciting and dramatic than our own daily lives. Of course, this is not a new phenomenon. Certainly, the early Greek myths and tragedies, the plays of Shakespeare, and the plethora of dramas, festivals, and celebrations created by humans over time all indicate that our desire to be entertained is not new. What is new, however, is the ubiquitous nature of this entertainment in modern life and the ways in which technology enables us to incorporate these spectacles into our daily lives. In today's world, teenagers can watch movies like *Rent* over and over again, virtually memorizing the script line for line. Fan fiction sites and blogs allow people to write about their favorite characters, and to immerse themselves in their worlds, as do computer simulation games.

Is it any wonder that actors routinely complain that fans confuse their onscreen persona with their actual personality? Fans frequently feel that they "know" people they have never actually met because they can list how many shoes the entertainer owns and their favorite colors, foods, and their vacation spots, based on interviews in the tabloid media. Witness the thousands of people who felt they had personally lost a friend after the death of Princess Diana, and responded by attending memorials, leaving flowers, and otherwise behaving exactly as they would have had they really known her. In another strange twist, given the realities of musical and digital recording, even when our favorite stars die, we can still re-watch videos of their performances and listen to their music over and over again. People who weren't even born when these stars performed can become obsessed with the lifestyles, talent, and personality (think Judy Garland, Frank Sinatra, Elvis Presley, and John Lennon) and subsequently feel as though they knew them. Following the death of entertainer Michael Jackson, search engines crashed as people sought information about his life and death.

This never-ending flow of entertainment also exposes us to a variety of emotions and lifestyles we might otherwise never encounter. On the one hand, these images are often glamorous, beautiful, and affluent. On the other, they can be seedy, depressing, and downtrodden, but in both cases they transport us out of our reality and often cause us to question just what that reality is. Our hairstyles, home decor, and clothing are constantly influenced by what we see in the media, as are our views of the lifestyles of people living in countries and circumstances that differ from ours.

CAN YOU BUY HAPPINESS?

The advertising world floods us with a ubiquitous, well-researched onslaught of messages designed to make us unhappy with our current lives and motivated to pursue shopping, travel, exercise, diet, and entertainment options, all at the expense of our self-esteem and pocketbooks. In the past, people's sense of the world was based on comparisons to people

A Paris shopping mall decorated for the Christmas holiday encourages a "buying-friendly" mood in customers.

around them. Today, no matter where you live or how affluent you are, there is always going to be someone ahead of you, which makes it hard to achieve contentment.

Advances in the field of advertising in the last 50 years have also caused unprecedented changes in our lives. Throughout most of history, shopping was a luxury reserved for the rich. This is not to say that sales practices were unknown. Door-to-door salesmen and peddlers certainly sought to influence people's purchases, as did catalog and newsprint adds. However, the systematic study of how best to make people buy products really emerged in the past century. Advertising agencies, marketing specialists, and targeted selling began to emerge. Books were written on how to engage people in conversation, or how to give them a small gift, like a pen or name labels in order to make them feel indebted enough to buy something from you.

The idea of malls, devoted to enticing people into one site to shop, eat, and seek entertainment, also emerged in the past century. It is no surprise that most malls and stores have convoluted floor plans to ensure that you get disoriented, thus making you more likely to be exposed to things you might want to buy. In grocery stores, it is standard practice to put staple items like milk and meat in the back of the store, forcing customers to walk by the chips, candy, and soda on every trip. The use of lighting, color, air conditioning, and even fragrances to influence purchasing behavior all came into vogue. Stores even began to develop themed departments like the bridal area and the toy area, and restaurants strove to create a themed experience in which the setting, food, and music all created a "buying-friendly" mood.

Marketers also began studying how to make people aware of their products. They began using focus groups to see what sorts of innovations and packaging people were most drawn to. Advertisers spend millions of dollars designing television and radio ads, creating magazine inserts with actual fragrance samples, coming up with product tie-ins such as baseball caps and t-shirts, associating their products with sporting and entertainment events, erecting traditional and electronic billboards, and inserting ads on line.

While it is actually very hard to quantify how many ads the average person is exposed to in a single day, estimates range from 1500 to over 4000. Although most of us believe that we are not at the mercy of this purchasing pressure, the fact remains that given the choice, we usually prefer brand name to generic products, recognize hundreds of advertising slogans and tunes, and often regret impulse purchases.

The science of advertising also addressed how advertisements are targeted. It is no accident that toy and cereal ads are rife during Saturday morning cartoons, cars and beer during sporting games, and clothes and fragrances during Hallmark television programming. With the advent of computers that can track our purchases and create large databases, so even the catalogs that come to our homes and ads that pop up on our computer screens are tailored to our age, gender, and prior purchasing history.

MEDIA AND CELEBRITY CULTURE

Of course, entertainment programming also influences our view of the world. Watching happy, attractive, well-dressed families who live in beautiful homes and drive great cars can serve to set up unrealistic expectations about how we should be living. I have often joked that although I enjoy sitcoms about families like the Huxtables from *The Cosby Show* and/or young singles like on the show *Friends*, I have never understood when they had time to earn the money to support their lifestyles since they spent almost all of their time sitting around talking to each other!

Reality programming, including live contests such as *American Idol*, *The Biggest Loser*, and *Dancing with the Stars*, and home and personal makeovers such as those featured on HGTV and the Style networks have also given us all the sense that there is always something more we could strive to do in order to improve our appearance or our lives. Part of the problem is a phenomenon called adaptation, which refers to the fact that on a sensory and cognitive level, humans quickly become accustomed to or adapt to input. At a very basic level, this allows your eyes to adjust to the dark when you walk into a dark theater. However, it also means that even as babies tire of playing with the same toys over and over, we prefer a variety of foods and toys, and we quickly adapt to new technology and lifestyle changes.

When I was a poor graduate student, I lived in a student apartment furnished with cinderblock bookcases, ancient carpet, and used furniture. If I had known then that I would live in a four-bedroom house filled with belongings, I would have seen that as the height of luxury. Of course, now I find myself comparing our house to other people's homes and to television and magazine images and wondering when we can repaint, or update the blinds or get new furniture. In short, as our lifestyle changes, we quickly adapt and typically find it very hard to backtrack.

IS ELECTRONIC ENTERTAINMENT MAKING US DUMBER?

The same thing happens in regard to entertainment and lifestyle changes. A hundred years ago, families entertained themselves by playing musical instruments, reading, games, and with local parties. Nearly all of us have heard people describe the joys of simple holidays characterized by family gatherings and simple gifts. However, few Americans today can imagine entertaining themselves without television, movies, radio, and computers. In fact, even the content of such electronic programming has changed significantly over time.

In the fascinating book *Everything Bad Is Good for You* (2006), author Steven Johnson explores the increasingly complex nature of television programming and computer games. It is his assertion that as our exposure to media has risen we have become increasingly sophisticated media consumers. Johnson systematically compares the plot and structure of early television shows such as *I Love Lucy* to later shows such as *Hill Street Blues* and then to programs such as the *West Wing* and *The Sopranos*. In these analyses, he illustrates how shows have changed from simple plots that are resolved in a single episode to convoluted, complex stories that carry over from show to show, season to season, and even jump across shows, and

The dilemmas presented on *I Love Lucy* are simplistic to our modern sensibilities.

move about in time. It is his claim that early television viewers would be baffled by the complexity of modern programming, but that it is this density that motivates us to watch such shows over again online, or on videos or DVDs.

He also compares simple early video games like Pong to the complex, simulated games available now and argues that the interactive nature of today's computer game actually challenges the human brain to perform in new and complicated ways. He further argues that because this type of entertainment is interactive, it requires more complex cognitive involvement than reading, that time-honored mental activity. He even asserts that the advent of social networking and blogging actually offers us a chance to interact in new and innovative ways, which are also cognitively challenging. As proof of his contention that changes in media technology and programming have not been all bad for us, he highlights the fact that during the time that media usage has skyrocketed, IQ scores have been steadily increasing as well. He does however, acknowledge that some of the skills being fostered by the Internet are better suited to the process of sifting through huge amounts of information than of sustaining interest in less interactive sources of information such as books or lectures.

ON OVERLOAD OR BORED?

The most ironic thing about the complex, entertaining world we live in is the fact that boredom is still common and may actually be on the rise. In the book *Still Bored in a Culture of Entertainment*, Richard Winter (2002) explores the fact that the electronic overload we experience today may itself lead to boredom because it causes us to periodically shut down as a response to being overloaded. Winter argues that as entertainment sources have become more sophisticated, we have continually raised the standards. As a result, its producers must continually endeavor to be more sensational to hold our attention, and the real, mundane world in which we live seems more and more boring compared to the fantasies we experience in books, movies, television, and games.

STARRING IN OUR OWN PERSONAL REALITY SHOWS

In his book *Life: The Movie*, Neal Gabler (2000) argues that we all now actually view our lives as an unfolding movie script, in which we are constantly striving to build an image of ourselves and assessing how others see us. This phenomenon is augmented by the reality movement and the rise of celebrity culture, such that many people are actually living their lives in front of cameras. Even those of us who are not celebrities have become accustomed to seeing our own images in digital pictures, videos, on websites, etc. While I still tend to put on an uncomfortable smile when I know my picture is being taken, my daughters are not self-conscious about it and frequently spend time with their friends snapping pictures of each other on their cell phones and cameras. They immediately post these pictures on Facebook. I suppose I shouldn't be surprised by their comfort with picture taking, given the paparazzi-like scenes we parents have been creating since they were born, making videos of their every smile, step, school performance, or athletic event. I can still remember the crowd of parents jockeying for video position when their three-year-old's Mothers' Day Out class performed a Christmas show.

GREAT EXPECTATIONS

When I was a young therapist, I spent a year working at a VA hospital. Often, groups of World War II and Korea veterans would talk about how materialistic the young people of today had become. What struck me was how many of them would end up stating some variation of the theme that kids today "want everything right away. When I was young, we were dirt poor, but we didn't know any better, so we were happy." The irony is that these comments are absolutely accurate. When most or all of the people you compare yourself to live pretty much the way you do, it doesn't create an expectation gap. However, in a world driven by media images of the good life and unbelievably focused advertising, it is much easier to come to feel that somehow we are missing out!

Robert Samuelson, an economist and author of *The Good Life and Its Discontents* (1997), asserts that the combination of the economic affluence which followed World War II and the attendant technological changes increased our exposure and access to goods and services. This has resulted in artificially inflated expectations regarding our lives and lifestyles. In turn, when these expectations are not met, we experience stress, frustration, and a loss of trust in public institutions—including politicians, major companies, the press, and academics—creating a downward spiral.

Martin Seligman (2002), a prominent psychologist who has spent much of his career studying helplessness and optimism, wrote an article in 1988 entitled "Boomer Blues," in which he argued that the combination of affluence, technology, and media exposure had resulted in a population of individuals who expect more from life than ever before. It is no longer enough to have a job that pays the bills: We want a job that pays well, provides benefits, challenges us, has room for upward mobility, and hopefully comes with a corner office and a window. We don't just want a simple, affordable house—we want one with all of the latest appliances, color schemes, furniture, and decorative features we see in magazines and on television. In fact, if you try to sell a house right now you will probably be told that you need to stage the property by painting the walls clean neutral colors, replacing flooring and fixtures, and hiding away any clutter or evidence that you actually live there, so it will look like a stage set, not a working home. On the social front, we want large groups of attractive friends who do fun things in exciting places, fulfilling relationships with beautiful partners who earn lots of money, and perfect children who excel in school, sports, and social skills. To showcase all this success, we often want hair and skin makeovers, designer clothes, shoes, and purses, luxury cars, and impressive second homes

Bill Clinton

and vacation destinations. In effect, learning to expect so much success and prosperity from life actually results in much higher chances of our being disappointed on at least one front.

At the same time, according to poll data—and caused in part by our ever increasing knowledge of the failures of famous people—the press have eroded our sense of confidence in social organizations, including the government and judicial system, politicians and political organizations, religions, academic and medical institutions. For example, compare the public's views of Presidents John F. Kennedy and Bill Clinton. Although both had affairs while in office, the Secret Service and the media did not reveal that fact during Kennedy's time, while Clinton's actions were made very public and had a major impact on his career. In the same vein, we all know far more about the failings of reli-

U.S. President John F. Kennedy (right), U.S. Attorney General Robert Kennedy (left), and actress Marilyn Monroe, on the occasion of President Kennedy's 45th birthday celebrations at Madison Square Garden in New York City.

gious leaders than ever before, which has made it hard for many people to see their churches or other places of worship in the same light.

While most of us would not wish to go back to a time when the media withheld such information from us, it is certainly harder to trust organizations or to have heroes when we know so much about their failings and foibles. According to Seligman, the combination of expecting so much more from life with increasing distrust of social structures leaves people feeling that they are solely responsible for their successes or failures, and have few supportive structures to turn to if things go wrong. He attributes rising rates of depression, anxiety, and suicide over the past half century to this combination of factors.

Recognizing that the exponential increase in information available to us today is both helpful and harmful is the first step to learning to manage the impact of the media on our attitudes, expectations, and emotions. Consciously managing our exposure to information and monitoring and choosing our reactions to what we see can allow us to manage this very modern source of stress. Perhaps it can be said that when it comes to the media, the old saws like "ignorance is bliss" and "no news is good news" might be more prescient than we know.

WHAT DO YOU THINK?

1. How much time do you think you spent following coverage of the events of 9/11 the week it happened?
2. Do you find yourself avoiding the news altogether or feeling that you need to have it on all the time to "stay in touch?"
3. How often do you compare yourself or your lifestyle unfavorably to things you see in the media?

REFERENCES

Deighton, L., & Schwartzman, A. (1979). *Airshipwreck*. New York: Holt, Rinehart & Winston.

Gabler, Neal (2000). *Life: The Movie: How Entertainment Conquered Reality*. New York: Vintage.

Goldstein, J. (1998). *Why We Watch*. London: Oxford University Press.

Gomery, D. (2008). *A History of Broadcasting*. New York: Wiley-Blackwood.

Johnson, S. (2006). *Everything Bad Is Good for You: How Today's Popular Culture Is Actually Making Us Smarter.* New York: Riverhead Trade.

Koch, H. (1970). *The Panic Broadcast.* New York: Avon. New York.

Moeller, S. D. (1999). *Compassion Fatigue: How the Media Sell Disease, Famine, War and Death.* New York: Routledge.

Mooney, M. (1975). *The Hindenburg.* New York: Bantam Books.

Moran, J. (2001). *Five Hundred Years of Printing.* New York: Oak Knoll Press.

Pillow, D. R., & McNaughton-Cassill, M. E. (2001). Media exposure, perceived similarity, and counterfactual regret: Why did the public grieve when Princess Diana died? *Journal of Applied Social Psychology, 10,* 2072–2094.

Samuelson, R. (1997). *The Good Life and Its Discontents: The American Dream in the Age of Entitlement.* New York: Vintage.

Seligman, M. E. P. (1988). "Boomer Blues," *Psychology Today* (October), 50–55.

Seligman, M. E. P. (2002). Positive psychology, positive prevention, and positive therapy. In C. R. Snyder & S. J. Lopez (Eds.), *The Handbook of Positive Psychology* (pp. 3–12). New York: Oxford Press.

Silver, R. C., Holman, E. A., McIntosh, M. P., & Gil-Rivas, V. (2002). Nationwide longitudinal study of psychological responses to September 11. *Journal of the American Medical Association, 288, 10,* 1235.

Slovic, P., Peters, E., Finucane, M. L., & MacGregor, D. G. (2005). Affect, risk, and decision making. *Health Psychology, 24,* S35–S40.

Winter, R. (2002). *Still Bored in a Culture of Entertainment.* New York: IVP Books.

CHAPTER 4

TIME: IF TIME IS MONEY, THEN IS SLEEP TIME?

KEY POINTS

- The perception of time is a function of how many options you have for ways to spend it.
- Multitasking actually decreases efficiency.
- Sleep is not a luxury; it is essential for physical and mental well-being.

IS TIME CONSTANT?

"What time is it?" is such a common question that we barely register it consciously as we check our wrists, cell phones, computer screens, clocks, bells, and buzzers to verify the time. We live in a world where two-minute waits at stoplights infuriate us and the few seconds it takes for our computer to boot up or a recorded phone message to get to the beep make us impatient. Therefore, knowing the time seems almost as routine as breathing. However, this has not always been the case. Throughout most of recorded history, time perception was a function of the changing of the seasons and the movements of the sun. People went to sleep when it was dark, and woke up when it was light. If you have ever tried to sew or read by firelight, you quickly realize that it is neither easy nor efficient. During our early hunting, fishing, and agrarian history, knowing the exact time of day did not provide any particular advantage. Hunting was always an unpredictable process driven more by the seasonal availability of prey than by the structured measurement of time. Likewise, growing and harvesting crops was an ongoing process marked by broad growing patterns that encompassed days or months, not hours. The study of changes in the night sky has long been a staple of long-distance sailors, although their interest was focused more on where they were than on what time it was.

IS TIME ACCURATE?

Physically, our bodies track time as well. Studies suggest that many of our hormones and neurotransmitters cycle in 24-hour patterns called circadian rhythms. The fact that we often feel sleepy at the same time every night or that teenagers have trouble falling asleep at night and waking up in the morning is a function of these patterns. Likewise, if you have ever felt groggy after traveling across time zones or after the switch to daylight savings time or have experienced a temperature spike at night, you have been at the mercy of your own circadian rhythms. Clearly, at one level, time is a function of the natural world.

Throughout history, though, people have struggled to find accurate ways to measure time using the stars or the sun. The use of sundials and other structures to mark time via shadows and lines dates back to ancient times. Over 300 years ago, Christiaan Huygens, a Dutch scientist, created the first known working pendulum clock that allowed him to measure the time with an error rate of less than one minute per day. In the 19th century, the vibration of quartz crystals was utilized to build even more accurate clocks that did not use gears or swinging parts. Relying on the fact that atoms and molecules resonate in stable ways over time, scientists eventually developed atomic clocks using atoms of cesium, hydrogen, or rubidium to keep time (Gleick, 2000).

As timekeeping became more accurate, the need to standardize time also emerged. The British first attempted to standardize railroad times in the 1840s, and similar attempts were made in the United States by transportation and military entities. Later, a system of world time zones was developed by using the meridian (an imaginary circle around the earth) that passed through Greenwich, England (as the prime or initial time) and adjusting time zones approximately every 15 degrees around the world to create a 24-hour global day.

In the meantime, the accurate measure of time began to figure more and more in the lives of individuals. Cities adopted bells to mark prayer times and the passage of time as well as to convey messages. Factories installed whistles that let workers know when to go to work, when to break for lunch, and when the workday was done. As technology advanced, owning a watch became a sign of prosperity. This is still evident in turn-of-the-century pictures of individuals and families in which a watch draped on a chain across the front of a man's suit is clearly visible. Today, many of us never leave the house without a watch, which we use as a workhorse, as well as a fashion statement and a status symbol. In fact, in some circles, the quality of a person's Rolex watch is still seen as a significant sign of power and influence.

TECHNOLOGY AND TIME

Younger individuals, who have grown up in the digital age, tend to rely more on their cell phones, iPods, and iPhones to mark time. When I look out over the podium in a typical classroom today, at least half the students have propped a phone, set to vibrate, on their desk. That way they can not only tell what time it is, but also see who is texting them at any given time! In my Stress Management classes, I often ask students to count the number of clocks in their homes. Even students who live in apartments tend to report at least ten, taking into account clock radios, stereos and televisions, microwaves, ovens, and computers, while those of us who live in larger houses can easily reach 25 or more. If you live in a part of the country that is subject to power surges, you may already have complained about this as you moved around the house checking to see which clocks need to be reset after the power goes out.

And of course, we now care very much about the minutiae of minutes and seconds, as we rush to get the kids on the school bus, to thaw dinner without burning it in the microwave, or to beat the traffic light so we won't be late to school or work. Rather than marking the time by seasons or physical rhythms, most people in

Western cultures feel driven by their clocks. Commuter rail and airlines publish arrival and departure times in tiny increments, time clocks calculate how many minutes you worked, and athletes and race car drivers often win or lose by seconds or even fractions of seconds. Gone are the days when viewers could tell who won a swim race or a track meet visually. Instead, Olympic commentators give us running analyses of how competitors' times compare to those who swam before them and where they stand in the race. Final victory is often determined electronically and visually checked repeatedly through instant replays to see who flicked a finger or a toe faster.

THE PERCEPTION OF TIME

My own life often seems dominated by a mere five to six minutes, the amount of time I am often running late to leave for work, to get to class, or to pick up the kids. Despite the fact that I know I am going to encounter traffic and have trouble finding the perfect parking place, I often behave as though I live in a virtual world where none of those things will happen! This leaves me making the 20-minute drive to work with one eye on my watch, and another on the car radio, fuming at the people around me who don't know where they are going or make me miss a light. Although I know consciously that all I have to do to resolve this situation is to leave earlier, in practice I would need to get up sooner, meaning I would need to get to bed earlier, leaving something undone that I would try to finish in the morning, and the cycle begins. It turns out that our perception of time and the actual passage of time have a complex relationship.

If you have ever spent time in prison or in a hospital bed or a slow-moving line in the bank, you know there are situations where time seems to move incredibly slowly. Likewise, if you have ever raced against a deadline to finish a project or catch a flight, you are aware that there are other instances when time literally seems to be flying by. Although in reality the actual passage of time is constant in both cases, as human beings our experience of time is a function of how our brain works. This means that our perception of time, like our perception of what we see or hear, is as much a product of how the brain processes it, as it is an external event (Musser, 2001; Eagleman et al., 2005).

Not surprisingly, the brain's perception of time involves a variety of complex processes (Rao, Mayer, & Harrington, 2001). It appears that sensory input such as auditory and visual signals contributes to our sense of time in conjunction with memory and thought. After all, understanding speech involves recognizing and separating sounds in a coherent, timely way, and driving or even walking involve the timed sequencing of visual and motor functions. Several brain structures are involved in this process. These include the basal ganglia, a collection of neurons involved in the coordination of movement, and the cerebellum, a cauliflower-like structure located at the base of the brain thought to play a key role in the coordination of hand and eye movements. The stumbling and slurring of words seen when people drink alcohol is a direct manifestation of the depressive effects of alcohol on the cerebellum. Tetrahydrocannabinol (THC)—the active ingredient in marijuana—has been shown to be related to time perception.

Specifically, in some people, THC decreases cerebellar blood flow, and they will experience significant altera-tions in time sense (Mathew, Wilson, Turkington, & Coleman, 1998). The parietal lobe coordinates sensation and perception; the temporal lobes, which are involved in attention and auditory perception, have also been implicated in time perception. Some researchers have even argued for a logarithmic relationship between time perception and increasing age (Kenney, 2009). Damage to the parietal lobe can disrupt both memory and speech. However, recent research suggests that rather than centering brain time in one site, the brain actually tracks time through a cascade of reactions. Given the importance of accurate timing for physical survival and the ability to navigate a complex, changing world, it is not surprising that time sensation is a multifaceted process.

Despite these advances in our understanding of how the brain experiences time, there are still many things we don't understand. Under extreme stress, time perception may speed up or slow down. During dreams, time often behaves in odd, unusual ways, collapsing or expanding at random. There are people who can think about the time they want to wake up in the morning and actually do so, and many of us can guess the time very ac-curately, even when we aren't near a clock. Even animals, as many pet lovers will attest, seem to be able to track time, such that they start begging for food at their usual dinner time or heading for bed at approximately the same time every night. Scottish researchers have even shown that hummingbirds can be trained to return to specific artificial flowers for food on different time schedules (Zimmer, 2008). Clearly, our social environment, experiences, and thoughts also shape our sense of time.

CULTURE AND TIME

In Western cultures, time tends to be viewed as an absolute entity that shapes and structures our activities. In less technological cultures, time still tends to be seen in more seasonal, environmental terms. Psychologist Robert Levine (Levine, West, & Reis, 1980) studied the speed of life around the world. He and his research-ers measured the accuracy of clocks in public places, how fast pedestrians walked, and how long it took to buy a stamp. Perhaps not surprisingly, Switzerland was the fastest country in his survey, while Mexico and Indonesia were among the slowest. Levine goes on to talk about what he calls "event time," or the tendency in less industrialized countries to mark time by events such as when the cows gather instead of by "watch time." Consequently, Americans get impatient if someone is late by as little as 12 minutes, while individuals in the developing world may tolerate lateness measured in hours or days. Clearly, our expectations about timeliness play a role in these responses. In a culture where people feel rushed, have access to accurate measures of time, and view lateness as a sign of disrespect, lateness has different implications than in a country where travel is difficult and erratic and people, in the absence of rigid methods of timekeeping, judge its passage more subjectively.

NEVER ENOUGH TIME

As discussed in previous chapters, a central characteristic of modern life is the omnipresent sense that there is too much to do, and not enough time to do it. Despite the fact that the goal of many technological advances has been to save time, the reality has been that these labor-saving devices have frequently altered our expecta-tions about how long things should take or how often we should do them, and so do not actually create more open time. While people used to wait days for the delivery of return mail, we are now impatient if we don't get an answer back within the hour. Our standards for how clean our homes should be have increased, such that the amount of time women spend on housework has not decreased nearly as quickly as was expected when dishwashers, washing machines, and vacuums first became popular.

Similar changes have occurred in regard to information. Although we have far greater access to information of all sorts, we have also changed our standards for what is timely or current. For example, news information is updated hourly, not daily as in the past, and stories that are a year old are often considered obsolete. The easier it is to acquire information, the harder it has become to process and sort through the unrelenting flow of data. In response, many of us spend as much time sifting through incoming information as we do accomplishing our actual jobs. And as each technological advance purports to help us control this flow of tasks and information, the new device contributes to the spiral by generating new demands (Eriksen, 2001). Some studies suggest that middle managers spend as much as a third of their time on email (Pratt, 2006). Ironically, as we spend more time trying to manage the flow of information we deal with on a daily basis, marketers and advertisers are spending their time finding ways to make sure that we still notice their products. To navigate this morass, we tend to try to speak faster, think faster, eliminate waste, and generally increase the speed at which we function.

There is even an argument that speed has become contagious. In the late 1960s and 1970s, two cardiologists, Meyer Friedman and Ray Rosenman (1974), identified a pattern of behavior among their patients who had experienced heart attacks, which they called Type A behavior. These Type A individuals were competitive, impatient, hostile, and driven. They tended to multitask or try to do more than one thing at a time and to feel that they never had enough time to do all that they needed to do. In early studies, the presence of this behavior pattern appeared to be related to the risk for subsequent heart attacks. Although the pattern did not hold up consistently over time, it became apparent that hostility and anxiety were good predictors of adverse health outcomes, at least in some people. In the meantime, with or without the hostility, many of us are reporting a sense of time urgency, and feeling pressure to accomplish more in less time. Just watching the number of people who are driving, talking on the phone, and putting on makeup simultaneously is enough to make me tired!

TIMELY CHOICES

The variety of choices we have for how we spend our time has also increased exponentially. As detailed in the books *The Era of Choice* (2005), by Edward C. Rosenthal, *The Paradox of Choice* (2003), by Barry Schwartz, and *The Progress Paradox* (2003), by Greg Easterbrook, people have never had more options for how to spend their time and money. Warehouse-style grocery store aisles offer walls of choices on cookies and crackers, home repair stores are stocked by people on small moving equipment, malls provide acres of shopping, eating, and entertainment, multiplex movie theaters offer round-the-clock viewing, and television stations no longer play the "Star Spangled Banner" and go off at midnight, but instead feature hundreds of niche channels 24 hours a day. In essence, no matter what you decide to do or buy in the modern world, by default you are missing out on other opportunities or choices. Of course, to pay for all these choices, many of us are working longer hours, which in turn limits our time and increases the sense that we don't have time to do all the things we want to do.

In both academics and the workplace, the number of choices available continues to increase, with the end result that many students feel totally stymied by the pressure to pick the perfect major or career. Workers often feel that as soon as they leave school their skills are obsolete, so they have to continually train and retool to remain competitive. Relationship-wise, we seem to have more means of getting in touch with each other than ever before, but less time to actually spend together. Many families are on the run from the moment they get up until they fall asleep, coordinating work, school, and extracurricular activities, eating in the car and firing off emails, text messages, voice mails, and tweets with abandon. As Dalton Conley writes in his book *Elsewhere, U.S.A.* (2009), many Americans feel most at home in their cars shuttling between one place they are supposed to be and another. Calling while en route to say that you are on your way to a meeting or appointment has almost become an accepted way of handling an overbooked schedule.

TIME VERSUS SLEEP

As if being too busy is not enough, many of us are also struggling to manage impossible schedules from a sleep-deprived state. Surveys show that as many as 56 percent of Americans report that daytime sleepiness is a problem for them. Given the fact that most of us require approximately eight hours of sleep a night, this probably doesn't surprise you. Research on sleep suggests that once electricity became readily available, the temptation to skimp on sleep became universal. Not only has electricity made it easy to continue activities after dark, but it has also provided the fuel for alternate means of stimulation. In addition, stimulation from radios, televisions, and computers can help us fight sleep, and alarm clocks ensure that we wake up before our bodies are fully rested. In addition to being uncomfortable, sleep deprivation can also be dangerous. Some researchers suggest that sleepiness causes just as many car accidents as alcohol and that up to 37 percent of drivers report that they have fallen asleep at least once while driving. Air traffic controllers, pilots, ship captains, emergency room staff, EMTs, and military personnel have all been shown to make more errors when tired, sometimes with disastrous results—as evidenced by the *Exxon Valdez* and Three Mile Island accidents, both believed to have been caused in part by operator fatigue (Dinges, 1995).

The increase in accidents caused by sleep deprivation seems to stem from our diminished ability to pay attention, especially to repetitive stimuli, to concentrate on the information at hand, and to make good judgments. These findings are somewhat paradoxical, however, in that we don't really understand why we need to sleep in the first place. Although we know that all mammals sleep, including certain breeds of dolphins that sleep with only half of their brains at a time, we have never been as sure of the purpose of sleep as we are of the reasons we eat, drink, or breathe. Despite the fact that sleep deprivation is so aversive that it is often used as a torture technique (as recently as in Guantanamo Bay, where detainees were reportedly deprived of sleep for up to 11 days), it is not clear whether people actually die of sleep deprivation. However, after periods of extended sleeplessness, they often report irritability, emotionality, and even delusions and hallucinations. Long-term sleep deprivation has also been linked to obesity, as the body appears to respond to the lack of sleep as a trigger for storing energy in the form of fat (Patel et al., 2006).

SLEEP AND THE BRAIN

Ironically, in order to understand how sleep works, we rely on measures of the electrical activity going on in the neurons in the brain, using electrodes placed on the outside of the skull. The results suggest that sleep is characterized by two distinct stages. Prior to falling asleep, our brain waves start to slow and become relaxed. During Stage 1 sleep, the EEG shows irregular low-voltage waves interspersed with bursts of energy called sleep spindles and K-complexes also emerge during Stage 2 sleep. In Stage 3 and Stage 4 sleep, collectively known as slow-wave sleep, heart rate, breathing, and brain activity continue to slow and become more syn-

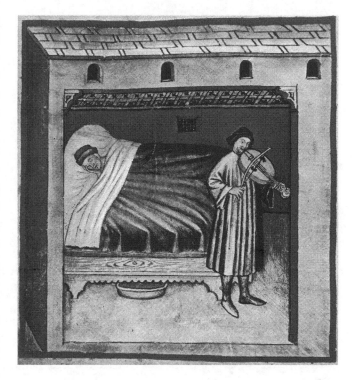

chronized. After about an hour of sleep, people begin to cycle back through these stages in reverse order. However, instead of entering Stage 1 sleep, the brain enters yet another stage, called paradoxical or rapid eye movement sleep (REM), characterized by a series of distinctive features. During REM sleep, EEG recordings show irregular, low-voltage, fast waves indicative of neuronal activity, while at the same time the muscles of the body are extremely relaxed, but heart rate, blood pressure, and breathing are variable, and the eyes, while closed, flicker and move. If you have ever watched a sleeping dog or cat twitch or moan while lying on the floor you have probably seen a period of REM sleep. When you wake people up during a REM period, they report dreaming 80 to 90 percent of the time. Although it has been shown that people can dream during other stages of sleep, the dreams that occur during REM sleep tend to include visual imagery and complex plots. In a typical night of sleep, people will cycle through Stages 1 to 4 of deep sleep and then a REM period four to five times a night. Earlier in the night we tend to spend more time in the deep sleep stage, while later in the night the dream periods last longer (Fuller, Gooley, & Saper, 2006).

In a normally functioning brain, the control of our patterns of wakefulness and sleep includes input from a network of neurons that run up from the hind- to the mid-brain, called the reticular formation. In addition, a small structure called the locus coeruleus found deep in the brain increases wakefulness via the neurotransmitter norepinephrine. A neurotransmitter called alternately orexin or hypocretin, also maintains arousal. Still other pathways from the hypothalamus regulate the release of acetylcholine from the basal forebrain, an area near the hypothalamus, which increases arousal, while other basal forebrain neurons release GABA, an inhibitory transmitter which is essential for sleep.

Another compound called adenosine is thought to inhibit the basal forebrain cells that trigger arousal and thus promotes sleep. After sleep deprivation, adenosine builds up and contributes to sleepiness. Prostaglandins also build up during the day and then decline during sleep. During immune responses to illness or infection, the body increases the release of prostaglandins and thus our sleepiness. REM sleep involves both the transmitters serotonin and acetylcholine and is characterized by electrical activity in the areas of visual, perceptual, auditory, and motor areas of the cortex and in the emotional parts of the brain called the limbic system—all triggered by signals from the pons, a deeper portion of the brain. The muscle paralysis seen during REM sleep is thought to prevent us from acting out our dreams. In fact, when people don't experience this relaxation, a disorder called REM without atonia, they frequently hurt themselves and others while dreaming because they physically act out their dreams. Of course, the superchiasmatic nucleus (SCN) and melatonin also contribute to our feelings of sleepiness, in part by helping maintain our circadian patterns in approximate 24-hour cycles (Vitaterna, Takahashi, & Turek,1991).

WHY DO WE SLEEP?

In spite of these advances in our understanding of how sleep occurs, we are still struggling with the why. It has long been suspected that the purpose of sleep, at least in part, is to conserve energy. Among animals who rely on vision, this would occur at night, while those that operate in the dark using their sense of hearing or smell would sleep during the day. However, sleep also appears to play a role in memory. When people sleep after studying, their recall and performance is significantly better than people who engage in other activities or are sleep deprived. Recent research suggests that after learning a motor skill, the parts of the brain that were active during the task are active again during sleep. It is as though their brains are practicing or consolidating the skill (Dement & Vaughan, 2009).

Perhaps even more intriguing than the purpose of sleep in general is the question of why we experience REM sleep and dreams (Dement & Vaughan, 2009). If you take a person into the lab and wake them up whenever they show REM sleep brain wave patterns, their overall sleep pattern will be increasingly disrupted and in particular will show large increases in the amount of time they spend in REM sleep overall. It has been suggested that REM sleep is involved in the consolidation of memory and furthermore plays a role in the processing of our daily experiences, especially their emotional content. Interestingly, when we are dreaming, there is arousal in parts of the brain (such as the amygdala) that are typically involved in emotions and in visual processing areas, but not parts of the prefrontal areas, which are involved in creating memories; therefore, we often forget our dreams and subsequently claim that we were not dreaming at all. However, even people who argue that they never dream will report dreams if they are awakened during a REM cycle.

Clearly, sleep is a very complex process involving the interactions of electrical and chemical signals throughout the brain, which evolved over thousands of years of life driven largely by the light/dark cycles of the natural world. In the past century, we have altered this pattern drastically without paying much attention to how it was impacting our sleep and our brains. Ironically, the electrical patterns in our brains are disrupted by the electrical patterns in our environments, in ways we are just starting to understand (Dement, 1997).

SLEEPING OUR LIVES AWAY

To further complicate the process, it turns out that sleep/wake cycles change with age and our emotional state (Mindell, 1999; Hansen et al. 2005; Ancoli-Israel, 2005). For example, most young children go to bed early and easily wake early as well. However, adolescents frequently prefer to stay up late and have more trouble waking up. As adults, people may be classified as either larks or owls, depending on their preferred sleep/wake pattern. Larks tend to go to sleep and rise earlier than owls and report that they are at their best mentally in the morning. Owls, on the other hand, tend to prefer to stay up late and sleep in and show increased mental alertness and activity much later in the evening than larks. Despite the cultural pressures of school and work times—and the temptations of our electronic environment—these patters appear to be firmly anchored in our genetic makeup and are difficult to change. In response to data indicating that teenagers on the whole are less alert in the morning, many high schools have shifted to later start times and report increased school performance and decreased tardiness (Mindell, 1999).

As a lifelong owl raising a daughter who has shown owl tendencies since babyhood, I am very sensitive to these distinctions. During college and graduate school I was perfectly happy studying from 8:00 in the evening until 2:00 or 3:00 in the morning, starting my workday around 10:00 a.m. However, when the twins came along, my husband and I went into a five-year-long sleep deficit free fall. No matter what we tried, the girls would not sleep on the same schedule. To make matters worse, our little owl, who barely napped and routinely fought falling asleep, wanted someone to stay awake with her when she couldn't sleep. One tortured night I finally took her downstairs so her dad and sister could sleep and fell asleep myself, in the middle of the family room floor. I awoke a couple of hours later to find that the *Barney* video she had been watching had turned to fuzz and she had been crawling back and forth from her toy box to get blocks, books, and toys, which she had been using to outline my body and pile on my stomach. It was years before she reliably slept through the night, but what really saved us was her learning to read, which enabled her to occupy herself when she couldn't get to sleep. As a teenager constrained by her high school and extracurricular schedule, she still struggles to fall asleep earlier in the evening, even after taking melatonin in an attempt to shift her circadian cycle.

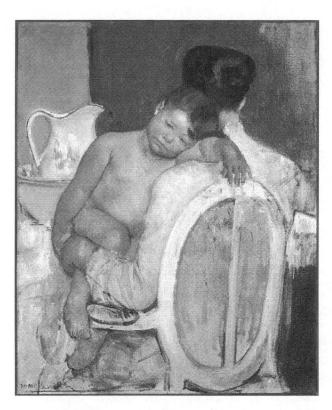

Woman Sitting with a Child in Her Arms, oil on canvas by Mary Cassatt, c. 1890.

Unfortunately, disrupted sleep is actually a problem for a huge number of Americans. In addition to sleep problems caused by jet lag and nocturnal work patterns, stress, depression, anxiety, exercise, diet, and pharmaceuticals are all known to alter sleep. Difficulty sleeping is a diagnostic criteria for depression, which is often characterized by waking in the middle of the night or waking earlier than you wish to and being unable to go back to sleep. Anxiety, on the other hand, often results in difficulty falling asleep, as can other forms of stress. Surprisingly, overall sleep deprivation, or simply awakening depressed individuals each time they enter REM sleep, can actually ameliorate their symptoms, suggesting that some sort of dysregulation of REM sleep is a component of depression.

Exercising too close to bedtime, eating and drinking foods high in sugar and caffeine, and taking medications for conditions ranging from colds and allergies to sleep problems can all influence our sleep patterns.

Sleep disorders, such as periodic limb movement disorder (sometimes called restless leg syndrome) and sleep apnea, a disruption in breathing while sleeping, can both result in frequent night awakenings, which the sleeper may not even be aware of. Nevertheless, these disruptions result in daytime tiredness, diminished attention, and difficulty with reasoning and impulse control. Unfortunately, we live in a culture where many people believe that sleep is expendable and even see tiredness as a badge of honor and importance. Given the toll that tiredness takes on our health and ability to function, perhaps we should all start to reconsider this belief!

CHOOSING HOW TO SPEND YOUR TIME

But what are our choices for managing time without borrowing from our sleep pools? Unfortunately, there is no simple answer. You may notice the fact that we talk about managing time, not curing our time deficit, as few of us are actually willing to give up the conveniences of modern life that have contributed to this crunch. If we assume that electricity and technology are likely to be part of our lives for quite some time, the first step is figuring out exactly how you are spending your time, much like people learn to pay attention to what they are eating before starting a diet, or tracking how you spend your money before creating a budget.

There are a number of ways to analyze how you spend time, ranging from keeping detailed lists to purchasing commercial time management planners. However, one simple way is to draw a circle, and then divide it into pie-shaped segments (Howe & Simon, 1995). Each piece of pie should indicate the percentage of a typical day you spend in activities including—but not limited to—work, school, studying, commuting, child care, exercise, house or yard work, shopping, cleaning, etc. The actual content of your day may vary, and you may even need to prepare different circles to represent weekend or weekday schedules, but the key is to determine what you are doing now. The second step is creating a similar drawing to represent your ideal use of time, which indicates how you would like to be spending your days. For some people, this task is easy, for others it is difficult to figure out exactly what they would like to be doing. Once you have drawn these circles, the next step is to analyze if and why your actual and ideal circles don't match. This includes thinking about the motivations behind your choices and potential barriers to change. In many cases, tasks that take up large portions of our time, such as working or driving, cannot be easily changed since we have bills to pay, and can't simply move our house or office to suit our needs. However, other tasks may be more amenable to change.

For example, if you are spending more time than you would like watching television, it can be very helpful to figure out whether this is occurring because you are avoiding other tasks, feeling bored, or simply like watching television. Other factors that must be considered when thinking about time management include the value we put on types of activities, how much we enjoy the things we are doing, and how important we feel they are. If we are spending lots of time during the day doing things we don't like doing to please someone else, that can be a key to the need for change. An exercise that often works for my students is to go back to the circles they drew and to rate each activity on three different dimensions. Using a scale from 1 to 7, with 1 the lowest rating and 7 the highest, they indicate how much they enjoy each activity on the list, how proficient they are at the task, and how important they think the task is. More than one of my students have been shocked to realize that they are spending large chunks of their day doing things they don't like and don't value, rather than focusing on the things they do well and do value. In his book *Authentic Happiness*, Martin Seligman (2003) makes a pitch for finding ways to use our skills to accomplish things we are passionate about as a means of finding happiness.

Social factors may also contribute to our failure to spend time the way we want to. Often, people find themselves engaging in activities to meet the needs of others. While this is an inevitable component of work, school, and child care, the key is learning to differentiate between those things you truly need to do and those things you are doing because it is hard for you to say no. While being assertive can seem scary in the short run, the ongoing stress and resentment engendered by not doing so also takes a toll. In his fascinating book, *Stumbling on Happiness* (2006), psychologist Dan Gilbert explores the ways in which we anticipate and plan for future events. According to his research and that of others, one of the problems is that it is very hard for us to project how we will feel in the future independently of how we are feeling currently. For example, have you ever struggled to pack for a journey to a place that was significantly colder or hotter than where you are when you are packing? It can be extremely hard to anticipate needing a parka when you are sweating.

Likewise, we often think that if we can only meet a particular future goal such as getting a job or earning a degree, we will be happy. However, when we finally get there, it often feels anticlimactic. According to Gilbert, this is because we have changed during the interval of time it took us to achieve the goal, so it no longer meets our needs in the same way. For example, in graduate school there were months when my husband and I actually ran out of money before our next paycheck. As hard as it is to imagine now, that was back in the days when grocery stores and fast food restaurants didn't take credit cards. I can remember scraping together change to get food. One memorable week, we celebrated because we got a very late wedding check, which carried us through. At that time, I couldn't have even imagined making as much money as we do now, although with a mortgage, two cars, two kids, and a fleet of pets, the reality is that I often feel just as stressed about money as I did back then. In terms of time management, this translates into thinking differently about how our current choices will affect us in the future. According to Gilbert, when agreeing to future activities, we need to think not just about why we should do something (I like the person asking me the favor; I don't want to annoy my boss; I should volunteer at my kids' school if I am a good parent, etc.), but also how we will actually be able to do it (Do we have time off that day; are we already overcommitted; how much will it cost, and so forth).
If you have ever found yourself saying that something "seemed like a good idea at the time," you have already acknowledged your tendency to make decisions based on the why and not the how of the project.

EARLY OR LATE

Your personal approach to time also matters. In addition to being characterized as larks or owls, people can also be categorized according to whether they view time as monochronic or polychronic (Kaufmann-Scarborough & Lindquist, 1999). In short, people who are monochrones see time as discrete and fixed. They prefer to have schedules and to accomplish one task at a time, placing a high value on punctuality. Polychrons, on the other hand, see time as continuous, prefer to work on two or more projects at the same time, view deadlines as arbitrary, and worry more about interpersonal relationships. As a lifelong polychron, I make lists, which I continuously amend and change as my activities and the demands of those around me change. I routinely assume I can get a lot of things done at a time, and consequently am often late for meetings and appointments.

In fact, one of my friends describes this approach to time management as "magical thinking," based on the idea that time will somehow conform to my to-do list regardless of the reality of the time line. Figuring out how to manage your own approach to time based on your time tendencies and personality is a key part of this process.

In my stress management class, I have started describing time management as the effort to keep a three-legged stool even. One of the legs is punctuality, another productivity, and the third personableness. In my observation and experience, most of us tend to rely on two of the legs more than the other. For example, since I value productivity and being personable, I will stop and talk to someone in the hall on the way to a meeting or finish a project, knowing that the decision will make me late. However, I have other colleagues who will resort to rudeness in the need to meet their punctuality needs and still others who are personable and punctual, but don't necessarily get a lot done. The key, then, seems to be figuring out how to keep the stool "level" enough to meet your needs by balancing your efforts across the three areas. Often this involves consciously reevaluating our expectations and cognitions about how we spend our time and applying the social skills and time management techniques we will discuss in later chapters. If you are chronically late, struggling with stress in your relationships, or feeling like you aren't getting enough done, you may want to take some time to think about how you are balancing your efforts across these three areas.

WHAT DO YOU THINK?

1. Make a list of all the tasks you do in a typical day and rate how productive, urgent, and enjoyable each activity is to you.
2. What tasks or activities would you like to add or subtract from your daily list?
3. Do you frequently feel like you have been busy all day, but not accomplished anything?

REFERENCES

Ancoli-Israel, S. (2005). Sleep and aging: Prevalence of disturbed sleep and treatment considerations in older adults. *Journal of Clinical Psychiatry* 66, 9: 24–30.

Conley, Dalton. (2010). *Elsewhere, U.S.A.: How We Got from the Company Man, Family Dinners and the Affluent Society to the Home Office, BlackBerry Moms and Economic Anxiety.* New York: Pantheon Books. Paperback Edition: Vintage Books.

Dement, W. C., & Vaughan, C. (2009). *The Promise of Sleep: A Pioneer in Sleep Medicine Explores the Vital Connection Between Health, Happiness, and a Good Night's Sleep.* New York: Delacorte Press.

Dement, W. (1997). What all undergraduates should know about how their sleeping lives affect their waking lives. Sleepless at Stanford, *www.stanford.edu*

Dinges, D. (1995). An overview of sleepiness and accidents. *Journal of Sleep Research*, 4, s2, 4–14.

Durmer, J. S., & Dinges, D. F. (2005). Neurocognitive Consequences of Sleep Deprivation,11 , 118 *Seminars in Neurobiology*, 25 (1), 117–129.

Eagleman, D. M., Tse, P. U., Buonomano, D., Janssen, P., Nobre, A. C., & Holcombe, A. O. (2005). Time and the brain: How subjective time relates to neural time. *Journal of Neuroscience, 25* (45), 10369–10371.

Eriksen, T. H. (2001). *Tyranny of the Moment: Fast and Slow Time in the Information Age.* London: Pluto Press.

Easterbrook, G. (2003). *The Progress Paradox.* New York: Random House.

Fuller, P. M., Gooley, J. J., & Saper, C. B. (2006). Neurobiology of the Sleep–Wake Cycle: Sleep Architecture, Circadian Regulation, and Regulatory Feedback. *Journal of Biological Rhythms*, 21 (6), 482–493.

Friedman, M., & Rosenman, R. H. (1974). *Type A Behavior and Your Heart*. New York: Knopf.

Gleick, J. (2000). *Faster: The Acceleration of Just About Everything*. New York: Pantheon.

Gilbert, D. (2006). *Stumbling on Happiness*. New York: Knopf.

Hansen, M., Janssen, I., Schiff, A., Zee, P. C., & Dubocovich, M. L. (2005). The impact of school daily schedule on adolescent sleep. *Pediatrics* 115: 1555–1561.

Kaufmann-Scarborough, C., & Lindquist, J. D. (1999). Time Management and Polychronicity: Comparisons, Contrasts and Insights for the Workplace. *Journal of Managerial Psychology, Special Issue on Polychronicity,* 14, 3/4, 288–312.

Kenney, J. M. (2009). *Logtime: The Subjective Scale of Life. The Logarithmic Time Perception Hypothesis.* http://www.kafalas.com/Logtime.html

Levine, R. V., West, L. J., & Reis, H. T. (1980). Perceptions of time and punctuality in the United States and Brazil. *Journal of Personality and Social Psychology,* 38 (4), 541–550.

Mathew, R. J., Wilson, W. H., Turkington, T. G., & Coleman, R. E. (1998). Cerebellar activity and disturbed time sense after THC. *ScienceDirect.com*

Mindell, J. A. (1999). Developmental features of sleep. *Child Adolesc Psychiatr Clin N Am.* 8, 695–725.

Musser, G. (2011). Time on the brain: How are you always living in the past, and other quirks of perception. *http://blogs.scientificamerican.com/observations/2011/09/15/time-on-the-brain-how-you-are-always-living-in-the-past-and-other-quirks-of-perception*

Patel, S. R., Malhotra, A., White, D. P., Gottlieb, D. J., & Hu, F. B. (2006). Association between reduced sleep and weight gain in women. *American Journal of Epidemiology, 164* (10), 947–954.

Pratt, A. (2006). Email overload in the workplace: A multi-dimensional exploration. *Orange Journal,* http://orange.eserver.org/issues/5-1/pratt.html

Rao, S. M., Mayer, A. R., & Harrington, D. L. (2001). The evolution of brain activation during temporal processing. *Nature Neuroscience* 4, 317–323.

Rosenthal, E. (2005). *The Era of Choice: The Ability to Choose and Its Transformation of Contemporary Life.* Cambridge MA: MIT Press.

Schwartz , B. (2003). *The Paradox of Choice: Why More Is Less.* New York: Ecco.

Seligman, M.E.P., (2003). *Authentic Happiness.* New York, NY: Free Press.

Simon, S. B., & Howe, L. W. (1995). *Values Clarification.* New York: Grand Central Publishing.

Vitaterna, M. H., Takahashi, J. S., & Turek, F. W. (2001). Overview of circadian rhythms. *Alcohol Res Health,* 25 (2), 85–93.

Zimmer, C. (2008). The Brain: How Your Brain Can Control Time. *Discover* Magazine.

CHAPTER 5

NATURE AND DOWNTIME: WHAT DOES QUIET SOUND LIKE?

KEY POINTS

- ✦ Most Americans spend very little time outdoors.
- ✦ We are asking our brains to do things that humans never did before.
- ✦ In today's busy world, people must actually schedule time to relax.

HOW NOISY IS MODERN LIFE?

The backdrop to modern life is so noisy that most of us aren't even consciously aware of it anymore. Radios, televisions, computers, beeps, ringtones, vacuums, jackhammers, heaters and air conditioners, plane and automobile engines, people on cell phones, Muzak, dogs barking—the list is seemingly endless. This is not to say that life was silent in the past. Weather, animals, and humans interacting certainly still make a considerable amount of noise, as is evident in many of the less developed parts of the world. However, in the absence of electronic advances, those noises are not sustained and amplified. The amazing thing is how quickly most of us have adapted to the constant stream of noise and activity around us. In fact, if you stop for a minute right now you might be surprised to notice how many sounds you weren't even consciously aware of hearing. If the sounds are low, and you aren't trying to concentrate on something difficult, this may be no problem for you. But if you find you need to concentrate, the situation changes. Certainly, many harried parents have surprised themselves by yelling "be quiet, I can't think," in a noisy room or car. The reality is that there is a limit to how much information our brain can process simultaneously, and the modern world frequently pushes us to that threshold both physically and mentally. In fact, research suggests that high levels of noise are associated with poor sleep and also linked to cardiovascular and immunological problems (Ising & Kruppa, 2004; Ising & Prasher, 2012).

An illustration of Buddha meditating under the Bodhi tree.

CAN YOU HEAR YOURSELF THINK?

Early studies of sensory perception suggest that the nervous system is extremely sensitive to changes in our external environment as measured by our auditory, visual, olfactory, and kinesthetic senses. These complex processes involve input from sensory organs such as the ears, eyes, nose, and skin, conveyed via neuronal pathways to dedicated areas in the brain which process and decode these signals. Structures such as the thalamus route sensory information to specialized areas in the brain, which decode their messages. For example, auditory information is processed, at least in part, in the temporal areas of the cortex, particularly in the left side of the brain, while visual information is processed in the occipital area at the back. Essentially, everything that we think or experience is actually the result of our brain's ability to process a series of synchronized electronic and chemical signals linked to memory, emotional, verbal, and musical processing areas of the brain. In fact, this is why strokes and other head injuries can disrupt sensory process such as vision or hearing without disturbing the eyes or ears at all. If the brain areas that receive input from these sensory organs are not working properly, then it is as though you are recording your son's baseball game with a video camera that has no capacity to store the memory.

LIGHT KEEPS GETTING IN OUR EYES

Of course, noise is only one of the sensory stimuli that assault us in modern life. Lights, signs, billboards, murals, and graffiti all compete for our attention on a daily basis. Driving presents our brain with a cacophony of signals, ranging from the cars around us to traffic signals to the lights and dials on the dashboard. Tracking and responding to this input is a full-time job, even if we aren't talking on the phone or listening to the radio. In order to process so much information and sensory input, the brain attempts to organize information into categories or patterns so it can respond automatically. Throughout much of human history, this was a useful strategy for deciding whether a berry was poisonous or an animal was dangerous as quickly as possible. Such rapid decision making is actually a crucial ability in a fast-moving world, but processing such information takes attention and energy, which can be disrupted or disruptive if we try to do too many things at the same time. Not surprisingly, drivers tend to show elevated stress levels while driving (van den Haak, van Lon, van der Meer, & Rothkrantz, 2010).

As discussed in Chapter 4, our body performs best on an approximately 24-hour hormonal, or circadian, cycle, which is regulated by light. When this cycle is disrupted by work or stress or travel, people can feel irritable or depressed and may have trouble concentrating. For example, people who live in northern parts of the world, including the northern states of the United States and Alaska, have long realized that the short days and long nights they experience during the winter months can result in seasonal depression. Formal studies of mood and light exposure have identified a condition called seasonal affective disorder (SAD), which may seriously affect as many as 2.7 percent of the population of North America and could impact many more of us in milder ways (Lam & Levitan, 2000). SAD, which is characterized by a long-lasting depression, is actually treated through exposure to very bright light produced by medical light boxes. This is thought to help the body regulate melatonin levels.

The plethora of light sources found in the typical American home may also contribute to the trouble many people have sleeping. Ironically, studies regarding sleep and insomnia indicate that exposure to artificial light at night causes sleep problems. Such light may stem from streetlights or home lighting, but may also be related to the number and variety of blinking lights, clocks, and indicators many of us have in our bedrooms.

Artificial light may also have a negative impact on our well-being. Both the fluorescent and incandescent lights commonly used in residential and commercial settings fail to replicate the full natural-light spectrum, despite their brightness. Not surprisingly then, people often prefer to work in offices and buildings that offer windows and natural light. Such settings have been shown to decrease eyestrain, headaches, and overall stress levels and to increase productivity. We are more likely to experience stress in settings with more artificial light (Leather, Pyrgas, Beale, & Lawrence, 1998). Natural light increases attention and alertness,

Natural light pours in from a skylight at a Toronto shopping mall.

especially when performing boring or routine tasks. Some researchers have even found that absenteeism, and employee turnover are decreased in offices that offer natural light. For example, one survey indicated that 35 percent of office workers at one company reported that working in a space with no windows was their biggest work-related difficulty, while in another study, 96 percent of respondents said they preferred to work in natural light (Edwards & Torcellini, 2002).

Similar findings regarding light preferences have also been reported among students and teachers, and natural light has even been related to increased achievement scores on standardized tests. This may be particularly important in an era when the emphasis on school performance and test results has caused many schools to reduce the amount of time children spend outside. Studies in Wal-Mart and Target stores even suggest that people spend more time in stores featuring daylight. A number of medical studies have indicated that people were less likely to get depressed and to recover more quickly from surgery if their hospital room had a window (Joseph, 2006). Finally, exposure to vitamin D from sunlight has long been known to protect people from a disease called rickets, which disrupts bone growth and causes muscle weakness. Ironically, as our knowledge of the link between sunburn and skin cancer led to increases in sunblock use, some physicians are now arguing that many Americans are not getting enough sun exposure to maintain the level of vitamin D their bodies need and so are at risk for fatigue and depression (Heaney, 2005).

Clearly, our bodies and brains are predisposed to function most effectively in the presence of natural light. Of course, not all of us work or live in settings where natural light is available. Fortunately, the incorporation of green spaces and plants in our environment has also been shown to improve psychological well-being. Even walking through an arboretum has been shown to boost memory and attention, as opposed to walking through an urban setting. In settings without windows, people also indicate a preference for art or posters depicting natural scenes or for artificial windows which provide views of nature scenes (Fjeld, 2002; Eisen, 2008). Light, color and even exposure to nature can improve health and increase rates of recovery in hospitalized patients (Ulrich, 1984; Oberacher, 2002; Franklin, 2010).

THE COLOR OF OUR WORLD

Even the color a room is painted may influence mood and behavior (Kopec, Stone, & English, 1998; Kopec, 2006). Performance on tasks that require recall and alertness seem to improve in red rooms or with red stimuli, while relaxation and creativity seem to be more common in blue environments (Mehta & Zhu, 2009). The fact that we often describe colors in terms of feelings or temperatures may play a role in these relationships. Colors of longer wavelengths such as red tend to be seen as warm, while those of shorter wavelengths such as blue are seen as cool. Of course, as with most studies of human behavior, such abstractions are likely to be influenced by personality, experience, and culture. People who are particularly sensitive to color may respond more strongly than others, feeling either overstimulated or depressed by certain color combinations. Social factors are also key. In the West, black often depicts darkness or evil, while in some Eastern cultures black is seen as lucky. In the West, white is thought to symbolize purity at weddings and red has been viewed as a sexually suggestive color, while in China red is seen as the symbol of wedding joy and prosperity. In our rapidly changing, globally connected world, some of these associations may change, but the fact remains that we are often attempting to live and work in spaces that are far removed from those our bodies evolved to thrive in.

THE ANIMAL WORLD

Another feature of modern life now being recognized often by mental health professionals is our connection—or lack thereof—to animals. Archaeological studies suggest that dogs and humans have existed synergistically for thousands of years, providing protection and food for each other. Likewise, it appears that cats became domesticated as agriculture and food storage became prevalent because of their ability to reduce rodent populations. Similarly, the use of horses, elephants, and other large animals for transportation and muscle and the domestication of cows, sheep, goats, and birds for use as sources of milk products, eggs, and meat, date back centuries. However, with industrialization and specialization, many of us live far from the origination of our food sources and have never dealt with or cared for large animals. This does not mean, however, that animals no longer play a major role in our lives. In fact, six out of ten Americans own at least one pet, with dogs and cats leading the list followed by birds, small animals such as hamsters, and fish (Gallup, 2009).

Although caring for pets can be costly in terms of time and money, it turns out that pets provide a variety of benefits to humans (Morey, 2006; Beck, 2008). Petting a dog lowers heart rate and blood pressure, and owning a pet can help to alleviate loneliness, which along with depression has been implicated as a causal factor in heart disease (Allen, Blaskovich & Mendes, 2002). The introduction of therapy dogs into nursing homes, hospitals, and prisons has been shown to improve mental health. Research is also ongoing regarding the ability of dogs to detect and warn people of imminent seizures or even the presence of cancer, as detected by smell. Evidence even suggests that caring for a pet such as a bird can increase elderly people's sense of control and well-being and that watching fish swim in an aquarium can induce calm and relaxation.

NATURE CAN BE NURTURING

So what is emerging is a picture of a society in which people are experiencing ever increasing levels of sensory and cognitive stimulation while being cut off from many natural sources of connection and well-being.

Not only do we spend hours sitting in chairs staring at computer screens, but we do it in artificially lit, temperature-controlled rooms, with limited opportunities to view the natural world. In addition, we now spend much of our travel time in enclosed climate-controlled cars, trains or planes, and may spend little or no time outdoors during our work week. Contrast this to our grandparents' lives, where large amounts of time were devoted to growing and harvesting food, walking or riding animals for transportation, and regulating our activity cycles by natural light. In essence, we have increased the volume, quality, and quantity of sympathetic stimulation we want our nervous systems to process, while simultaneously decreasing the amount of time we have available for parasympathetic activation. Walking, gardening, and washing clothes by hand all offer moderate physical activity with ample time to think and contemplate, which rushing from our offices to our cars to grocery stores, malls, and Laundromats simply do not provide.

Not coincidentally, many of us now strive to assign time in our schedules for exercise, relaxation, meditation, or contemplation, which we often carry out in artificially controlled environments while lamenting that we really don't have time to do so. Further, we add sensory clutter to these activities in the form of television, music, and communication devices. Polls suggest that in many American homes, the television is on virtually all the time, serving as a backdrop to people's daily chores, homework, and mealtimes. Additionally, many of us deliberately schedule activities to allow ourselves to talk on the phone while folding clothes or preparing dinner or to listen to music or other input while exercising. When asked why they combine such activities, people tend to cite boredom and lack of time to process all the information they feel they need to. This would seem to be a contradiction in terms, unless we back up and look again at how the nervous system processes information.

WHY WE CAN'T TURN AWAY

In the natural world, the sensory nervous system is constantly feeding information to the brain to enable us to navigate effectively, find food, and avoid prey. When stimuli are repetitive, we tend to habituate to them—and then essentially tune them out. When stimuli are novel or changing, we attend to them in order to determine what they mean for us. This is why a sound or a smell that initially bothers us a great deal may not even enter our conscious awareness after a period of time. It is also why an unexpected sound, for example, a creak when you think you are in a house alone, can be so startling.

It also accounts for the fact that it is easy to lose track of repetitive tasks because we habituate to them and so stop attending. If you are counting pennies, this may simply mean you have to start over; however, if you are tracking blips on an air traffic control screen which represent actual planes in the air, losing track can have much larger consequences. When the stimuli you are watching are constantly moving or changing, it is easier to continue to pay attention; it is even difficult to switch your focus to something else. Picture your cat watching the birds in your backyard, with total concentration, even if you flick at his tail.

In a sense, this is what happens to us when we are watching multimodal electronic stimuli such as computers or televisions or when we are doubling up on the input we are receiving by watching one stimulus and listening to another. Research suggests that humans are particularly attuned to both auditory and visual components. Psychologists Kubey and Csikszentmihalyi (2002) argue that the combination of visual and auditory inputs on your television screen make it singularly addicting. As a result, we walk into a room and lose track of what we are saying or doing because the screen so captures our attention. Furthermore, it can be hard to separate from the stimuli because each time we start to leave, the picture on the screen changes, drawing our attention back. Just about all of us can remember sitting and watching a show or commercial that we didn't even like, but were somehow unable to leave. Paradoxically, we don't actually interact with television, so in spite of its addictive quality, it is essentially a passive activity.

Overload Addiction

To complicate the picture even further, the very volume of stimulating information we are exposed to in a given day actually contributes to our habituating to that level of input, such that we subsequently require even more stimulation to feel the same level of excitement. In a sense, sensory and emotional stimulation appear to work in the same way as certain drugs do. For example, alcoholics and illegal drug users will often tell you that as time goes on they find that they become tolerant to certain amounts of a substance and have to increase their dosage to get the same high. Something similar happens with entertainment, in that we are rarely entertained by the same input over and over. Even infants exposed to mobiles will habituate to something they see repeatedly (Rovee-Collier, 1999).

Is it any wonder, then, that television, movies, and even news shows continue to increase their violent, sexual, and exotic content in an effort to attract and hold our attention? By exposing us to a never-ending array of exotic, glamorous, exciting people and lifestyles, the media also contributes to a sense of boredom based on the feeling that our everyday lives and activities are far less entertaining or worthwhile than the fictional depictions we see on the screen. All of this is not to say that our grandparents were necessarily happier with their lives than we are. However, their daily existence tended to move at a slower pace that included more time spent outside, more physical exercise, and fewer arbitrary deadlines. In addition, they were not constantly bombarded by advertising and electronic input designed specifically to capture their attention and change their behavior to benefit someone else's financial or behavioral agenda.

But I Saw It on Television

The sensational, ubiquitous nature of the modern news media is another factor. A populace constantly exposed to negative stories about crime, war, disaster, and atrocity is not likely to view the world as a safe and welcoming place. Numerous studies in the past two decades indicate that people increasingly rate the world as dangerous and believe that crime is on the rise, even when crime statistics themselves proved otherwise. It seems that in the absence of personal experience, people tend to base their judgments on what they see and hear in the media. This can result in a phenomenon sometimes called the optimism gap, which refers to the fact that people will rate the safety, efficacy, and general state of well-being of their own community or nation as far greater than that of places they are not familiar with, even when their perceptions are consistent with reality.

For example, in a study conducted in my lab, participants were asked to rate their own communities and the country in general on a variety of indicators including crime, corruption, drug use, and school and personal safety (McNaughton-Cassill & Smith, 2002). As predicted, higher levels of television viewing were associated with elevated ratings of risk and danger for the nation as a whole but not one community in particular. It appears that when rating our own communities, we have access to a broader data set. We may know about a crime that happened in our neighborhood, but also be aware of how the neighbors helped, or we may know that some of the teachers at our child's school are bad but others are highly dedicated and competent. When judging settings where we have no personal experience on the other hand, we tend to assume the worst—because that is predominantly what we hear in the news.

Ironically, overall crime rates have been dropping in the United States for decades, and yet many people aren't aware of this fact. As the mother of young children, I constantly found myself telling other parents that I thought they should be more concerned about their child's safety riding a bike without a helmet, swimming, and riding in a car than about their being abducted by strangers. Nevertheless, in the past and even today, surprising amounts of time at parenting and PTA meetings are devoted to talking about stranger danger, teaching your child not to talk to people they don't know, and even to purchasing bracelets or dental IDs in case a child is kidnapped.

The irony of this is that in spite of all the media coverage of the abductions of Polly Klaas and Elizabeth Smart, the vast majority of child kidnappings involve family members, friends, or custody struggles. In addition, the children abducted by strangers are almost never toddlers. Typically, they are teen girls who are runaways or living in other types of unsafe settings. The fact is that your child is statistically more likely to be hit by lightning than to be kidnapped by a total stranger (Louv, 1991; Stokes, 2009). Regardless, many parents, scared by the perceived threat, struggle to teach their children to protect themselves and seriously curtail the amount of time these kids spend outdoors or in unstructured settings.

Growing up in the 1960s and 1970s, everyone I knew walked to and from school unless it was pouring rain. By the time my daughters went to school in the late 1990s, the line to drop off and pick up kids outside the school caused significant traffic jams in our neighborhood. While I understand that this may in part be a reflection of complex family schedules, many of the parents I spoke with cited stranger danger as a reason they didn't let their kids walk or bike to school. After school, my sister and our friends played outside for hours at a time. In the summer we went back out after dinner and roamed the neighborhood until dark, played ball in the street, and floated in and out of each other's yards and houses.

Today, such freedom is almost unimaginable. If kids aren't participating in organized sports, music, language, or other classes, they are at home doing homework. Elementary school-age children rarely escape their parents' immediate surveillance, and middle school and high school kids check in with their

Nowadays, children are sedentary and spend the majority of their time indoors. Their outdoor exercise is mainly limited to organized sports.

parents electronically throughout the day. Not surprisingly, one unanticipated outcome of these changes is the fact that children get less exercise, which contributes in part to our growing obesity problems. Another is that many kids have almost no personal interactions with the natural world and often don't even know what they are missing.

ARE THE WOODS STILL THERE IF WE AREN'T IN THEM?

In his book *Last Child in the Woods*, author Richard Louv (2008) explores how American families have moved from rural settings, where children worked and played outside virtually every day, to closed units, where both the children and their parents shuttle between homes and cars with little daily contact with nature. Louv attributes these changes to a variety of factors, including suburban sprawl, which limits the availability of natural play sites, fear of litigation, leading many neighborhood associations and property owners to regulate and discourage free play on their lands, exaggerated fears of the dangers of strangers, and of exposure to nature, fanned by graphic news coverage of rare kidnappings or injuries in natural settings. According to Louv, rising rates of stress, obesity, and even mental illness among the young may be due in part to this pattern that he has taken to calling nature-deficit disorder. According to his research, both children and their parents would benefit from increased contact—and subsequent familiarity with—nature, through schools, camps, and park programs. He also argues for bringing natural history studies back to the public schools and leaving more parks undeveloped to provide for wildlife habitats and corridors and to give more people access to natural settings (Louv, 2012).

DOES NATURE MAKE YOU SMARTER?

Interacting with the real world also brings other benefits. Some research suggests that attention and concentration improve in natural settings; this is relevant to the increases being seen in the diagnosis of ADHD in Western cultures. Further, the ability to solve practical problems in the real world can still have survival value. Every year the news is filled with stories of people who died because they went driving in the desert without water or sunscreen, tried to walk away from a snowbound car without adequate clothing, drowned while trying to cross a swollen stream or river, or didn't realize a tornado could be so strong! Spending most of our time as we do in climate-controlled worlds watching televisions, and using computers and other electronic devices can lull us into a false complacency. Because disaster responders can overcome all odds on television, it is easy to overestimate our control over the natural world. If you have ever tried to plug a small leak, prevent an umbrella from turning inside out in a storm, or jump off a roof or wall, you have probably learned that water is relentless and gravity is real. However, this is knowledge we gather through experience, so raising a generation of children without giving them the opportunity to learn to solve practical, physical problems can be a real problem in itself.

WHEN DISASTER STRIKES

After Hurricane Katrina, most of us watched in disbelief as the levees broke and an entire city flooded. Urban city dwellers suddenly found themselves wading through polluted, snake-infested water. People struggled to find drinking water and food and railed against the slow responses of disaster responders and authorities. Although the scope and complexity of this disaster was unique—and the suffering very real—what was most striking was how quickly the entire technological and physical infrastructure deteriorated and how very unprepared people were to cope without the modern amenities. Despite nationwide efforts by groups like the Red Cross to get people to plan for natural disasters with their families, the reality is that most Americans have neither the supplies nor the knowledge necessary to survive on their own for even a few days. Contrast this to many of our ancestors, who cleared land, grew food, and lived directly off the land. While going off the grid is not a feasible option for many of us, increasing our familiarity with the natural world can be a matter of life and death.

THE SPIRITUAL SIDE OF NATURE

Besides providing physical benefits and increasing psychological well-being, exposure to nature also seems to be strongly related to spirituality. Throughout the ages, literature has been filled with links between spirituality and natural settings. From the Bible to Native American stories, to Thoreau and Whitman, to the Dalai Lama, there are human accounts of spiritual experiences involving mountains, forests, deserts, oceans, lakes, and rivers. The feelings of being one with nature or the universe or mankind are often reported in conjunction with time spent in the wild. Visiting huge mountains or canyons or bodies of water seems to inspire awe in many of us, which paradoxically can also be generated by observing the miniature complexity of an ant hill or a beehive or the delicacy of a flower or a leaf.

McWay Falls, Big Sur, California.

Not surprisingly, there are those who argue that such experiences are simply the result of physiological changes in oxygen levels in the mountains or ions in the water, or that nature simply offers an opportunity for people to get out of their normal mental ruts. However, others believe that the brain may indeed be wired for spirituality, which can be triggered by beauty in nature, art, music, or architecture or by prayer, meditation, or relaxation practices. The parietal lobes in the cortex, responsible for processing sensory information, and the prefrontal lobes of the brain have all been implicated in spiritual experiences. Specifically, the parietal lobes show decreased activity during prayer and meditation, which may account for the reduction in the sense of space and time associated with these practices. Activity in the prefrontal cortex and even changes in the size of the thalamus, a sensory relay situation, have also been observed in relation to prayer and meditation. Furthermore, religious practices and spirituality have been associated with better physical and mental health and longevity (Seeman, Dubin, & Seeman, 2003; George, Larson, Koenig, & McCullough, 2000).

Going Back to Nature

In short, it becomes increasingly apparent that the more technological and structured our lives have become, the more our exposure to the natural world has diminished. While there are certainly benefits to not having to struggle to maintain the temperature of our homes or to raise crops and animals for food, or to travel on foot no matter the weather, there are downsides too. By depriving children of time to explore nature, we limit their understanding and appreciation of how the physical world works. By working long hours in artificial settings, we increase our own chances of depression and stress and of the feeling that we are disconnected from the real world. By structuring our time and emphasizing productivity, we miss opportunities to think, create, and experience the spiritual benefits of looking at the bigger picture of our lives.

Fortunately, unlike dieting or exercise, bringing nature back into our lives doesn't have to be difficult. Increasing the quality and amount of natural light in our homes, growing houseplants, maintaining small gardens, or even container gardens on a balcony, can help us reconnect to nature. Getting a pet or a fish tank, or volunteering at an animal shelter walking dogs or socializing cats for adoption, can offer us the health benefits of interacting with animals. Watching the stars or the clouds from our porch or patio can help, as will taking short walks around the neighborhood or workplace. Taking nature classes, guided walks, or participating in outdoor activities can benefit those who have little exposure to the natural world. Revisiting hobbies such as hiking, skiing, or camping can help those of us who have spent time outdoors reconnect with how it feels. In short, making nature a priority in your life is likely to pay off in ways you may never have imagined (Clay, 2001; Fjeld, 2012; Fuller et al., 2007).

What Do You Think?

1. When was the last time you spent a whole day in a natural setting?
2. How much natural light are you exposed to in a typical day?
3. Do you argue that you are too busy and stressed to take time to relax?

References

Allen, K., Blaskovich, J., & Mendes, W. B. (2002). Cardiovascular reactivity and the presence of pets, friends, and spouses: The truth about cats and dogs. Psychosomatic Medicine, 64, 727–39.

Beck, A. M. 2008. The human-animal bond: Essential elements in veterinary education. *Journal of Veterinary Medical Education*, 35(4): 476.

Clay, R. A. (2001). Green is good for you. *Monitor on Psychology*, 32(4), 40–42.

Edwards, L., & Torcellini, P. (2002). *A literature review of the effects of natural light on building occupants* (Technical report). Golden, CO: National Renewable Energy Laboratory.

Eisen, S. (2008). The stress-reducing effects of art in pediatric health care: Art preferences of healthy children and hospitalized children. *Journal of Child Health Care*, 12 (3), 173–190.

Fjeld, T. (2002). The effect of plants and artificial daylight on the well-being and health of office workers, schoolchildren, and health care personnel. *Seminar Report: Reducing Health Complaints at Work*. Plants for people, International Horticultural Exhibition, Florida.

Franklin, D. (2012). How Hospital Gardens Help Patients Heal. *ScientificAmerican.com*. http://www.scientificamerican.com/article.cfm?id=nature-that-nurtures

Fuller, R. A., Irvine, K. N., Devine-Wright, P., Warren, P. H., & Gaston, K. J. (2007). Psychological benefits of green space increase with biodiversity. *Biological Letters*, 3, 390–394.

Gallup Polls (2009). Americans and their pets. http://www.gallup.com/poll/25969/americans-their-pets.aspx

George, L. K., Larsons, D. B., Koenig, H. G., & McCullough., M. E. (2000). Spirituality and health: What we know, what we need to know. *Journal of Social and Clinical Psychology*; Spring 2000; 19, 1; Psychology Module p. 102.

Heaney, R. P. (2005). The Vitamin D Requirement in Health and Disease. *The Journal of Steroid Biochemistry and Molecular Biology*, 97, 13–19.

Ising, H., & Kruppa, B. (2004). Health effects caused by noise: Evidence from the literature from the past 25 years. *Noise Health*, 6, 5–13.

Ising, H. & Prasher, D. (2012). Noise as a stressor and its impact on health. *Noise Health*, 2, 5–6.

Joseph, A. (2006). *The Impact of Light on Outcomes in Healthcare Settings*. Center for Health Design, August 2006. http://www.healthdesign.org/chd/research/impact-light-outcomes-healthcare-settings

Kaplan, R., & Kaplan, S. (2008). Bringing out the best in people: A psychological perspective. *Conservation Biology*, 22(4), 826–829.

Kopec, D., Stone, N. J., & English, A. J. (1998). Task type, posters, and workspace color on mood, satisfaction, and performance. *Journal of Environmental Psychology*, 18, 175–185.

Kopec, D. (2006). *Environmental Psychology for Design*. New York: Fairchild, Publications, Inc.

Kubey, R., & Csikszentmihalyi, M. (2002). Television addiction is no mere metaphor. *Scientific American*, 286, 74–80.

Kubey, Robert. (1996). Television dependence, diagnosis, and prevention, in *Tuning in to Young Viewers: Social Science Perspectives on Television*, edited by Tannis M. Williams, Thousand Oaks CA: Sage, 221–260.

Lam, R. W., & Levitan, R. D. (2000). Pathophysiology of seasonal affective disorder: A review. *Journal of Psychiatry and Neuroscience*, 25(5): 469–480.

Leather, P., Pyrgas, M., Beale, D., & Lawrence, C. (1998). Windows in the workplace: Sunlight, view, and occupational stress. *Environment and Behavior*, 30, 832–858.

Louv, R. (2008). *Last Child in the Woods: Saving Our Children from Nature-Deficit Disorder*. Chapel Hill, NC: Algonquin Books.

Louv, R. (2012). *The Nature Principle: Reconnecting with Life in a Virtual Age*. Chapel Hill, NC: Algonquin Books.

Louv, R. (1991). *Childhood's Future*. Boston: Houghton-Mifflin.

McNaughton-Cassill, M. E., & Smith., T. S. (2002). My world is OK, but yours is not: The optimism gap and stress. *Stress and Health*, 18, 1, 27–33.

Mehta, R., & Zhu, J. (2009). Blue or red? Exploring the effect of color on cognitive task performances. *Science*, 324, 5915.

Morey, D. F. (2006). Burying key evidence: The social bond between dogs and people. *Journal of Archaeological Science*, 33, 158–175.

Oberacher, L. (2002). Colour and light: Orientation and well-being in health care facilities. In *Proceedings of International Colour Association Meeting*. Color & Textiles, Maribor, Slovenia, pp. 48–55.

Rovee-Collier, C. (1999). The Development of Infant Memory. *Current Directions in Psychological Science*, 8(3), 80–85.

Seeman, T. E., Dubin, L. F., & Seeman, M. (2003). Religiosity/spirituality and health. *American Psychologist*, 58, (1), 51–63.

Stokes, M. A. (2009). Stranger danger: Child protection and parental fears in the risk society. *Amsterdam Social Science*, 1 (3), 6–24.

Ulrich, R. S. (1984). View through a window may influence recovery from surgery. *Science*, 27, 420–421.

van den Haak, P., van Lon, R., van der Meer, J., & Rothkrantz, L. (2010). Stress assessment of car drivers using EEG analysis, 11th International Conference on Computer Systems and Technologies, *Proceedings of the 11th International Conference on Computer Systems and Technologies*, pp. 473–477.

CHAPTER 6

DIET AND EXERCISE: RUNNING ON EMPTY?

KEY POINTS

- Throughout history, malnutrition was a bigger threat than obesity.
- Worry about weight is ubiquitous in Western countries.
- We still don't even know what a healthy weight is for a given person.

FEEDING FRENZY

Few topics engage the attention of Americans more on a daily basis than diet and exercise. In my Psychology and Health classes, I routinely ask students to select a health-related behavior they would like to work on changing during the course. Semester after semester, close to three quarters of the class select some variant of eating less, eating a more nutritious diet, or exercising more. And most strikingly, these choices are not limited by age, ethnicity, or even gender. During discussions, 20-year-old Caucasian females, 30-year-old Hispanic males, and 40-year-old African American women bond over their issues with food, weight, and activity.

Ironically, malnutrition was—and in many parts of the world, still is—a greater problem than obesity. In hunter-gatherer societies, food availability tended to cycle, leading to periods of feasting, which alternated with periods of famine. Among the poor, diseases such as scurvy, caused by the lack of vitamin C, and beriberi, caused by

A modern cafeteria (below) offers a wide variety of foods, regardless of season or location. Compare this with the typical diet of a stone age man (right). How has the convenience of food choices affected our current obesity epidemic?

thiamine deficiency, disrupted growth and development resulting in malformation and even death. Of course poor nutrition
also weakens the body and diminishes the efficiency of the
immune system, leaving people more susceptible to illness and
disease in general.

Of course, over the course of history, people's food options
were more limited even when it was available. In early human
society, diet was constrained by what was naturally available
in the area, effectively limiting the variety of foods available to
people. Substances such as salt and spices that could preserve
and enhance the taste of food were rare and expensive. Of
course, there were always a few people who were wealthy
enough to eat as much as they wanted, and paradoxically, obesity actually came to represent prosperity in some cultures. The
problem in today's world, of course, is that those of us living in
Western cultures rarely suffer from too little access to food, and
instead are surrounded by an amazing array of cheap, easy, and
enticing food choices.

Prior to World War II, many people in rural settings grew
and raised their own food, and only ate out when traveling. Although people in the cities had greater access to food
through stores and restaurants, choices were still limited by
the season, cost, and the difficulties of transporting fresh food.
With the advent of electricity, refrigeration, rail commerce,
and the interstate highway system, all of that changed rapidly.
Have you ever wondered why so many cities in the Southwest
had stockyards near the railroad tracks? In San Antonio, these
yards were used to corral cattle brought in from all over the state
prior to shipping them to Chicago and other northern cities to
be butchered. The cows were transported live to prolong their
freshness. Of course, now we have become accustomed to grocery stores featuring huge arrays of meat and produce, shipped
from all over the world by plane, train, and truck. In addition,
changes in food preparation and manufacturing have exponentially increased the variety of processed food we have available.
While many of us don't think twice about the floor-to-ceiling
shelves of cereal and chips in our local supermarket, they actually represent advance in food preparation and advertising that
weren't even dreamed of a hundred years ago.

Patterns in dining out have changed significantly as well.
While dining in restaurants in the past was primarily the
domain of the rich and those who were celebrating big events,
today it is simply another expression of our driven lifestyles.

Dining in Italy throughout history—a
thermopolium in Pompeii offered an early
version of fast food to diners (c. 79 A.D.),
travelers in the 1800s enjoyed meals at
osterias like this one in Rome painted by Carl
Heinrich Bloch (1866), and diners today
enjoy food at an outdoor café in Rome (2006).

Most surveys indicate that Americans eat out four to five times a week, with fast-food restaurants leading their choices. Such restaurants—characterized by rapid delivery, large portions relative to price, and a heavy emphasis on sugar, fat, and salt—have become a mainstay of many American families.

The appeal of the food we eat in drive-through and other restaurants is not an accident, either. Large chain restaurants conduct constant, ongoing research on recipes, portion sizes, and the efficacy of their advertising. By the time an entrée is listed on their menu, they already know it will be attractive to customers. Of the hundreds of ads we see a day, a large portion involves food and beverages, many specifically targeting children. Commercial and fast foods have even crept into public school cafeterias, raising concern about what we are feeding and teaching our children.

A BIG PROBLEM

Not surprisingly, many researchers have linked these changes in diet, dining, and advertising to rising rates of obesity in America. Obesity, in turn, has been associated with negative health effects, ranging from heart disease and diabetes to joint problems and asthma (Mokdad et al., 2001; Kulie et al., 2011). However, it turns out that the story is actually far more complex and involves not only food availability but genetic and biological factors, emotional and cultural components, and factors such as sleep and exercise. For example, the Pima Indians here in the United States have extremely high rates of diabetes, indicating that it is the interaction of their genetic makeup and modern life that contributes to the development of this disease. To complicate things further, there is significant disagreement about how best to measure obesity, what healthy weight guidelines should be, and how harmful obesity actually is to health (Gaesser, 2002). No wonder many of us throw our hands in the air and go eat some chips or a bowl of ice cream!

The debate regarding how much of our body weight is the direct result of our genetic makeup has raged for decades (Campos, 2004). Studies suggest that adopted children's weights resemble those of their biological parents rather than those who raised them, regardless of the eating habits seen in the adoptive families. In comparison to fraternal twins, identical twins are far more likely to share eating preferences and behaviors and even to require the same amount of stomach distension (fullness) to signal satiety.

Studies of Native American groups such as the Pima Indians also shed light on the genetic links to obesity (Knowler, Bennet, Hamman, & Miller, 1978). The Pima Indians, native to Arizona and Mexico, have very high rates of obesity and diabetes as well. Recent research suggests that as a result of several genes, these individuals have a heightened tendency to conserve energy, which is probably due to the fact that they survived for centuries in a harsh environment where food wasn't readily available throughout much of the year. When people with this sort of energy-conserving metabolism find themselves living in the food-rich modern environment, they are at high risk for obesity.

A series of studies conducted by Ancel Keys and his colleagues after World War II (Keys, Brozek, Henschel, Mickelsen, & Taylor, 1950) addressed the biology of obesity as well. Using conscientious objectors who volunteered to participate in research in place of military service, they put normal weight young men on diets designed to reduce their weight by 25 percent. Initially, the men lost weight quickly, but over the three months of the study they had to keep reducing their caloric intake in order to continue losing weight. Over the course of the study, they also became irritable, angry, and food obsessed and even started to avoid physical activity and to neglect personal hygiene. At the end of the study, the men went on a diet to regain the weight, with many of them actually reaching a new weight slightly higher than their original.

In another series of studies, prisoners in a Vermont prison volunteered to gain 20–30 pounds by increasing their food intake and decreasing their exercise levels (Salans, Horton, & Sims, 1971). Interestingly, no matter how hard they tried, not all of the men were able to reach their target weights. One individual was unable to gain the weight despite consuming 10,000 calories a day. At the end of the study, most of the prisoners were able to return to their original weight, although the rates at which this happened varied. The two who had the most difficulty losing the weight came from families with a history of obesity. It turns out that age, gender, fitness level, and current weight all impact how efficiently your body processes and stores the nutrients you eat. Recent studies even indicate that the types of bacteria found in an individual's gut are a factor in how they digest and absorb food.

So how does our body maintain and regulate body weight? As we all know, food consumption starts in the mouth, where enzymes in the saliva begin to break down food. In the meantime, the taste buds on our tongues detect and send signals to the brain regarding the types of food we are eating (Beckman, 2004). It turns out that we have five types of taste receptors: sweet, sour, salty, and bitter, with a fifth receptor that detects cheese/meat, named after the Japanese word umami. Because of these receptors, humans—who are omnivores—can balance their food intake across a variety of categories and avoid foodstuffs that might be unripe, spoiled, or poisonous. As a result of a specific process called conditioned taste aversion, we are particularly wired to avoid foods that have previously made us ill (Reilly & Schachtman, 2008). Ironically, sometimes this conditioned aversion occurs even when we know the food itself wasn't responsible for our illness. For example, pregnant women, as well as people who suffer from car or sea sickness, may learn to avoid foods they ate before they got ill, even when they knew the food was not responsible for the nausea.

Of course, the taste of food also contributes to its reinforcing properties. It is no accident that fast food is often either sweet or salty. So how does the brain figure that out, and how does it respond to what we eat? After leaving the mouth, food travels down the esophagus to the stomach, where it is broken down by acids and enzymes. The stomach also conveys messages to the brain regarding the stretching of the stomach walls and even the nutrient content of food. The small intestine (duodenum) absorbs nutrients from the food and also releases hormonal signals such as cholecystokinin (CCK) that limits eating. Once food is broken down, it is typically released into the bloodstream in the form of glucose, a key sugar. Both the body and the brain use glucose, which is converted into glycogen in the liver and fat in fat cells, as a means of storing excess energy. When blood glucose levels fall, these stored reserves can be accessed. These processes are controlled by two hormones, insulin, and glucagon, released from the pancreas. The cells in the body require insulin in order to use glucose. So, when blood glucose levels are high, insulin is released, allowing cells to use the energy. As insulin levels increase, appetite decreases. As blood glucose levels fall, insulin drops, cells aren't getting as much energy, and hunger increases. At that point, glucagon triggers the conversion of some of the stored glycogen back to glucose for the body's use. When this system is disrupted, the results are dire.

In Type 1 diabetes, the so-called childhood diabetes, the pancreas stops making insulin, which means the body is unable to use or store glucose. Although patients can take medications or injections to replace their natural insulin, it is difficult to fine tune the system. Consequently, many diabetics experience serious heart, kidney, neurological, and eye problems. Type 2 diabetes typically occurs in adults and is caused by an insensitivity to insulin, rather than its absence (Ahmad & Crandall, 2010). It can be treated with insulin as well, but often responds well to weight loss and increased exercise. Cleverly, cells in the brain do not require insulin to use glucose, meaning that glucose in the blood is available to the brain on a constant basis, which is crucial to survival, of course.

The issue of how and when we stop eating is still only part of the process. How does your body regulate weight over the long run? It appears that we also have a complex biological mechanism for regulating our weight (Geary, 2004). The fat cells of our body produce a peptide called leptin that signals the brain to eat less, and become more active. Another chemical signal, called ghrelin, released from the stomach when food is not present, appears to trigger a series of signals that result in hunger. Strains of mice that lack the genes necessary to make leptin end up gaining huge amounts of weight. Although a few humans have a similar disorder, in most humans taking leptin does not actually decrease their appetite or weight gain. However, many obese individuals have high levels of leptin, suggesting they might be insensitive to its effects (Klok, Jakobsdottir, & Drent, 2007).

MAYBE ALL OF OUR HEADS ARE FAT

Naturally, the coordination of all of these functions ultimately resides in the brain in a structure called the hypothalamus (Blevins & Baskins, 2005). In terms of food, the arcuate nucleus, a tiny subsection of the hypothalamus, receives both hunger and satiety signals, some of which are based on taste sensations. The lateral hypothalamus has been implicated in eating, and the paraventricular nucleus is thought to inhibit lateral hypothalamic eating signals. Yet another structure, the ventromedial hypothalamic area, is involved in meal frequency, weight gain, and insulin release. Clearly, regulating hunger, satiety, and body weight is a complex process (Broburger, 2005). Rather than rely on a single control system, the brain and body frequently utilize disparate mechanisms to ensure redundancy in the case of malfunctions. But the next time that someone tells you that weight control is merely a matter of limiting your caloric intake, feel free to laugh and tell them that we could only wish it were that simple!

As if the biology of food intake wasn't complex enough, our eating patterns are also subject to a variety of emotional, social, and cultural influences. Because food is a basic, primary reinforcer, eating is a soothing, comforting activity. Sucking is immediately calming to infants, even if they are sucking on their own thumb. The taste of sweet, fat, and salty foods also seems to be inherently satisfying, as evidenced by the fact we don't have to teach children to appreciate them—they do it automatically. It's a rare parent who doesn't occasionally offer their child a cookie or candy as a reward, and many of us continue to self-medicate with food when we are upset. Often, we turn to the same specific foods when stressed because we associate them with happier times. These "comfort foods" might be things our mothers made when we were sick, foods that remind us of happy people or places, or foods that we particularly savor. In my family, potatoes were a staple of every meal (influenced perhaps by the number of Irish ancestors in our family tree). Baked, boiled, fried, mashed, I like them all and to this day turn to mashed potatoes and gravy or a baked potato with butter when under duress. My husband, who is Japanese American, feels the same affinity for rice, and many of my Hispanic students in San Antonio report they are comforted by tortillas. Clearly, the food we are exposed to as children will take on meaning for

The Peasant Wedding by Pieter Brueghel the Elder (1526/1530–1569).

us as adults. Of course, this learning can go both ways, as adults who detest oatmeal—or broccoli or brussels sprouts or other things they were forced to eat as a child—will attest!

But eating is also a social custom. For thousands of years, food has been used to mark important dates and events in the life of a community. From weddings and funerals to feasts, religious ceremonies, and entertainment events, food often plays a central role. Frequently, the ritualistic manner in which food is prepared and the specific dishes served for an occasion are very symbolic. Even simple routines like making the same sorts of cookies for Christmas or eating popcorn at the movies lend continuity to our activities. Not surprisingly, food has also become a commercial enterprise, celebrated not just in ads and restaurants, but in magazines, cookbooks, and even television shows. The ease of purchasing prepared food and the size of restaurant portions also contribute to the tendency to eat too much. Simply having access to recipes and ingredients for dishes from around the world is actually an artifact of modern life that in the past was reserved only for the very rich. Nursery rhymes, often dating back hundreds of years, often talked about food such as "pease porridge hot, pease porridge cold, pease porridge in the pot, nine days old," and "patty cake, patty cake, baker's man, bake me a cake as fast as you can," indicating that a focus on food is certainly not a modern phenomenon.

However, the availability of so much food is a modern-day problem. Studies show over and over that both humans and animals will tire of a particular food but start eating again when offered something different. How many times have you declared yourself full when eating chips, only to turn around and eat a cookie when it is offered. Rats given access to a "supermarket diet," including cheese, salami, chocolate, condensed milk, and peanut butter, eat until they are very obese. Some research now suggests that diets high in fat and sugar actually disrupt satiety signals in the brain.

Ironically, another factor that contributes to increased eating is time of day. A number of studies have shown that people will eat because they think it is lunch or dinner time even if they aren't hungry, and that this will occur even when they are tricked into thinking it is earlier or later than it actually is. This has led to the theory that due to our time obsessions and highly scheduled days, we are losing contact with our physiological hunger and satiety cues, and so often eat more than we need to do. Our time-related sleep deficits may also matter. In recent years, it has been shown that sleep deprivation and weight gain are actually related (Patel, Malhotra, White, Gottlieb, & Hu, 2006). Apparently, as far as the body is concerned, lack of sleep triggers an increase in hunger, food storage, and weight gain. People who sleep less than five hours a night are almost twice as likely to develop Type II diabetes as those who sleep seven or more hours.

WHAT SHOULD WE WEIGH?

Given how much we know about why we eat, it would seem that defining the ideal weight for an individual would be fairly straightforward. However, this has not proven to be the case. According to Dr. Glenn Gaesser (2002), a professor of exercise physiology at the University of Virginia, the first formal attempts to quantify ideal or desirable weights began in the 1940s when a researcher at the Metropolitan Life Insurance Company tried to correlate body weight with health status. Based on initial analysis, it looked as though lower body weights were very predictive of good health. The problem with this conclusion, however, was the fact that it did not adequately control for age. Not surprisingly, people in their twenties had both the lowest body weights and best health. But this doesn't prove that the lower body weight was the reason for good health. In fact, the truth is that the variations in health were largely related to age, not weight. Ironically, when later studies actually charted health and weight in the same people over time, it turns out that the best mortality rates actually occur at higher rates than the traditional tables suggest, especially as people age.

Another means of measuring body makeup is the body mass index (BMI), calculated by measuring body weight in kilograms and dividing that number by height in meters squared. Using these standards, people's weight can be classified as desirable, under- or overweight, and obese. However, the actual numbers assigned to these cut-offs are under debate. Since BMI does not factor in age, gender, or ethnicity, many people have argued that it fails to accurately reflect a person's actual body weight status, especially among people who are very short, very tall, or very muscular. Even more confusing is the fact that in 1999, the BMI guidelines were changed such that people who weren't overweight the day before suddenly were.

**A painting of ballerinas by Edgar Degas (1834–1917).
What is the ideal body type and weight?**

Of course, changes in the desirability of a certain weight are not new either. If you were to go to an art museum and walk around with an eye to figuring out which sorts of body types were in vogue at any given time or place in history, you would quickly realize that the ideal body weight is a moving target (Haughton, 2004). From Botticelli's lush portrayals of Renaissance women to Degas's ballerinas, it is clear that the form society valued most was not a look that most women possessed the genetic or monetary means to attain. In today's world, that translates into female models and actresses who are far taller and thinner than the average American and who often maintain that look through extreme dieting, exercising and smoking—all practices that can end up hurting their health in the long run. Nevertheless, awash in a world of movies, television, and advertising, most of us have internalized these images and come to think of being thin as a mark of attractiveness, success, and good health. Although research in this area indicates that girls and women are most susceptible to the negative effects of the media on body images (Grabe, Ward, & Hyde, 2008), recent work indicates that boys and men are increasingly experiencing similar dissatisfaction in regard to the onslaught of all the heavily muscled models with 6-pack abs they see (Olivardia, Harrison, Borowiecki, & Cohane, 2004; Mazur, 1986).

Furthermore, research indicates that even Miss America winners and Playboy centerfolds have gotten thinner over time, while the average weights of Americans have risen (Garner, Garfinkel, Schwartz, & Thompson, 1980; Spitzer, Henderson, & Zivian, 1999). This is ironic given the number of beauty, diet, exercise, and clothing companies that are based on selling us products or services guaranteed to help us achieve these unrealistic looks! Gaesser actually argues that worrying about weight and subsequent efforts to lose weight by dieting set up patterns of weight loss and gain (the so called yo-yo effect), which make it harder to maintain lower weights because the body compensates for the diet (or fasting periods) by becoming more metabolically efficient. He also sites work that indicates that weight fluctuations are actually harder on the health than remaining at a steady, but moderately overweight, point.

This is not to say that the negative health effects of being overweight are negligible. People who are overweight are at risk for poor health outcomes, including Type II diabetes, the development of cancer and heart disease, gall bladder problems, and exacerbated joint pain (Ahmad & Crandall, 2010; Manson et al., 1990). The body dissatisfaction that comes with not feeling attractive, not believing that you meet the ideals of your culture, or experiencing negative or hostile responses to your weight can also contribute to low self-esteem, embarrassment, anger, anxiety, depression and controversy. Witness the floods of media coverage and commentary generated whenever there is a high-profile story about someone being denied an airline seat or a job.

Of course, the medical and weight loss industry has also invested a great deal of energy into arguing that a calorie is a calorie—thus, in order to lose weight, you simply have to eat less. However, as most dieters know, it is not that simple. Studies on the thermodynamics of burning calories, the content and type of food being consumed, the gene expression of the individual, and even the biology of the bacteria in your gut and your hormone levels indicate that for some people gaining or losing weight is easier than for others. This is not to say that we should all just give up. Decreasing the amount of fat and processed foods we eat and increasing fruit and fiber can have a significant positive impact on health (Ballantyne, 2009). However, dieting is not a benign practice. Studies repeatedly indicate that dieting is associated with stress and depression, and that a common response to such emotions is to seek comfort foods. When people do violate the diet by overeating, they experience guilt, setting up a frustrating, negative, emotional cycle. Clearly, dieting is neither simple nor easy.

YOU CAN BE TOO THIN

Unfortunately, some people choose to cope with weight issues by taking extreme steps. Binge eating, bulimic behaviors, and anorexia have received significant attention in recent years, amid claims that such disordered eating patterns are on the rise. Certainly, overeating and then using laxatives or making yourself throw up to avoid gaining weight may seem attractive in the short run. Among teens and college students, seeing someone else binge and purge is often the first step to developing your own eating disorder. However, the constant disruption caused to your gastrointestinal system by these methods eventually takes its toll. Constipation and damage to the throat, esophagus, and teeth have all been associated with bulimic behavior.

Anorexia, characterized by voluntary starvation and/or excess exercise, is actually one of the most dangerous psychological disorders (Kaye, Klump, Frank, & Strober, 2000). Anorexics who typically restrict their body weight to 85 percent or less of the weight expected for their height, experience skin, nail, and hair problems, digestive distress, a reduction or cessation of the menstrual cycle and reproductive abilities, osteoporosis, and heart difficulties, which can be fatal. The treatment for anorexia, enforced eating coupled with cognitive-behavioral and psychosocial support techniques, is often stymied by the patient's refusal to acknowledge that they are too thin and that their behaviors are harming their health. Although young women are at higher risk for anorexia, it does occur in men as well, and rates have been on the rise.

To be sure, eating disorders are not the only extreme steps people are willing to take for appearance. Plastic surgery, artificial tanning, tattoos, piercings, and using steroids to enhance fitness have all become staples of modern life, despite their mixed success record. Clearly, in the modern, media-driven world, comparing ourselves to others makes it difficult to be comfortable with how we look, and some of us are willing to risk our health and well-being to try to live up to those models.

THE FIT-OR-FAT CONTROVERSY

Ironically, thinness isn't even necessarily a sign of health. Recent studies suggest that much of the research on obesity and health has confounded fatness and fitness (Gaesser, 2002; Stevens, Evenson, Thomas, Cai, & Thomas, 2004). In reality, people who are active physically typically have better health as measured by blood pressure, cholesterol, and triglyceride levels, reduced heart disease, better respiratory function, stronger bones, stronger muscles, less dangerous falls, decreased stress, depression, and anxiety—even if they are actually overweight. The fact that people who are overweight are less likely to exercise confuses the picture, but as a general rule it is better to be fit and overweight than thin and sedentary.

The key, then, becomes figuring out why people find it so hard to exercise on a regular basis. In part, this is due to the fact that our daily lives no longer demand routine exercise in the form of walking, gardening, cleaning, and generally being active. Instead of having to be active to survive, we often struggle to find time to work exercise into our daily routines and may find it inconvenient to take time out from work and our daily lives to run, swim, dance, or ride our bikes.

Furthermore, it can be hard to stay motivated to pursue strenuous routine exercise when the goal is long-term health, as gains in fitness and appearance are not obvious in the short run. Fortunately, there are solutions to this conundrum. One is to incorporate more routine exercise in our daily schedules. Parking at the back of a parking lot, taking the stairs, sweeping floors, gardening, and other day-to-day activities can have a beneficial impact on fitness. Studies comparing the health of people who exercise for 30 minutes a day in three ten-minute increments of routine activity to the 30–40 minutes of aerobic exercise many of us have come to associate with adequate exercise suggest that even the less-rigorous activity regime increases fitness and health (Schmidt, Biwer, & Kalscheuer, 2011).

Another approach is to go back to the role of exercise in childhood. As kids, exercise is more likely to be a means to an end. We run, play, and dance for the fun of it. As we get older and pursue sports, we may condition and train, but our goal is to excel in our chosen sports or activities, not simply to stay fit. However,

as we get older, our opportunities to play and exercise for fun diminish. This occurs partly because we have less time, but it is also the case that in many sports the opportunity to compete diminishes as we get older.

If you like to play tennis or golf or to run, swim, or bike, you may still be able to compete in your sport in your age group. But if you were a gymnast or an ice skater or loved dodgeball, football, volleyball, or other team sports, you may have to search for venues in which to play after you leave high school or college. In our culture of youth, there is also a tendency to feel that if you didn't start a sport as a youngster you will never be good or that if you were good at the sport when you were younger, it would be too frustrating to watch your skills diminish. The truth, however, is that there is satisfaction in performing physically at any level. As you age, you may not be able to do all the things you did when you were younger, but with advances in technology, ranging from high-performance running shoes to enhanced training machines, some skills are easier to acquire. If you must compare yourself to others, it can help to compare your skills to those of other people your age or to take up a sport you have never done before, so that the progress you make is measured against your current—not your past—self. As an added benefit, exercise even appears to enhance brain function (Cotman & Engesser, 2002).

In short, many aspects of modern life make it difficult for people to maintain the body weight and levels of fitness they would like (Langhans & Geary, 2010). Constant access to enticing food, diminished opportunities for exercise, time pressure, and even sleep deprivation play a role. Certainly, most of us do not want to go back to our pretechnological levels of physical activity. But perhaps focusing on increasing fitness regardless of weight, finding ways to exercise more the way we did when we were younger, and being more cognizant of the impact of unrealistic media images on our self-esteem can enable us to find ways to be happier in the bodies we have. If that, in turn, enables us to spend more energy taking care of those bodies, rather than spending so much of our psychological energy wishing for something different, so much the better.

WHAT DO YOU THINK?

1. How many times have you started or planned to start a diet and then not followed through? Why did you quit?
2. Would you be happy at a weight that was healthy for you even if it did not match your appearance ideal?
3. Do you believe it is possible to be fit and still fat?

REFERENCES

Ahmad, L. A., & Crandall, J. P. (2010). Type 2 Diabetes Prevention: A Review. *Clinical Diabetes*, 28: 53–59.

Ballantyne, C. (2009). Weight-loss winner: A diet high in fiber, low in calories. *ScientificAmerican.com*

Beckman, Mary. (August 2004). A Matter of Taste. *Smithsonian*, 35(5), 24, 26.

Blevins, J. E., & Baskin, D. G. (2000). Hypothalamic-brainstem circuits controlling eating. In Devlin, M. J., Yanovski, S. Z., & Wilson, G. T. (2000). Obesity: What mental health professionals need to know. *American Journal of Psychiatry*, 157, 854–866.

Broberger, C. (2005). Brain regulation of food intake and appetite: Molecules and networks. *Journal of Internal Medicine*, 258: 301–327.

Campos, P. (2004). *The Obesity Myth: Why America's Obsession with Weight Is Hazardous to Your Health*. Reed Elsevier.

Cotman, C. W., & Engesser-Cesar, C. (2002). Exercise enhances and protects brain function. *Exerc Sport Sci Rev*, 30(2), 75–79.

Gaesser, G. (2002). *Big Fat Lies*. Carlsbad CA: Gurze Books; First Trade Paper Edition.

Garner, D. M., Garfinkel, P., Schwartz, D., & Thompson, M. (1980). Cultural expectations of thinness in women. *Psychological Reports* 47:484–491.

Geary, N. (2004). Endocrine controls of eating: CCK, leptin, and ghrelin. *Physiology & Behavior 81*, 719–733.

Grabe, S., Ward, L. M., & Hyde, J. S. (2008). The role of the media in body image concerns among women: A meta-analysis of experimental and correlational studies. *Psychological Bulletin*, 134(4), 460–476.

Haughton, N. (2004). Perceptions of beauty in Renaissance art. *Journal of Cosmetic Dermatology*, 3, 229–233.

Kaye, W. H., Klump, K. L., Frank, G. K. W., & Strober, M. (2000). Anorexia and Bulimia Nervosa. *Annual Review of Medicine* 51, 299–313.

Keys, A., Brozek, J., Henschel, A., Mickelsen, O., & Taylor, H. (1950). *The Biology of Human Starvation*. Minneapolis: University of Minnesota Press.

Klok, M. D., Jakobsdottir, D. S., & Drent, M. L.(2007). The role of leptin and ghrelin in the regulation of food intake and body weight in humans: A review. *Obesity Reviews, 8*, 21–34.

Knowler, W. C., Bennet, P. H., Hamman, R. F., & Miller, M. (1978). Diabetes incidence and prevalence in Pima Indians: A 19-Fold greater incidence than in Rochester, Minnesota. *American Journal of Epidemiology, 108* (6), 497–505.

Kulie, T., Slattengren, A., Redmer, J., Counts, H., Eglash, A., & Schrager, S. (2011). Obesity and women's health: An evidence-based review. *J Am Board Fam Med.* Jan–Feb; 24 (1): 75–85.

Langhans, W., & Geary, N. (Eds.), (2010). Frontiers in Eating and Weight Regulation. *Forum Nutr. Basel*, Karger, 63, 133–140.

Manson, J. E., Colditz, G. A., Stampfer, M. J., Willett, W. C., Rosner, B., Monson, R. R., Speizer, F. E., & Henekens, C. H. 1990). A Prospective Study of Obesity and Risk of Coronary Heart Disease in Women. *New England Journal of Medicine*, 322: 882–889.

Mazur, A. (1986). U.S. trends in feminine beauty and overadaptation. *The Journal of Sex Research, 22*, 3, 281–303.

Mokdad, A. H., Ford, E. S., Bowman, B. A, Dietz, W. H., Vinicor, F., Bales, V. B., & Marks, J. S. (2001). Prevalence of Obesity, Diabetes, and Obesity-Related Health Risk Factors. *JAMA*, 289(1), 76–79.

Olivardia, R., Harrison, G. P., Borowiecki, J. J., & Cohane, G. H. (2004). Biceps and body image: The relationships between muscularity and self-esteem, depression, and eating disorder symptoms. *Psychology of Men & Masculinity*, 5, (2), 112–120.

Patel, S. J., Malhotra, A., White, D. P., Gottlieb, D. J., & Hu, F. B. (2006) Association between reduced sleep and weight gain in women. *American Journal of Epidemiology, 163*, (10) 947–954.

Reilly, S., & Schachtman, T. R. (2008). *Conditioned Taste Aversion: Neural and Behavioral Processes*. Oxford University Press.

Salans, L. B., Horton, E. S., & Sims, E. A. H. (1971), Experimental Obesity in Man: Cellular Character of the Adipose Tissue. *Journal of Clinical Investigation, 50*, 1005.

Schmidt, W.D., Biwer, C.J. & Kalscheuer, L.K. (2001). Effects of Long *versus* Short Bout Exercise on Fitness and Weight Loss in Overweight Females. Am Coll Nutr, 20 (5), 494-501.

Spitzer, B., Henderson, K., & Zivian, M. (1999). A comparison of population and media body sizes for American and Canadian Women. *Sex Roles.* 700 (7/8): 545–565.

Stevens, J., Evenson, K. R., Thomas, O., Cai, J., & Thomas, R. (2004). Associations of fitness and fatness with mortality in Russian and American men in the lipids research clinics study. *International Journal of Obesity*, 28, 1463–1470.

CHAPTER 7
SOCIAL SUPPORT: ARE YOU SUPPORTED BY A NETWORK OR CAUGHT IN A WEB?

KEY POINTS

+ Social support is necessary for human survival and well-being.
+ The components of effective social support vary across individuals and by gender.
+ Changing gender roles and marital norms have disrupted many traditional sources of social support.

SOCIAL SURVIVAL

One of the most complex concepts in psychology is social support. Infants automatically orient toward faces, probably because bonding with caregivers is essential for their survival (Simion, Valeza, Umilta, & Barba, 1998). Children raised in extreme conditions often exhibit life-long social difficulties. For example, many of the children adopted from Eastern European orphanages have difficulty bonding with subsequent caregivers; in other cases, they are indiscriminate about whom they interact with, whether it is a long-term caregiver or a stranger. When very young children are separated from their mother or caregiver, they may withdraw from others, show disruptions in sleep and eating, and even alterations in motor behavior. This syndrome, called anaclitic depression, is reversible, but only if the mother returns or another supportive caregiver steps in.

Certainly, animals also rely heavily on social support for both physical and mental functioning. Prey animals often live in herds or groups and may have complex social mechanisms for posting lookouts, warning each other of danger, and protecting young. Most of us have seen *National Geographic* specials showing zebras, antelopes, or prairie dogs posting guards so the rest of the group could sleep or eat. Although not all predatory animals hunt in packs, certainly some, including lions and wolves, do so, and animal species ranging from elephants to chimpanzees combine efforts to care for their young. Social interactions in the form of grooming, licking, and removing lice and bugs are also key markers of status in many animal groups and can indicate bonding, acceptance, and hierarchy status. Researcher Harry Harlow (Harlow, Dodsworth, & Harlow, 1965) also demonstrated that small chimps deprived of a live mother showed a preference for a soft mannequin rather than a wire one, but still failed to develop normal social behaviors.

Clearly, social interactions are necessary for normal development. However, this is not surprising if you take into account the fact that learning to read and respond to other people's expressions may make the difference between surviving and dying. Successful mothers have to know whether their baby's expressions and cries indicate minor discomfort or are a sign of a serious illness or problem. From early childhood, we need to recognize threatening facial expressions so we can protect ourselves. It is no surprise that we tend to feel uneasy around people who don't show much facial expression, either because they are schooled in hiding their feelings or because of a facial injury or motor disorders that can disrupt the ability to smile, frown, squint, etc. When playing sports or games like poker, being able to deceive your opponent can give you an edge. Some research even suggests that those individuals who frequently make errors in judgments about others' expressions are more likely to be bullied (McKown, Gumbiner, Russo, & Lipton, 2009).

EMOTIONAL INTELLIGENCE

Studies in the field known as emotional intelligence suggest that being able to recognize your own feelings, as well as those of others, and learning how to convey your needs and to meet theirs is crucial for success—not just in intimate relations between your family and friends, but for professional success (Goleman, 2006; Mayer & Salovey, 1997; Grewal & Salovey, 2005). Those people who are good at social interactions rise higher in organizations and are more successful in their work than those who have the same education or job skills, but are less socially skilled. Research on the detection of emotions suggests that across cultures, humans tend to judge the same expressions as friendly, happy, sad, or mad. Researchers have failed to find any cultures where a smile indicates unhappiness and a frown pleasure.

Assuredly, technology has not always helped us in our quest to communicate effectively. People have long known that conversations on the telephone are hampered by our inability to read each other's nonverbal signals. When talking in person, we pay close attention to how people stand, where they are looking, and what they are doing with their hands and faces (Manusov & Patterson, 2006). In fact, research has repeatedly shown that if the things a person says and the tone of voice and body language they use when they say it don't match, we will trust the nonverbal cues. Just remember the last time someone crossed their arms and scowled at you while saying, "I AM NOT MAD AT YOU" to see what I mean. When we cannot see these clues, it is easy to misunderstand the speaker's intent, with the result that we mistake a joke for sarcasm, or to fail to recognize a plea for support, or an attempt at self-deprecation. Online or in texts, some of the same problems occur. Despite the development of smiley face emoticons, it can still be difficult to know what someone else is trying to convey. In fact, to avoid that, many of us find ourselves adding comments in parentheses like NOT and LOL to make sure the person we are communicating with gets our drift.

Cognitive science researcher Donald Norman has written extensively about how humans interact with technology and machinery and how these interfaces can be extremely frustrating. In his book *Turn Signals Are the Facial Expressions of Automobiles* (1993), he talks about the fact that at least some of the frustration and rage we experience when driving stems from how difficult it is to judge the intentions and motives of other drivers, since we can't see their body language. Although we can use turn signals and brake lights to signal our next move, we may not always do this reliably, and it still does not give those around us a sense of what we are doing. Isn't it true that you are much more likely to be tolerant of someone who slows down or turns in front of you if you know that they are lost, than if you think they are doing it as a power play against you? Have you ever found your anger diminishing if another driver waves in apology after cutting you off? However, in the absence of words, shrugs, smiles, and other ways in which we convey our intentions to others when we deal with them face to face, it is easier to assume that the other driver's motivations are negative and to respond negatively as a result.

THE SOCIAL BRAIN

So, how and why are we wired to need social support? What happens if your brain is not good at recognizing or managing emotions? Over the past 20 years, advances in the ways in which we study the brain have revealed some interesting things. As mentioned earlier, the limbic system, located below the forebrain, seems to play a key role in generating emotions in response to incoming input from the thalamus and the cortex. Increased limbic system activity has been linked to emotions ranging from love and empathy to anger and disgust. Structures called the amygdala and the insula seem to play key roles, although the specific mechanisms of how these areas generate emotions are still under study.

The discovery in the 1990s of mirror neurons may be a key to these explorations (Rizzolatti, Fogassi, & Gallese, 2006). Mirror neurons, found in the cortex of the brain, fire when we enact goal-directed motor activity like picking up a pencil or throwing a ball. What makes them interesting from a social point of view is that they also fire when we watch someone else perform a motor act. It has been hypothesized that it is mirror neurons that enable us to learn by imitation—which, of course, begins with babies responding to their parents and continues across the life span as we attempt to learn to walk, drive, hit a golf ball, or make a quilt—by watching someone else do it first. But in addition to simply echoing that movement in isolation, mirror neurons also seem to help us understand the intent or emotion behind the action. Pictures of brain activity made with

functional magnetic resonance imagery or (fMRI) scans suggest that inhaling a bad smell or seeing an expression of disgust on someone else's face activates the same mirror neurons in the insula of the cortex. In short, we can literally feel someone else's disgust or pain or joy, thanks to motor neurons. To carry the story even further, research in a number of labs suggests that disorders such as autism, in which individuals seem to lack the ability to recognize, respond, or empathize with other people's emotions, are characterized by dysfunctions in their mirror neuron systems. While it is sometimes possible to teach autistic children to recognize the behavioral expressions of emotions on

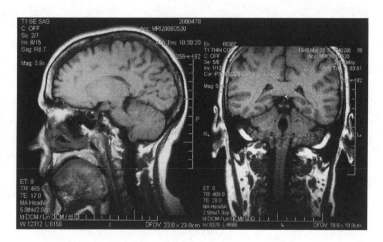

An MRI scan of the brain and head.

others' faces (mean, smiles, frowns, etc.) they do not seem to have the ability to do this spontaneously. In a way, it may turn out to be the case that autistic individuals are deaf to emotional cues, in much the same way that deaf individuals cannot pick up and process auditory signals (Piggott et al., 2004). In both cases, learning to cope successfully with other people may require the development of alternative ways to communicate each other's needs and responses.

Another type of neuron, called a von Economo neuron after the Vienna researcher who first identified it in 1881, has also been implicated in the experience of socially related emotion (Allman et al., 2010). These neurons are much larger than most other neurons and are found only in the anterior cingulate cortex and the frontal insula of the brain. Structurally, they are long and thin and have only one dendrite at each end. This means they look significantly different from other neurons, which have a long axon on one side and a number of dendrite branches on the other. So far, these neurons have been found only in humans, great ape species, and in elephants and whales; all have large brains and live in complex social groups. Consequently, it is suspected that these neurons, which carry signals very rapidly, play a role in generating social emotions, including love, trust, guilt, embarrassment, and even humor. In short, they seem to enable us to monitor our own feelings, and to recognize the feelings of others, by allowing us to interpret emotionally charged situations rapidly. Elephants even share child care and appear to mourn the loss of group members. Primates and humans recognize themselves in a mirror (which most other animals, including very young humans, can't do), interact in complex social hierarchies, groom and care for their young for years, and communicate with each other about emotions and threats in ways that promote the survival of the individual and the group. In fact, a human neurodegenerative disease called frontotemporal dementia, characterized by the loss of social understanding and erratic emotional resources, is also accompanied by the loss of about 70 percent of the von Economo neurons in patients (Seeley et al., 2006). While there is clearly still a great deal to learn about the ways in which such cells work, it does not appear to be a stretch to argue that social support is such a crucial aspect of human functioning that our brains are literally wired to promote and facilitate our social and emotional interactions.

DO YOU REALLY LIVE LONGER IF YOU HAVE FRIENDS?

Research on health and psychological well-being also indicates that the relationship between social support and health is complex, but that social contacts definitely impact our overall health and well-being (Roy, 2011; DeSilva, McKenzie, Harpham, & Huttley, 2005; Gallo, Troxel, Mathews, & Kuller, 2003). The Alameda County study conducted in 1979 found that low levels of social support were correlated with higher death rates (Houseman & Dorman, 2005). Subsequent research has shown that marriage in general is predictive of good health, but that men benefit more than women from being married. Other studies suggest that for women their degree of satisfaction with the relationship is crucial, such that only women who report that they are very satisfied with their marriage show significant health benefits (Antonucci & Akiyama, 1987).

The question of whether social support can buffer or somehow moderate the effects of stress is relevant. Although numerous studies suggest that the lack of social support may contribute to higher levels of stress and depression, it is also possible that people who are very stressed or depressed actually drive away sources of support, as people get frustrated trying to help them. In some cases, social support can also have a negative impact. If you are trying to quit drinking or smoking and many of your friends are still using, they may actually interfere with your efforts to change. Certainly, teens often run the risk of associating with friends who introduce them to self-defeating habits such as drug use, or skipping school, while those who associate with friends who are active in church, athletics, or their education are much less likely to fall into such habits.

A number of cultural factors also contribute to our perceptions and responses to social support. In his book *Stress, Culture, and Community* (2004), Dr. Stevan Hobfoll distinguishes between communal cultures and their emphasis on interdependence and individualistic cultures that emphasize the accomplishments of the individual. Communal values, which often characterize Asian cultures and have also been seen as key to understanding many Hispanic, American Indian, and even Jewish commune groups, emphasize placing the needs of the group over your own. In such a community, personal success and acclaim—especially if they require ignoring the needs of others—are not sought after or rewarded. Self-sacrifice and taking care of others is reinforced instead. An emphasis on independence, on the other hand, has characterized many western European and North American cultures. In the United States, we tend to venerate individual accomplishments, often above all else.

As a faculty member at a university that is over 50 percent minority, I sometimes see how this plays out in real life. When I was a student, my parents emphasized school performance above all else. If that meant missing family activities to study, holding back sad news until after I had taken a final, or moving to another state to excel, they were all for it.

However, the messages many of my Hispanic students receive from their families differ. I have seen good students drop out of school to work to support their families, miss finals to attend family events, and even consider not taking scholarships to attend graduate or medical school in another state, because of the value they place on family unity. Given that there are pros and cons to both approaches, the question is not so much whether one approach is better than the other, but rather, whether the social support you receive matches what you expect. When discrepancies occur between these two  things, it causes rifts in friendships, marriages, and families. While such differences in perception certainly can and do occur between people who hold the same cultural values, the problem is exacerbated when people of different backgrounds fail to recognize or acknowledge how they differ in terms of social expectations.

Somewhat surprisingly, college students tend to report relatively high levels of stress and depression. In an increasingly complex economy, many students find themselves in distress. Trying to balance the demands of academia with financial and personal concerns can take its toll (Chang, 2006; Friedlander, Reid, Shupak, & Cribbie, 2007). Certainly, social connections can provide both the emotional and instrumental support necessary to manage these stressors.

WHAT MAKES SOCIAL SUPPORT SUPPORTIVE?

Given that from birth, social support seems to be crucial to survival for humans, it is somewhat surprising that it has been so difficult for us to define what it actually is. Early researchers in the field recognized that there are multiple aspects of social support. In some situations, it can take the form of physical security or protection. Certainly, phrases like, "I've got your back" and "birds of a feather flock together" imply it has long been recognized that there is strength in numbers. Social support may also include material or instrumental support. When we are sick or ill, we may need other people to bring us food or to take us to the doctor. If we are short of money or stranded in our car, having someone lend us money or pick us up can make a huge difference.

To be sure, there are certainly other key aspects of social support. When you are upset, you may not need someone to do something for you physically, but you may want them to listen to you, to help you make a decision, or to calm you down. Sometimes you might also want their advice, especially if you are facing a situation with which they have more experience. Just about all of us who have children have called our parents, friends, or physicians to try to figure out if our child's behavior or symptom was something normal or something we should worry about.

Psychologists Carolyn Cutrona and Daniel Russell (1987) have argued that there are actually six components of social support. The first is guidance, defined as the provision of information or guidance—for instance, asking a friend how they like the gym they belong to before joining. The second is reliable alliance, or the assurance that others can be counted on for help. An example would be knowing someone could lend you money or drive you to the doctor if you are desperate. The third, reassurance of worth, is based on the recognition of competence. After a breakup, friends often step in to remind you of your good qualities and of why the breakup wasn't entirely your fault. Another is emotional closeness, or intimacy, and reflects how much you trust and share feelings with this person. The fifth is social integration or sense of belonging, which can range from defined groups such as a sorority or a church, to subgroups among your friends at work, to sharing an alliance with other fans of your favorite sports team. Finally, the opportunity for nurturance is defined as having the opportunity to help others. Research among the elderly in nursing homes suggests caring for a plant or pet actually improves mental health. As you can see, this view of social support is based on the idea that your social support needs will vary across situations and that different people may provide for different needs.

This raises another issue, though, which is often referred to as the quality versus quantity debate. In a nutshell, the question is whether it is better to have a lot of people in your social support network, some of whom you may not know very well—or is it better to have a smaller, more intimate group? It turns out that this is a fairly individualistic preference. More external individuals often thrive in big groups, while more internal folks may find being in contact with too many people stressful. However, the common factor across different personalities seems to be whether the support they are offered matches their need and their perceptions of the help they thought would be offered. Evidence also suggests that happiness can spread within a social network over time (Fowler & Christakis, 2008).

Of course, this brings us back to the issue of expectations as well. All of us have probably known people who don't ask enough from their significant others, as well as those who ask for too much. People who are dealing with depression, anxiety, and substance abuse may even drive away their social support providers because they are so needy or difficult for people to help. Paradoxically, not having social support can also be a risk factor for those disorders. In some cases, having a large network can even increase stress. Some studies of middle-aged women indicate that being the center of a large family network may actually generate stress since they spend so much time caring for others, and do not receive enough support in return to meet their own needs.

NOT ALL SOCIAL SUPPORT IS CREATED EQUAL

Gender is another factor that influences social support. Clearly, being pregnant and caring for a newborn require different skills than hunting or fighting. Although men certainly can care for babies and women can hunt and will definitely fight to protect their offspring, there may be some neurological and physiological differences in males and females that impact their social support preferences. After looking at data from both animals and humans under stress, psychologist Shelley Taylor (2006) realized that there are differences in both the stress and social responses that individuals make. While we all experience the hormonal fight-or-flight response discussed earlier, males also show testosterone responses and an increase in hostility and aggression under stress. Female aggression, on the other hand, is less hormonally and more cognitively linked. Consequently, especially among animals, aggression in females is much more closely linked to defensive rather than offensive behaviors. Females under stress release oxytocin, a hormone crucial to maternal bonding, ensuring that females stay to protect their young from danger, rather than fleeing to protect themselves. Stressed mother rats will often groom and lick their pups, so soothing the babies and themselves.

Human females have also reliably been shown to gravitate toward being with others, especially females, when under stress, ranging from health to work to relationship issues. As a result of such findings, Taylor (2006) and her colleagues concluded that women are less likely to fight or flee under stress than men because they prefer instead to do what Taylor called tending or befriending others. I hadn't really noticed how strongly I gravitated toward my mother, sister, and girlfriends when stressed until my husband and I were planning our wedding. As is typical, we were on a budget and trying to accommodate many different expectations. I remember my husband-to-be midway through the process commenting on the fact that on a given evening, I might call two or three people to relate the same story about my latest frustration. For me, talking to other people was a way of coping, while for him, continuously talking about the situation was frustrating. It turns out that we are not alone.

Linguist Deborah Tannen (1987; 1990) has been studying conversations between girls and boys and men and women for much of her career. What she finds is that women use conversation as a means of building rapport and intimacy and of negotiating with others, while men are more likely to use conversations as a means of conveying information and establishing status. Even among young children, Tannen finds that girls spend more time talking about feelings and relationships, while males focus on games and rules.

Clearly, such gender-based distinctions make sense in the context of how we respond to stress. However, it is also the case that misunderstandings generated by these different styles, or judging others' speech style by the standards of the opposing gender, can be stressful. When experiencing stress such as infertility, the loss of a child, or the loss of a job, couples often find they want to deal with the situation differently. A woman often wants to talk about her feelings and responses and to share her experience with others. If her husband doesn't want to talk about it, the woman may feel hurt or that he doesn't care about the loss as much as she does. Men, on the other hand, often feel that repeatedly talking about the subject just makes them more upset, and so may try to tune out or avoid such conversations to cope.

Several years ago, I was involved in a research project offering psychological support groups to military couples going through IVF treatment (McNaughton-Cassill et al., 2000). The groups, which met weekly, were designed to help couples cope with the stress of going through the medical treatment and to manage their larger feelings about experiencing trouble conceiving a wanted child. Ironically, by the end of the study, we found that while women enjoyed the groups and were more likely to attend regularly, their husbands actually showed greater psychological improvement afterward. This difference was related to the fact that most of the women had a network of other women they were talking to about infertility outside the group, while many of the men had never talked about the issue with anyone outside of their immediate family. As a result, talking to other people going through the same trauma was especially helpful to them.

FAMILIES—SOURCES OF SUPPORT OR STRESS?

The issue of gender-based differences in communication may well be exacerbated by some of the lifestyle changes we have been discussing throughout this book. Since World War II, there have been significant changes in the structure and function of American families. Women are far more likely to be working outside the home, at least part-time. Men are more likely to take an active role in child care. Divorce levels have been on the rise. However, not all of our perceptions about the changes in our families and marriage are exactly accurate. Despite our collective belief that before World War II, most families resembled the Waltons, and during the 1950s and 1960s they were the Cleavers or the Cunninghams, and in the 1970s the Huxtables or the happily blended Brady Bunch, marriage in America has always been a complex, messy institution.

According to Stephanie Coontz in her book *The Way We Never Were* (2000), the reality is that over the course of history, marriages were often economic arrangements designed to promote survival. Family members often worked long hours to provide a subsistence living, and children were expected to start contributing as soon as they were able by helping with household chores, food production, child care, or even outside employment. During the colonial era, high mortality rates and childbirth-related deaths resulted in as many as half of all children losing at least one parent before they turned 21. By the 1800s, a bimodal family pattern was emerging, such that wealthy families were able to promote the idea of protecting women and children from hard work by hiring other poor women and children to work as servants, factory workers, and hired help.

During the first half of the 20th century, the pressures of the Depression and the World Wars often resulted in increased mobility of family members looking for work, which persists into this century as well. And yet over half of American adults see or talk to a parent at least once a week; rates which exceed those of earlier decades. Additionally, 90 percent of Americans marry at least once, and 70 percent of those who divorce remarry. However, after five years of marriage, more than a fifth of all couples have separated or divorced—a number exceeding that of virtually all other Western cultures. In short, Americans marry more and divorce more than people in other comparable cultures and so experience a significant number of life transitions (Cherlin, 2009).

This, in turn, has led to a great deal of debate about the impact of divorce and remarriage on children in particular. Some studies have found greater percentages of behavioral and school problems, higher rates of depression and anxiety, and increased relationship problems on the part of children of divorce. Others, however, argue that such findings are biased because they failed to compare children from divorced families with their cohorts in unhappy families that did not break up. They also failed to take into account the impact of living with and sharing the biological tendencies of parents who are depressed, and have substance abuse problems or other mental issues which may have been partly to blame for the divorce in the first place. Nevertheless, dealing with the financial, logistical, and emotional issues raised by physically separating a family are significant (Wallerstein, 2001). Often, divorced families are forced to relocate, change schools or jobs, and to otherwise disrupt their existing social networks, in addition to the ruptures in their family support system. Divorced parents who turn to their children for emotional support may also inadvertently stress their children by depending on them too much or making them feel caught between their two parents' views of the situation.

Part of the problem when modern marriages fail is that we have been socialized to view the search for a romantic partner as a quest to find the "perfect person" who will meet all of our economic, emotional, and sexual needs. Throughout history and in many parts of the world today, the idea of marrying for love and romance was foreign—and an impossibility. Couples often married people they hardly knew to enhance the status or finances of the family. In many parts of the world today, arranged marriages continue to exist and even to flourish. This is certainly not the case though, in the movies, television shows, fairy tales, romance novels, magazines, and the music playing as the backdrop in our lives. The idea of romantic love and finding a partner who essentially meets all of your emotional needs is firmly entrenched in modern society (Fisher, 2002). In fact, researchers Holmes and Johnson (2009) argue that our expectations about the ease with which we will find our "soul mates" have been raised too highly by the pat relationships we see on the screen (Segrin & Nabi, 2002; Shapiro & Kroeger, 1991). Despite the typical Disney movie portrayal of love and marriage (Tanner, Haddock, Zimmerman, & Lund, 2003), it is unrealistic to assume that two people will mesh emotionally over our ever increasing lifespan. The idea that one person will share all of our interests and be able to meet all of our needs is certainly flawed.

Although studies of marriage success suggest that sharing comparable values and goals are important, it is also increasingly apparent that being able to communicate and resolve conflict in nondestructive ways is key. In good marriages, partners also tend to have both shared and individual interests and friends, and to respect each other's differences. This may entail reassessing our expectations about what sorts of emotional and social support we expect from our partners, what we are willing to give back in return, and finding multiple ways to meet our social needs without undermining our marriages and partnerships in the process. The fact that more and more women are entering college and the workforce also means they can support themselves and their children, and so may feel less obligation to stay in an unhappy relationship. In addition, the availability of a wide variety of family planning options mean couples have far more latitude in deciding when and if to have children. Dealing with the nuances of nontraditional single-parent families, as well as the myriad other ways in which families can blend, including gay couples and those who choose to cohabit without getting married, may well be one of the defining issues of the 21st century.

ALONE IN A CROWD

Of course, changes in the types of support we expect and receive from marriage have been paralleled by changes in many other areas of our lives. Books such as Robert Putnam's *Bowling Alone* (2001) suggest that many American social institutions are changing too. Far fewer Americans belong to social or civic groups or attend church regularly, and yet many people continue to volunteer in their communities and to report that they consider themselves spiritual or religious (Blum, 2008). The rise of megachurches, which offer social incentives, including contemporary music, singles groups, financial and parenting aid, and athletic opportunities indicate that many churches are seeking ways to make their offerings attractive to people who already have so many entertainment options available to them. Others argue that many of us now attempt to meet our social needs through our workplace interactions and rely on colleagues for practical and emotional support. Many worksites promote such interactions by providing child care, exercise, and other social activities to entice and retain workers.

SOCIAL NETWORKS VERSUS SOCIAL ISOLATION

The rise of technologically-oriented social networking is also altering the social world as we know it (Wei & Van-Hwei, 2006; Bryant, Sanders-Jackson, & Smallwood, 2006; Bonbrake, 2002). Certainly, the way we instigate and maintain relationships has changed drastically in the last 100 years (Ellison, Steinfield, & Lampe, 2007; Whitty, 2007). Meeting in person, and exchanging written messages are no longer the only two options. First, phone calls allowed people to communicate across long distances, then cell phones and the Internet came along and made it possible for people to talk to virtually anyone anywhere at any time. For those of us old enough to remember the days of the single-phone home, cell phones are still amazing. It is difficult for today's teenagers to imagine trying to manage their social lives on the family phone, which was typically tethered to the kitchen wall. If people weren't listening to the conversation they were telling you to hang up so they could make a call. Long distance calls were a different proposition in those days as well. Not only did the phone companies charge by the minute, but those rates varied. The ritual of calling home on Sunday afternoons or waiting up until 11:00 to talk to the person you were dating seems totally foreign today, and it made it harder to remain close to people who did not live near you or share your daily life. However, some research indicates that while internet use decreases social loneliness, it may not be a substitute for emotional connection (Moody, 2002).

When I was in school, friends were the people I saw regularly, typically because I worked or went to school with them. If a family moved or someone switched to a different school, they were virtually lost from your life. When we found out that my daughter's middle school fed into three different high schools, I felt bad about them losing contact with friends they had known for years. What I didn't realize was that, due to technology, they would be able to stay in touch with those friends while adding new ones to their circle. Instead of having a social life revolving exclusively around one school, they attended dances, plays, and sporting events at multiple schools, blending friends in ways that simply were not possible with our more limited technology.

Despite the convenience and connection afforded by the telephone, it didn't take long for its insistent, demanding ring to become a source of irritation. Whether disrupting family dinners, generating late-night fear, or triggering misunderstandings because of poor connections, phones didn't always make our lives easier. When answering machines and voice messages joined the cavalcade, we all had to learn to record greetings and messages, and now we dread having to listen to a backlog of recordings if we haven't been around for a while. As cell phones became ubiquitous, people began to complain about being forced to listen to strangers' conversations and about people giving precedence to phone calls over live conversations. Now it is almost impossible to imagine not being able to coordinate plans and carry on conversations as we go about our daily lives. With texting, we can even exchange information on a continuous basis without having to actually talk or respond to each other verbally.

Although the researchers who developed the Internet were motivated by the desire to be able to communicate with other academics, few anticipated the seemingly never ending growth of personal communication options it would spawn. From email to instant messaging to Facebook, Skyping, Google, and YouTube, the Internet has become a central facet of modern life. Not only do we talk to our friends and family, but we shop, apply for jobs, date, and follow world events, often in real time, online. The catch, however, is that communicating through technology isn't the same as talking face to face.

Much of our personal communication is influenced by non-verbal cues such as facial expressions, hand movements, and tone of voice. Although smiley face emoticons, acronyms like LOL, and conventions about the use of capitals, exclamation points, and bold fonts attempt to bridge the gap, it can still be difficult to avoid misunderstandings. The fact that electronic messages can be saved, forwarded, and altered also raises privacy issues and has given rise to phenomena like cyber bullying and spying on people through their electronic records. The rapid rise of technology has also created new generation gaps. The so-called "technology natives," or young people who have grown up in the Internet era, adapt rapidly to new forms of communication and, in fact, often reject older methods, including letter writing and real-time phone calls, preferring to text or communicate online. Older folks, sometimes called "technology immigrants," often adopt new means of communication more slowly, and the two groups may not always understand each other's attempts to communicate.

Not long ago my daughter, who is in her freshman year of college, sent me a text which read: "I GOT A 96 ON THE CHEM TEST!!! =D. My husband and I were baffled. How could a 96 be a D? Since she wasn't picking up her phone we texted her twin sister, who checked on Facebook and reported to us that the 96 was in fact an A. It turns out that the emoticon she had used was meant to signify a big smile. As a parent, I am happy that I don't have to wait for a weekly phone call to hear how my kids are doing. On the other hand, people who have received bad news or have been dumped or had private pictures or conversations posted publicly, often have understandably mixed feelings. It is no coincidence that the manners gurus who write books and newspaper columns are now devoting entire chapters to electronic etiquette. However, the arbitration of such questions is still a moving target. Most people seem to agree that breaking up with someone really shouldn't be done online. However, there is significant disagreement about whether a text message should count as a thank-you note, if hold-the-date emails actually constitute an invitation to a wedding, and whether cyber birthday cards are a thoughtful—or lazy—way to remember someone.

Another common source of conflict is the desire of older folks to talk in person and of younger folks to prefer text messages (Pew, 2003). I suspect it is the rare parent who hasn't sent a text, in capital letters, asking their child to CALL THEM. Surveys of teens, however, suggest that they tend to see texts as perfectly polite, attentive means of communicating and view phone calls as intrusive bids for attention, which should only be used in urgent situations. Since talking in real time does require emotional energy and can't be done in all circumstances, it occurs to me to wonder whether this is actually a logical adaptation. In a world characterized by excessive sensory input and high levels of social connectedness, limiting conversations to text would seem to be an effective way of conserving social energy, maintaining control over your time, and even allowing yourself to formulate responses at a more leisurely pace than that afforded during regular conversation.

As with the other forms of technology we have discussed, it is unlikely that our reliance on electronic forms of communication is going to decrease—in fact, in many ways it has opened multiple doors. However, in the interest of maintaining healthy social links, avoiding confusion, and limiting the intrusion of electronic input on real-time social interactions, we may well have to rethink their roles in our lives. Do we really have to respond immediately to each message we receive? Are there some conversations that are better conducted in person? How do we want to preserve our privacy? How sure can we be that we have interpreted someone's cyber message accurately? The trick in the modern world seems to be finding a way to harness social media in ways that promote contact and connectivity without diminishing the quality of our relationships and interactions.

WHAT DO YOU THINK?

1. If you had a broken leg, how many people do you think would help you with practical tasks like driving and getting groceries?
2. Who would you be most likely to call if you got very upset?
3. Do you think electronic means of communication are making people closer or creating distance between them?

REFERENCE

Allman, J. M., Tetreault, N. A., Hakeem, A. Y., Kebreten, F., Manaye, K. S., Erwin, J. M., Park, S., Goubert, V., & Hof, P. R. (2010). The von Economo neurons in frontoinsular and anterior cingulate cortex in great apes and humans. *Brain Struct Funct.*, 214: 495–517.

Antonucci, T. C., & Akiyama, H. (1987). An examination of sex differences in social support among older men and women. *Sex Roles*, 17, 11–12.

Blum, D. (2008). 26% of Americans Volunteer. Philanthropy.com/news/updates

Bonbrake, K. (2002). College students' Internet use, relationship formation, and personality correlates. *CyberPsychology & Behavior*, 5(6), 551–558.

Bryant, J. A., Sanders-Jackson, A., & Smallwood, A. M. K. (2006). IMing, text messaging, and adolescent social networks. *Journal of Computer-Mediated Communication*, 11 (2), 10.

Chang, E. C. (2006). Perfectionism and dimensions of psychological well-being in a college student sample: A test of a stress-mediation model. *Journal of Social and Clinical Psychology* 25, 1001–1022.

Cherlin, A. J. (2009) *The Marriage-Go-Round: The State of Marriage and the Family in America Today*. New York: Knopf.

Coontz, S. (2000). *The Way We Never Were: American Families and the Nostalgia Trap*. New York: Basic Books.

Cutrona, C. E., & Russell, D. (1987). The provisions of social relationships and adaptation to stress. In W. H. Jones & D. Perlman (Eds.) *Advances in Personal Relationships* (vol. 1, pp. 37–67). Greenwich, CT: JAI Press.

De Silva, M. J., McKenzie, K., Harpham, T. & Huttley, S. (2005). Social capital and mental illness: A systematic review. *Journal of Epidemiological Community Health*, 59(8): 619–627.

Ellison, N. B., Steinfield, C., & Lampe, C. (2007). The benefits of Facebook "friends": Social capital and college students' use of online social network sites. *Journal of Computer-Mediated Communication*, 12, 1143–1168.

Fisher, H. (2004). *Why We Love: The Nature and Chemistry of Romantic Love*. Holt Paperbacks.

Fowler, J. H., & Christakis, N. A. (2008). Dynamic spread of happiness in a large social network: Longitudinal analysis over 20 years in the Framingham Heart Study. *BMJ* 2008; 337:a2338.

Freidlander, L. J., Reid, G. J., Shupak, N., & Cribbie, R. (2007). Social support, self-esteem, and stress as predictors of adjustment to university among first-year undergraduates. *Journal of College Student Development*, 48, 259–274.

Gallo, L. C., Troxel, W. M., Mathews, K. A., & Kuller, L. H. (2003). Marital status and quality in middle-aged women: Associations with levels and trajectories of cardiovascular risk factors. *Health Psychol.*, 22(5): 453–463.

Goleman, D. (2006). *Emotional Intelligence: Why It Can Matter More Than IQ* (10th anniversary edition). Bantam.

Grewal, D., & Salovey, P. (2005). Feeling smart: The science of emotional intelligence. *American Scientist*, 93, 330–339.

Harlow H. F., Dodsworth, R. O., & Harlow, M. K. (1965). "Total social isolation in monkeys." *Proc Natl Acad Sci USA*.

Hobfoll, S. (2004). *Stress Culture and Community*. New York: Springer.

Holmes, B. M., & Johnson, K. R. (2009). Where fantasy meets reality: Media exposure, relationship beliefs and standards, and the moderating effect of a current relationship. In E. P. Lamont (Eds.), *Social Psychology: New Research*. Ch. 6, 117–134.

Houseman, J., & Dorman, S. (2005). The Alameda County Study: A Systematic, Chronological Review. *American Journal of Health Education* (Reston, VA: American Alliance for Health, Physical Education, Recreation and Dance, 36 (5): 302–308.

Manusov, V. & Patterson, M. (2006), *The SAGE Handbook of Nonverbal Communication* (pp. 219–236). Thousand Oaks, Calif.: Sage Publications.

Mayer, J. D., & Salovey, P. (1997). What is emotional intelligence? In P. Salovey & D. Sluyter (Eds.). *Emotional Development and Emotional Intelligence: Implications for Educators* (pp. 3–31). New York: Basic Books.

McKown, C., Gumbiner, L. M., Russo, N. M., & Lipton, M. (2009). Social-emotional learning skill, self-regulation, and social competence in typically developing and clinic-referred children. *J Clin Child Adolesc Psychol,*_38(6): 858–871.

McNaughton-Cassill, M. E., Bostwick, J. M., Vanscoy, S. E., Arthur, N. J., Hickman, T. N., Robinson, R., & Neal, G. S. (2000). Development of brief stress management support groups for couples undergoing in vitro fertilization treatment. *Fertility and Sterility* 74, 1, 87–93.

Moody, E. (2002). Internet use and its relationship to loneliness. *CyberPsychology & Behavior*, 4 (3), 393–401.

Norman, D. (1993). *Turn Signals Are the Facial Expression of Automobiles*. Cambridge MA: Basic Books.

pewresearch.org/pubs/1572/teens-cell-phones-text-messages

Piggott, J., Kwon, H., Mobb, D. , Blasey, C., Lotspeich, L., Menon, V., Bookheimer, S., & Reiss, A. L. (2004). Emotional Attribution in High-Functioning Individuals with Autistic Spectrum Disorder: A Functional Imaging Study. *Journal of American Academy of Child and Adolescent Psychiatry*, 43, (4). 473–480.

Putnam, R. (2001). *Bowling Alone: The Collapse and Revival of American Community*. Touchstone Books by Simon & Schuster.

Rizzolatti, G., Fogassi, L., & Gallese, V. (2006). Mirrors in the Mind. *Scientific American*, 295, 54–61.

Roy, R. (2011). *Social Support, Health, and Illness: A Complicated Relationship*. University of Toronto Press, Scholarly Publishing Division.

Segrin, C., & Nabi, R. L. (2002). Does television viewing cultivate unrealistic expectations about marriage? *Journal of Communication*, 52, 247–263.

Seeley, W. W., Carlin, D. A., Allman, J. M., Macedo, M. N., Bush, C., Miller, B. L., & Dearmond, S. J. (2006). Early frontotemporal dementia targets neurons unique to apes and humans. Ann Neurol. 60(6):660–7.

Shapiro, J., & Kroeger, L. (1991). Is life just a romantic novel? The relationship between attitudes about intimate relationships and the popular media. *American Journal of Family Therapy, 19*, 226–236.

Simion, F., Valeza, E., Umilta, C., & Barba, B. D. (1998). Preferential orienting to faces in newborns: A temporal-nasal asymmetry. *Journal of Experimental Psychology: Human Perception and Performance, 24* (5), 1399–1405.

Tannen, D. (1987). *That's Not What I Meant! How Conversational Style Makes or Breaks Relationships.* New York: Harper Perennial.

Tannen, D. (1990). *You just don't understand: Women and men in conversation.* New York, NY: Morrow.

Tanner, L. R., Haddock, S. A., Zimmerman, T. S., & Lund, L. K. (2003). Images of couples and families in Disney feature-length animated films. *American Journal of Family Therapy, 31*, 355–373.

Taylor, S. E. (2006). Tend and befriend: Biobehavioral bases of affiliation under stress. *Current Directions in Psychological Science, 15*, 273–277.

Wallerstein, J. (2001). *The Unexpected Legacy of Divorce.* New York: Vision Paperback.

Wei, R., & Van-Hwei, L. (2006). Staying connected while on the move: Cell phone use and social connectedness. *New Media and Society.* Thousand Oaks, CA: Sage Publications.

Whitty, M. T. (2007). Revealing the "real" me, searching for the "actual" you: Presentations of self on an Internet dating site. *Computers in Human Behavior* doi: 10.1016/j.chb.2007.07.002.

CHAPTER 8

CHANGING WITH AGE: DO YOU EVER FEEL YOUR AGE?

KEY POINTS

- ◆ Children are exposed to adult entertainment, advertising, and activities at increasingly younger ages.
- ◆ The teenage years are actually an artifact of modern life.
- ◆ People are living longer and staying more active than ever, while also worrying more about aging.

HAS CHILDHOOD EVER BEEN INNOCENT?

Accustomed as we are to ubiquitous images of precocious kids on television sitcoms and talk shows, it is difficult for us to even imagine a time when children were truly expected to be seen but not heard. Throughout much of history, youngsters were expected to begin earning their keep by caring for siblings, helping to raise food, or even working outside the home to earn money to support the family. For many families, education and time spent in school were seen as luxuries secondary to real work. Interestingly, our current tradition of holding school from fall through spring with a long summer break is a holdover from the days when families needed everyone to work during the warm months. As soon as they were old enough, they were expected to start their own families—but they were also to serve as their parents' pension and social security plans if necessary. In families caught up in an endless struggle for survival, the central goal of parenting was meeting their son or daughter's basic needs for food, security, and safety. Often, this left little time to worry about whether kids were happy, fulfilled, or popular. If there was energy left beyond that needed for survival, the emphasis seemed to be on making sure that they knew right from wrong and grow up to be contributing members of society. Families, buoyed by the GI Bill, were able to move to the suburbs and buy their own homes in unprecedented numbers. Despite the fact that many women worked during the war years, the need to provide work for returning soldiers resulted in most of their jobs being taken over by men. Women, who were then expected to become the primary emotional and social caregivers of their families, channeled their interests into maintaining flawless homes and raising perfect families. With Dad working outside the home and Mother focusing more and more of her energy on the well-being of their family, the concept of a carefree childhood truly took hold in the American imagination.

Television programs from the 1950s and early 1960s like *Leave It to Beaver* and *The Ozzie and Harriet Show* reinforced stereotypes about the role of the kids in the nuclear family. By the 1960s and 1970s, middle-class children were more likely to be taking dance and piano lessons than working in their families' businesses; by the 1990s, people began to worry about whether offering their offspring the chance to compete in sports year round while playing in the band or orchestra, learning a foreign language, taking a variety of summer science and computer enrichment camps in the summer, was too much structure. While such opportunities never were available to the less privileged, the sense that childhood was a crucial developmental period became a key component of parenting. The irony is that children are actually far more resilient than typically assumed (Masten, 2001).

The Adventures of Ozzie and Harriet, circa 1956.

PROTECTIVE, PAMPERING, PUSHY PARENTS?

Paradoxically, the more energy we have focused on making sure our sons and daughters become as accomplished and successful as possible, the more we have worried about how safe and healthy they are. At the turn of the century, as many as 15 percent of infants did not live to see their first birthday, and older children were at risk from illnesses such as measles, polio, and whooping cough, as well as the injuries common to people working on farms, in factories, and around animals. When I was growing up in the 1960s, kids rode their bikes with no helmets or shoes and sat in the backs of cars with no seat belts (I bet a few of you still remember sleeping on the shelf in the back window of your parents' old car). Most of us walked to school without supervision, and our parents knew we were home when we got there: they couldn't check up on us with cell phones and GPS units. Certainly, parents knew about the dangers of car accidents, kidnappings, and pedophiles, but having grown up themselves with relative freedom they didn't feel the need to watch their children constantly.

However, as the news media focused more and more on how dangerous the world is, many adults have decided that to keep their children safe, they need to drive them to and from school, teach them not to talk to strangers, and in some cases even to get ID bracelets or tooth bands to identify them if they are kidnapped. Unfortunately, such decisions have actually resulted in a generation of children who don't exercise enough, in part because they spend little time outside alone, and who are afraid to talk to strangers, even though they are far more likely to be kidnapped or abused by someone they know (Louv, 1991).

Paradoxically, parents who so judiciously protect their son or daughter's physical safety may, at the same time, be pushing them to excel at school and in extracurricular activities to such a degree they leave little time in their schedules for unstructured play, or even sleep. A perusal of many middle-class kid's schedules leaves little doubt that they and their parents need complicated planners simply to keep track of where they are supposed to be. The question, of course, is whether these activities are designed to allow the youngster to pursue their own interests and desires, or are they actually a reflection of the parents' need to be seen as a super parent or to make up for things they feel they missed in their own upbringing. Certainly, anyone who has ever taught a gymnastics or dance class or coached a baseball or soccer team has dealt with the parent who is attempting to live their own dreams through their children, often to the child's detriment. Ironically, individuals from less affluent backgrounds who have to struggle much harder to gain access to the resources necessary to realize their academic, athletic, or performance goals are far more likely to be personally invested in the process than those kids whose parents over-manage things for them.

Of course, not all individuals thrive under constant pressure. For every child that lights up on the stage or the basketball courts, there are others who agonize over their real or perceived failures and eventually end up hating the activity. Even those who do very well in school report that they find the constant pressure to achieve academically, to do well on standardized tests, and to focus on where they are going to go to college from an early age get stressed. I still remember the day my five-year-old twins came home from kindergarten and told me they had learned to color bubbles that day. I eventually figured out that they meant they had been taught how to color in the bubbles on the Scantron sheets used for standardized tests. That same year, they were paired up with "third grade partners" who were going to be taking the high-stakes reading test that determined whether or not you were allowed to move to the next grade. The kindergartner's task was to write a letter of encouragement to the third grader, presumably to bolster their confidence, and to make sure that the younger children realized how important it was going to be for them to study and do well on that test themselves. By the time they were in the third grade, one of my daughters started having strange episodes at school characterized by nausea, headache, and chills. I picked her up at school several times, only to find out that she felt better within an hour. The pediatrician finally figured out that she was having migraine headaches, which can be severe, but short-lived in kids. Unfortunately, this was not an isolated experience. More than one parent has told me about the stomachaches, headaches, and sleep difficulties their children experienced in response to stress at school. Over time, people who are unable to perform well in school may actually choose to give up, rather than to continue subjecting themselves to failure.

Well-meaning efforts to hold a child back early in school in order to improve their academic performance are not likely to succeed, unless the reasons the individual didn't perform well in the first place (learning disabilities, emotional issues, stress at home, poor instruction at school) are addressed. Ironically, holding children back in school actually correlates better with their failure to finish high school than any other academic measure. Childhood is a period characterized by major psychological and physical development. Striking a balance between challenging and protecting kids can be difficult, especially in today's complex world (Miller, 2009).

COMMERCIALIZING CHILDHOOD

As small consumers, kids are also inundated with advertising designed to sell everything from clothes and food to toys and entertainment (Calvert, 2008). The content of much of this advertising is based on dressing and treating children as small adults. The young actors on television shows for kids and tweens are often shown performing adult tasks such as entertaining at a hotel or making a webcast. Their clothes are chic, expensive, and adultlike, as is their language and knowledge of the world. They are often portrayed as being as smart as—or smarter than—their parents, who in many cases are absent or incompetent. Entertaining as these shows are, they suggest that being a kid gives them a special status. Children on television get to combine the benefit of not being totally responsible for their actions with enjoying the perks of adult-style autonomy, actions, and accomplishments. Perhaps it isn't surprising, then, that parents of toddlers often wonder where they learned to flip their hair and roll their eyes or to spit before throwing a baseball. In the meantime, the parents of preteens struggle to reconcile the fact that they want their children to act and dress their age, while at the same time asking them to perform sporting feats, dance and cheerleading routines, and musical events at decidedly adult levels. At the same time, children, encouraged and rewarded for being high achievers, often have difficulty relaxing or feeling safe in a world they have been taught is both demanding and dangerous.

WHO SAID THAT THE TEEN YEARS ARE THE BEST YEARS OF OUR LIVES?

As teenagers and young adults, these same children continue to feel (and believe) that they need to achieve in all areas of their life—or conversely, to rebel to assert their independence—while also trying to reconcile the mixed messages we as a society give them about sexuality, morality, obedience to authority, and autonomy. Physiologically, humans are ready to engage in sex and to produce babies somewhere in their early teens. Once boys have undergone puberty and girls have started their periods, their brains and bodies are actually signaling them hormonally to engage in activities designed to promote the survival of the species. Studies of teen brains and behavior suggest that the tendency to feel infallible, to take risks, and even to stay up late and sleep late in the morning reflect evolutionary pressures designed to get individuals to leave home, seek sexual partners, and begin to raise families of their own (Kuhn, 2006). Traditionally, this has happened in the middle and late teens in most cultures.

However, in the Western world, and especially in the past 50 years, two contradictory things have been happening. On the one hand, the onset of puberty has been steadily moving down, such that girls as young as 11 and 12 may be starting their periods. Explanations for this change range from improved nutrition and diet to exposure to food additives or other compounds in the environment, but the point remains that girls in Western cultures are physiologically ready for sexual activity at the onset of their teen years.

In the meantime, the complexity of society, the time required to complete high school, vocational, college, and advanced degrees has been steadily increasing (Setterson & Ray, 2010). While a young man who was virtually illiterate could support a family with a farm or trade 100 years ago, the inability to read and the lack of a high school diploma or equivalent is a serious deficit in today's economy. Skilled fields such as building, plumbing, car repair, etc., have become increasingly dependent on computer applications. Navigating our daily lives, managing complex equipment, and even the ability to read and do complex computations takes its toll on all of us (Norman, 2010).

Careers such as teaching and nursing have come to require more and more formal education as well as ongoing training to stay abreast of the field. The daunting number of career choices can also overwhelm today's students. I frequently work with students who freeze when faced with the prospect of having to pick a major and career from the vast array of choices. Not only are there more options than ever before, but most of them require significant commitments in terms of time and money, with few guarantees about what the job outlook will be in the four or more years it will take them to complete the degree. Professions such as medicine, law, science, and psychology now require an undergraduate degree as well as years of graduate training before practitioners are even allowed to enter the field. Most of us know that medical training requires four years of medical school plus several years more of training in specialty areas before people qualify as doctors. However, did you know that the average PhD-level biologist goes to school for an average of six years of graduate work, followed by two to four years of postdoctoral training before they are considered ready to work as an actual biologist at a university or company?

Such extended training periods are problematic in that they are expensive and also keep the student out of the workforce while they are learning. Additionally, in many fields simply getting the required degree does not ensure future employment in a complicated, ever changing economy. In short, what parents tend to perceive as slacking when a student doesn't seem to know what they want to do may in fact be a paralysis generated by the fear of letting others down or of making a mistake by choosing the wrong future path. This tendency to freeze may only be exacerbated by caring parents who have become accustomed to making, or at least being involved in, their child's every decision.

Ironically, the same parents who worried about their kids walking to school alone often have trouble letting go of their teenager's day to day lives. They may allow them to learn to drive, but still check on them throughout the day by cell phone. They may tell their teens that they should be responsible for managing their own time, money, and schoolwork, but then help them to finish late-night projects, fill the car with gas, argue with their teachers about grades, and insist on telling the teen what college they should go to, what they should major in, and even who they should socialize with while there. As a young faculty member, I was initially amazed by the number of parents of college students who called or emailed the university to inquire about their child's grades, bills, or conflict with a teacher. It eventually dawned on me that these parents were so in the habit of thinking of their child's accomplishments as their own, and of stepping in to help the child, that they weren't even really aware they were preventing the child from learning how to manage their lives on their own. These so-called helicopter parents have become so ubiquitous that universities now hold seminars on how to deal with the issue. Ironically, these same parents will often complain and express disappointment when their kids move back in after college or continue to borrow money from their parents to maintain the sorts of lifestyles they grew accustomed to at home.

As a result, we have created a stage in life where individuals who are biologically ready to separate from their parents are socially expected to stay in their homes and depend on them financially for far longer than ever before. During this time, we want them to excel academically and show increasing autonomy and responsibility for their own actions while still obeying our rules and relying on us to bail them out when they slip up. Although the family may believe that the teen's success in school, sports, or other activities is their job, they no longer have the sense that they are performing tasks that are essential for the immediate well-being or survival of their family. In fact, in families that fail to set or articulate explicit achievement goals for their teens, children may end up feeling entitled to the care and concern of their parents without internalizing the need to reciprocate with effort or accomplishments of their own.

To complicate things further, we have created a complex social expectation that the teen years are the last time in our lives when we are free to experience and enjoy a sense of freedom from responsibility. Despite the reality that high school is often a turbulent time filled with angst about our own identities, social connections, and future, movies and novels often portray these years as fun-filled carefree episodes in our lives. Rituals such as proms, high school football games, and Sweet Sixteen birthday parties are glamorized, leaving many teenagers—and their parents—feeling that they somehow missed out on all the fun.

The fact that teenagers by definition are young doesn't hurt either. Although few teenagers can see it at the time, many of us spend the rest of our lives wishing we were as thin, tan, or in shape as we were during those years. Living in a culture which worships a youthful appearance is paradoxical, in that there is no doubt we will all age and change over time, no matter how much we exercise, diet, or turn to plastic surgery. Although youth has long been a valued commodity because it represents health, the ability to procreate, and physical prowess, the insistence that people should resist the signs of aging has taken on a whole new meaning in the modern world. Admiring youth as you age gracefully, gaining weight, accepting wrinkles and gray hair, is a much different proposition than trying to look far younger than you are your whole life. Again, the media, through its portrayals of youth and beauty, plays a central role in encouraging us. The media literally sells us on the idea that we can somehow avoid aging if we try hard enough and spend enough money.

Where Are the Adults?

Adulthood also carries with it a number of stresses and strains. Even individuals who have managed to complete the necessary training or education in their chosen career field may find that they are unable to start at a salary that enables them to live at the same economic level as their parents. While the children of the 1930s and 1940s were almost always able to increase their standard of living relative to their parents, their offspring have not always been able to do so. It is a fact that as humans' experiences expand and grow, it is hard for us to go backward. When people of my generation went to college, we didn't have much trouble adjusting to shared dorm rooms with no individual phones or TVs, because we were used to sharing rooms with our siblings and sharing the family phone in the kitchen. However, when our kids go to college, they want individual dorm rooms with ample room to hook up their stereos, televisions, computers, and other electronic paraphernalia, not because they are intrinsically greedier than we were, but because that is the level they have come to expect in the homes we provided for them!

First Comes Love, Then Comes Marriage? Not Always

Negotiating the process of finding a partner in the modern world can also be stressful. Arranged marriages may lack the romance and sense of self-determination common of Western expectations, but they did and do ensure that those involved share at least some common cultural experiences and values. When marriage was largely an economic choice, having a wide variety of choices regarding your partner's personality and connection with you was less important. Today, we find ourselves expecting our partners to be attractive, successful, sensitive, and devoted to us, over increasingly long lifespans, with little guidance on how to find or engage such a person (Cherlin, 2009). If randomly meeting people at work, school, the gym, social events, and bars doesn't seem to be working, we can now try sophisticated chat room or dating services that offer to vet the person for us, so we don't have to waste time getting to know someone who would not be a good match for us. Even after we do find someone we deem compatible, getting and staying married is a complex process in a multicultural society, where people's experiences of family life and expectations for their partners often differ significantly and may be unrealistically shaped by the media. Although living happily ever after has long been a staple of fairy tales, I have always found it hard to believe that Cinderella would truly be happy in the long run with a prince who urges her to get him a drink of water, even after she lets him know that her stepmother will be angry at her if she does! The reality is that conflict is inevitable in long-term relationships and that communication and conflict resolution are key to negotiating the changing stages of

Children place large demands on parents' time and the family finances which could lead to diminished marital satisfaction.

marriage. However, few of us expect this process to be as hard as it is. When entering marital therapy, both young and old couples frequently express confusion about how their "fairy tale romance" could have deteriorated so much. After the glow of dating and falling in love wears off, the stress of juggling jobs, finances, housework, and careers takes its toll. Sternberg and Sternberg (2008) argue that love is made up of passion, intimacy, and commitment, but that the ratios of these components change as the relationship develops. Surveys of happiness among married couples indicate that having young children in the house correlates with diminished marital satisfaction (Vaillant & Vaillant, 1993; Cowan & Cowan, 1999; Lawrence et al., 2009). Even when the couple wanted and planned for kids, the demands they place on their time, coping, and finances are enormous.

Of course such pressures are not new. However, it is important to note that over half of American mothers work outside of the home at least part time, and significant numbers of children are raised by a single parent, meaning that most parents are experiencing significant stress related to balancing their work and home life. Couple this with the pressure parents often feel to provide their kids with a perfect childhood, and the source of the stress becomes clear. Mothers raised in the feminist and postfeminist eras want—and expect—their husbands to participate in child care, yet often struggle sharing control of the process. At the same time that these young women are striving to be the perfect parent, they are also trying to compete and flourish in work environments that still lack adequate support for working mothers. Problems range from the lack of adequate maternity leave policies and places for nursing mothers to pump breast milk to limited options for quality day care. Negative attitudes by coworkers about mothers failing to pull their own weight on late nights, weekends, or other inconvenient schedules also add to the stress.

Working fathers find themselves pulled between the demands of their careers, which they see as crucial for the well-being of their family, and wanting to be more involved in their kid's care and upbringing than their fathers were (APA.org). Gender roles and expectations, of course, factor into all this as well. A study conducted by my colleagues Drs. Jo Meier Marquis and Molly Lynch and I (Meier-Marquis, McNaughton-Cassill, & Lynch, 2006) showed that among parents of young children, fathers do indeed do more house and yard work and child care than in previous generations. If you doubt this, just check out the pick-up line at your local elementary school. When I was growing up in the 1960s, fathers almost never came to school except for awards ceremonies, held in the evening after traditional work hours were over. At my daughters' school, the array of fathers in shorts, UPS uniforms, plumbing trucks, and suits attested to the fact that in families where both parents work, everybody has to pitch in.

However, the Meier-Marquis study revealed that mothers still tend to do more of the planning, scheduling, and worry work of managing the family. Fathers may take the kids to school or camp or the pediatrician, but it is still mothers who set up the schedules, track who is supposed to be where, and cover when kids get sick or plans go awry. Not surprisingly, many women resent this fact, even though they are, in reality, simply continuing to follow the patterns they most likely saw in their childhoods, where fathers often placed the highest priority on work while mothers were responsible for making home life flow smoothly. The strain of competing in the workplace and then running the household when they get home is reflected in the fact that studies of blood pressure suggest that men are likely to show decreases in blood pressure when they get home from work, while women are more likely to show an increase when they enter the house and inventory the things they still feel responsible for completing. Cutrona (1996) concluded that marital satisfaction is in large part a function of the match between the social support we expect—and actually receive—from our partners.

CAUGHT IN THE MIDDLE

Because training for and establishing yourself in a career takes longer to achieve now, people generally are waiting longer to have babies. Many couples are also finding themselves in the position of trying to care for their kids while juggling the needs of their aging parents. In a mobile society where people move quite often and marriages often end up disrupted by divorce or death, the issue of who will care for an aging parent becomes very salient. Research suggests that just as they are likely to take primary responsibility for child care, adult women are more likely than their brothers to take on the care of their elderly parents. While providing care for a sick or aging person can provide the opportunity to get closer to a parent, or to feel that you are paying them back for the care they gave to you, it can also be overwhelming. The costs of nursing homes and medical care for the elderly often exceed the resources of middle-class families. These can pose no-win choices about whether to give children opportunities such as camp or college, or pay for care for aging parents. Although television shows such as *The Waltons* often gave us the sense that in the past, multiple generations of families coexisted happily in the same home, sociological studies of families in the United States suggest that this was the exception, not the rule. People have often moved to seek economic opportunities in this country, leaving family members behind. However, we are living longer, although often with chronic health conditions that have altered the needs of the elderly. The demands these can place on working parents who are already stretched thinly in their personal and professional lives can be overwhelming.

AGING, A LUXURY NOT EVERYONE CAN AFFORD

Of course, living long, while a goal of most of us at least in theory, is not an unmitigated benefit itself. Finding ways to age gracefully in a youth-obsessed culture can be difficult (Gardner, 2006). Reconciling a lifelong emphasis on independence and self-sufficiency can be difficult when you are faced with illness, infirmity, or dementia. Dealing with the loss of friends and loved ones, as well as the diminishment of physical abilities, can be difficult. Nevertheless, most aging Americans don't fall prey to the dramatic hardships often portrayed in the media. Only a small percentage of the elderly end up living in nursing homes or in poverty. Many elderly individuals gradually find ways to adapt to the changes in their body, walking instead of running, adjusting the way they garden, etc., while still enjoying the activities they are able to do. Others, however, rail against the changes of old age and have difficulty reconciling their changing circumstances with their self-image. Making the decision to retire or move to a warmer or more inviting locale can be invigorating—or demoralizing. Retiring without adequately planning for how you will pay your bills, afford your pills, or fill your time can be a mistake. However, those individuals who find meaningful ways to occupy themselves through social interaction, part-time work, volunteering, or setting new goals may find that they feel better about themselves than ever (Vaillant, 2003). Certainly, stress and personal resources play a significant role in the aging process (Holahan, Holahan, & Belk (1984).

Again, the catch is managing to bridge the gap between what you expect from your life and the reality of what you are experiencing. Questioning who sets our expectations for each stage of life, setting new goals at each step of the way, and refusing to glorify or glamorize any age can all be helpful techniques. Contrary to popular assumption, most elderly individuals are not unhappy with their lives; many report greater happiness, peace, and satisfaction than their younger counterparts. In fact, overall levels of happiness seem to climb until age 30, dip somewhat in the forties and fifties and climb again after that, suggesting that for most of us, the best years are not all behind us

WHAT DO YOU THINK?

1. Do you believe many children are growing up too soon?
2. Are you bothered by the fact that many teenagers and young adults seem to be prolonging their dependence on their parents and delaying their entry into the real world?
3. How would you define aging gracefully?

REFERENCES

APA *The Changing World of the Modern Day Father.* http://www.apa.org/pi/families/resources/changing-father.aspx

Calvert, S. L. (2008). Children as Consumers: Advertising and Marketing. The Future of Children, *Children and Electronic Media, 18* (1),) 205–234.

Cherlin, A. J. (2009) *The Marriage-Go-Round: The State of Marriage and the Family in America Today.* New York: Knopf.

Cowan, C. P., & Cowan, P. A. (2000). When partners become parents : the big life change for couples. Mahwah, NJ: Lawrence Erlbaum Associates.

Cutrona, C. E. (1996). *Social Support in Couples: Marriage as a Resource in Terms of Stress.* Thousand Oaks, CA: Sage.

Gardner, M. (2006). The age of age obsession. ChristianScienceMonitor.com

Holahan, Holahan, & Belk (1984). Adjustment in aging: The roles of life stress, hassles, and self-efficacy. *Health Psychology, 3,* 315–328.

Kuhn, D. (2006). Do cognitive changes accompany developments in the adolescent brain? *Perspectives on Psychological Science, 1* (59).

Lawrence, E., Cobb, R. J., Roghman, A. D., Rothman, M. T., & Bradbury, T. N. (2009). Marital satisfaction across the transition to parenthood. *Journal of Family Psychology* 22(1), 41–50.

Louv, R. (1991). *Childhood's Future.* Boston: Houghton Mifflin.

Masten, A. S. (2001). Ordinary Magic. Resilience Processes in Development. *American Psychologist, 56* (3), 227–238.

Meier-Marquis, J. A., McNaughton-Cassill, M., & Lynch, M. (2006). The management of household and child care tasks and relationship satisfaction in dual-earner families. *Marriage & Family Review, 40:* 2/3, 61, 88.

Miller, Patricia. (2009). *Theories of Developmental Psychology.* New York: Worth Publishers.

Norman, D. A. (2010). *Living with Complexity.* MIT Press.

Setterson, R., & Ray, B. E. (2010). *Not Quite Adults.* New York: Bantam.

Sternberg, R., & Sternberg, K. (Eds.) (2008). *The New Psychology of Love.* New Haven, CT: Yale University Press.

Vaillant, C. O., & Vaillant, G. E. (1993). Is the U-curve of marital satisfaction an illusion? A 40-year study of marriage. *Journal of Marriage and the Family, 55,* 230–239.

Vaillant, G. E. (2003). *Aging Well: Surprising Guideposts to a Happier Life from the Landmark Harvard Study of Adult Development.* Boston: Little, Brown, and Company.

CHAPTER 9

THE FOUR CORNERS OF STRESS: SHARP ANGLES OR TURNING POINTS?

KEY POINTS

- Stress occurs when there is a gap between what you have and what you want.
- Sometimes, stress can be eliminated by removing the problem, but often the only option is to manage your responses to the event.
- Stress reactions involve thoughts, feelings, physiological responses, and actions.

GETTING A CORNER ON STRESS

The circumstances that cause stress vary but typically stem from discrepancies between what you have and what you want or expect in a situation. For example, losing a family member, not having enough money to cover your bills, not getting the grades you want, or dealing with poor health can all be conceptualized as discrepancies between the actual circumstances you are dealing with and what you imagine things could or should be like. Ironically, our ability to think abstractly can generate alternative views of the world. This can allow us to achieve great things, but also predisposes us to be unhappy with the gap between the way things are and the way we want them to be.

When people can change their actual circumstances, they diminish the gap and eliminate stress. As we discussed in Chapter 1, solving the problem by changing a situation is called problem-focused coping and is very effective when the stressful event is amenable to change. However, many stressors can't be easily changed. Watching a parent struggle with Alzheimer's disease or putting up with a difficult boss because you need the paycheck may require emotion-focused coping instead. This type of coping is characterized by attempts to deal with emotional responses to negative events that cannot be easily changed or rectified. However, emotion-focused coping is not always a beneficial approach. Avoiding a doctor's appointment because you are afraid to hear your test results may help you avoid anxiety in the short run. However, it may exacerbate your problems over the long run if it means you fail to get the treatment you need. Charles Holahan and his colleagues (2005) have demonstrated that over a 10-year period avoidant coping was associated with both increased levels of future stress, and depression. Consequently, making thoughtful choices about how you respond to stress is the key to effective stress management.

Stress responses can be assessed on four interactive dimensions: thoughts, feelings, physiological responses, and actions. The first step is to pay attention to your characteristic thoughts and feelings and physical sensations each time something stressful occurs in your daily life. Most people tend to respond to stressors with similar responses, many of which can be traced to the fight-or-flight response. Understanding how we think and feel when we are stressed allows us to bring a greater element of choice to our actions (Greenberg, 2011). So, how do you start the process?

ARE YOU WHAT YOU THINK, OR WHAT YOU FEEL?

The work of Aaron Beck, Albert Ellis, and Martin Seligman suggests that we can learn to identify and control thoughts and emotions if we put our mind to it. Often, things we do in response to stress, such as eating, drinking, smoking, or fighting, actually make the situation worse instead of better, so learning to thoughtfully choose actions can be a successful coping approach. Of course, humans have long been interested in how the mind and body interact. In 380 BC Plato wrote, "So the reason ought to rule, having the ability and foresight to act for the whole, and the spirit ought to obey and support it. And this concord between them is effected, as we said, by a combination of intellectual and physical training, which tunes up the reason by intellectual training and tones down the crudeness of natural high spirits by harmony and rhythm." In Act II, Scene II of *Hamlet*, Shakespeare has the lead character exclaim, "There is nothing either good or bad but thinking it makes it so." Freud, of course, distinguishes between our conscious life, our thoughts, and the unconscious layer of feelings, conflicts, and motives beneath our explicit awareness. His psychoanalytic theory actually postulates that good mental health is predicated on identifying and bringing to light these subterranean thoughts. However, expressing emotions (catharsis) and exploring the unconscious through free association and dream interpretation as Freud advocated, proved cumbersome and often ineffective.

As a result, theorists, led by Albert Ellis (2001), Aaron Beck (Beck , 2011), and later Martin Seligman (2006), suggest that thoughts can be classified in terms of their content and how they make sense of the things that happen in a person's life. Beck and Ellis argued that thoughts centered around approval, competence, and perfectionism—which they called dysfunctional thoughts and irrational beliefs, respectively—occur so automatically in some people that they are not even aware of how they are influencing their emotions and behavioral choices. Although their theories differed in some respects, both argued that learning to identify and replace these thought patterns with more rational alternative assumptions could alter the process significantly.

However, managing thoughts and feelings under duress is easier said than done. When faced with challenging events, our evolutionary tendency is to either fight for our lives or flee from the danger. In order to make this happen, the fight-or-flight response kicks in. Our heart rate and breathing increase, our body undergoes metabolic changes to increase our available energy, we feel stronger, but are less aware of pain, and generally focus all of our attention on coping. When the stressor is a physical threat, these responses are adaptive. Fighting to protect your young, hiding from a predator, or fleeing for your life makes sense. But in the modern world, most of the stressors we encounter are not immediate or physical. Often the things we are stressed about are far less tangible. Conflict with a partner, loss of a job, or financial problems rarely calls for a physical response; in fact, hitting someone, yelling, or hiding may exacerbate the problem. Certainly, most of us have had the experience of doing or saying something we later regret, but feelings have a way of swamping more rational responses in the name of survival.

CHICKEN OR THE EGG?

Ironically, early psychologists tended to view emotions as negative, destructive impulses that needed to be managed. Freud felt that the superego, or conscience, and the ego, our reality check, were necessary to keep the id from simply acting on any and all emotions and impulses. Other theorists spent a great deal of time trying to figure out whether thoughts or emotions occurred first. The James-Lange theory (Myers, 2001) proposed that emotions start in the sensory organs, or unconscious responses, which then trigger thoughts, rather than the other way around. In contrast, Walter Cannon (1915) argued that autonomic responses were not varied enough to distinguish emotions. They instead argued that sensory organs detect a stimulus and signal cortical and thalamic centers that in turn trigger emotional responses. In contrast, Stanley Schachter and Jerome Singer suggested that the variability seen in emotions implied that there had to be a cognitive aspect to their formation. Essentially, the brain has to make sense of the stressful event and then trigger the appropriate response.

We now know that emotions serve as a warning system and are crucial for normal functioning. When emotional function is disrupted, people have a great deal of trouble taking care of themselves or interacting with others. Think, for example, of people with Alzheimer's disease, who no longer remember or respond appropriately to their spouses, or of autistic children who don't read and react to emotions the way other children do. While the mechanisms of such diseases are still largely a mystery to us, we do know that emotional responsivity is a function of the limbic system.

This series of structures, deep in the brain, is crucial for the production of emotions, but is also in close communication with the cortical areas of the brain. In fact, some scientists compare the emotional centers of the brain to a car engine. When revved up it runs, unless you put the brake on. In the case of the brain, the cortex and prefrontal cortex serve as the braking system. However, their efficacy varies with the experience of the individual, their age, their mental status, and their brain wiring. An individual who has been abused may manage their emotions far differently than someone who was well nurtured as a child. Likewise, someone under the influence of alcohol or who is even very tired or very hungry may exercise different levels of emotional self-control than others. Finally, some psychological disorders themselves may reflect dysfunction in the braking or inhibitory system. Some research suggests disorders such as attention deficit and antisocial personality disorder occur as a result of faulty inhibitory circuitry, while obsessive-compulsive disorder and some forms of anxiety reflect an overly active braking system.

Clearly, our cognitive interpretations of events and our subsequent emotional responses may not always be accurate or helpful. When we revert to problematic automatic thoughts or to negative attributions about a situation, we may experience high levels of emotional distress. The irony is that it is actually difficult to recall or describe emotions without referencing thoughts and physiological sensation. Just for a minute, think about the last time you were very stressed. Try to label and describe how you felt. If you were angry, you are likely to remember feeling hot, tense, and ready to explode and may even localize the feelings in your body. For example, when some people are angry, they feel it in their stomachs, while others feel the tension in their necks or jaws. Likewise, common symptoms of anxiety include an upset stomach or a dry mouth, while depression often results in changes in appetite and sleep. In short, the thoughts, feelings, and physiological sensations that accompany stress occur virtually simultaneously and can be hard to differentiate.

LEARNED EMOTIONAL BEHAVIORS

Further complicating things is the fact that we do not tend to think of our internal, autonomic responses as being under our control—to some degree, this is a good thing. We don't really want to have to think about regulating our liver enzymes or maintaining our breathing. In some cases, these autonomic responses are influenced by experience. Over 100 years ago, a Russian physiologist, Ivan Pavlov, was studying digestion in dogs. To collect their saliva he put them in a harness-like apparatus, exposed them to food, and let them drool into a tube. By accident, he realized that over time the dogs began to drool as soon as they were put in the apparatus, even if no food was available. He went on to train them to salivate in response to lights, bells, and other stimuli that he paired with the food (Pavlov, 1927). It turns out that these same mechanisms work in humans. We learn to respond to certain cues in certain ways. Smokers, soda drinkers and a variety of other consumers condition themselves to have positive responses to the logo or brand name of their favorite product.

Conversely, many of us have inadvertently conditioned ourselves to avoid things we associate with negative outcomes. For example, if you have ever eaten a particular food and then felt nauseated, you avoid eating that food in the future. From a survival point of view, this conditioned taste aversion makes sense. Humans are omnivores, meaning we forage for and eat a variety of foods. If we eat something that is unripe or spoiled and it makes us sick, we want to avoid it in the future, so responding to that food item with disgust is useful. However, sometimes we learn to associate a certain food with nausea, even though we know objectively that it didn't cause our illness. Think of women who are experiencing morning sickness or travelers who get seasick. Even though they know that their symptoms would occur with a variety of foods, they often have difficulty overcoming the aversion they developed when a particular food was paired with the nausea. It turns out that the central nucleus in the amygdala is crucial to the development of conditioned responses.

CANCELING OUT NEGATIVE RESPONSES

Fortunately, it turns out that we can alter our responses to stress through a variety of mechanisms. Exercise and relaxation can dissipate muscle tension, measured breathing can slow heart rate and blood pressure, music can alter our emotional states, and changing our thoughts can calm our stomach and gastrointestinal system. In some cases, these actions work by allowing the body to physically act on fight-or-flight driven impulses; in others, they constitute actions that are incompatible with the fight-or-flight response. By definition, it is impossible to be anxious, agitated, and relaxed at the same time. Fortunately, we can learn to alter the largely unconscious physiological correlates of emotions without specifically understanding the underlying biology. In subsequent chapters, we will explore ways to identify and modify your characteristic cognitive, emotional, and physiological response patterns in order to enhance your ability to respond effectively to stress, but we still need to talk about your behavioral responses to stressful life events.

LEARNING FROM CONSEQUENCES

As we have previously discussed, humans tend to be problem solvers. If it is cold and we have the means to light a fire, we will do so. If the food we have is too hard to chew easily, we will cook it on the fire, and if the smoke from the fire becomes bothersome, we will find a way to divert it from us. However, we don't always have the resources or skills necessary to fix or avoid problems, and not all problems have a physical solution. In addition, some of our solutions may themselves cause other problems. If the fire we lit gets out of hand and starts a wildfire, being cold may no longer be a problem, but being homeless might be.

Not surprisingly, early psychologists devoted a great deal of time to thinking about how behaviors emerge and why they persist or disappear. The foremost thinker in this area, B. F. Skinner, postulated that behaviors can be specifically linked to the things that precede them (antecedents) and the things that follow them (consequences). According to Skinner, antecedents can stimulate a response, but the consequences determine whether or not a behavior is emitted again. Take, for example, learning to be polite. If a child who says "please" is consistently given a cookie, they will probably learn to use the word routinely. If they are swatted on the hand for just grabbing the cookie, they will learn not to do the behavior. Obviously, these two scenarios exemplify what we typically call reinforcement and punishment (Skinner, 1953 & 1976).

However, Skinner also described two other possible behavioral consequences. Sometimes we do learn to commit a behavior to remove something negative, which he called negative reinforcement. Taking an aspirin to minimize pain is a good example. In other cases, we learn to stop doing a behavior that results in our losing something we like, sometimes called negative punishment. When a teen is grounded for missing their curfew, it is an example of punishing a behavior by taking away something the individual values, namely, their freedom.

Occasionally, the outcome of a behavior includes elements of more than one type of consequence. For example, most people find getting a speeding ticket to be extremely aversive. First of all, it is embarrassing to be pulled over to the side of the road and chastised. This is classic punishment. But for most tickets, we also have to pay a fine or pay to take a defensive driving course. Both of these outcomes are examples of negative reinforcement, since the state is taking away something you value in order to change your behavior. Unfortunately, since there aren't enough police to catch every instance of people speeding, getting a ticket doesn't tend to deter people's speeding in the future. When the punishment is intermittent, we may gamble and go back to speeding. But if a reward is intermittent—and especially if we don't know when the next payout will come—we may continue to do the behavior long after we have been awarded. Think of people playing slot machines or the child of an abusive parent who keeps seeking approval from the parent, although it is delivered in an inconsistent manner.

But understanding the basics of behavior is not enough. We also have to consider the skills underlying the behavior and the value of the reward associated with that behavior. For example, I might believe that getting a gold medal in the Olympics is a great goal, but I also know that I don't have the athletic skills and ability necessary to compete at that level. Conversely, I

Jamie Gray, bites her Olympic gold medal after winning the women's 50-meter rifle 3-positions event August 4, 2012.

might have the skills I need to do a job, but be missing the requisite interest in the offered reward. It turns out that the things that motivate us vary between people, within people, and across situations. If I love chocolate, then being offered a piece of homemade chocolate cake might get me to clean up the table while someone else cooks. However, if I hate chocolate, I might well decide not to clean up the table because the reward isn't worth it to me. Finally, I might find that I don't know where any of the dishes go and so don't have the necessary skills to complete the task.

Often, when people get frustrated with their own behavior, whether they are trying to quit drinking or smoking or if they are procrastinating or avoiding something, they assume that the problem is either laziness or a lack of motivation. However, in practice people often lack the skills necessary to make the behavioral change. Students who are anxious may avoid studying not because they don't care how they do on the test, but because they care a lot and so get very anxious when looking at the material. Or it may be that they do not have strong study skills and so don't know how to effectively tackle a big project. In these cases, showing students how to identify what they fear, and helping them gain the skills they need to study more effectively or to feel more in control can make a huge difference.

Delayed Gratification

Figuring out what skills you need to manage stress can seem daunting, but whether you need to develop better study skills, learn how to quit smoking, or how to relax or exercise effectively can be the first step in behavior change. The hardest part of the process, though, is realizing that the new behavior, while not terribly rewarding in the short run, will pay off later. It turns out that being able to wait for something is a key component of coping and thriving in general. In the late 1950s, psychologist Walter Mischel (Mischel, Ebbesen, & Zeiss, 1972; Mischel & Ayudek, 2004) tested this premise using preschool children and marshmallows. In the experiment, children were left alone in a room with a treat such as a marshmallow, candy, or a cookie. The child was then told that they could eat the treat immediately, or wait a few minutes and then have two of them. Video tape of the children while they were waiting indicates that it was very hard for them to resist the treat, and in fact only 30 percent of the children were able to delay for the entire 15 minutes the experimenter was out of the room. The fascinating piece of this experiment is not that most young children are impulsive, but that having self-control while young is actually predictive of success, both personally and academically, 20 years later. When Mischel followed up on the 600+ children in his study, he found that the ability to delay gratification was significantly related to everything from classroom behavior to having higher SAT scores.

Are We Born This Way?

Such correlations however, don't explain why some children were able to wait and others were not. Is this sort of control, or willpower, an inborn trait or something that we can teach? Certainly, a large part of socialization in general involves teaching children to follow rules, wait their turn, and be fair to others, all of which require impulse control. But perhaps some of us find these tasks easier than others. In the personality literature, the concept of personality traits suggests that there are innate differences in how people approach the world (Pervin & John, 2001). The most commonly used personality measure to date, the Big 5 Personality Inventory, rates people on five statistically derived dimensions (Digman, 1990). These include neuroticism, defined as the tendency to experience emotional instability, anxiety, and sadness; extraversion is characterized by sociability, emotional expressiveness, and talkativeness; conscientiousness, which reflects self-control and orientation toward goals; agreeableness, or the predisposition to trust others, to be kind and engage in prosocial behaviors; and openness to new ideas and a broad range of interests: Each of these dimensions is seen as a continuum and is assumed to have a strong genetic component. However, the Social Investment theory argues that the particular expression of personality traits in an individual is a function both of their genetics and their life experiences, culture, and social milieu. Certainly, the irrational beliefs concept, as detailed by Ellis and Beck, implies that if people view the world as a threatening place and see discomfort or failure as unacceptable, one possible response is to give up on the goals or to quit trying. On the other hand, people who frame stressful events as challenges rather than threats and who assume that short-term discomfort may be worth a long-term reward (think dieting, exercising, studying) are more likely to persist and eventually to succeed in reaching complex goals.

What are your New Year's resolutions?

Obviously, changing thoughts, feelings, and behaviors is not an easy task. Simply looking at the number of people who fail to achieve their New Year's resolutions each January brings home that fact. There are clearly a number of factors that can either contribute to success or predict failure. When under stress, we tend to experience a complex combination of sensations, including visceral symptoms, uncomfortable emotions, agitated thoughts, and behavioral impulses that may or may not improve the situation. Many of us approach this tangled web with the belief that it is impossible to tease out the strands. Among my students and clients, I frequently hear people say "I can't change my feelings," "I have always been this way," and "that's just the way I think." However, the principles of Cognitive Behavioral therapy and stress management suggest that with a little bit of effort, we can decide to change patterns that are not working for us.

THE STORY OF OUR LIVES

In addition, recent work from clinical and cognitive psychology suggests that we are predisposed to look for the underlying causes of events, to try to make sense of the things that happen around us. When faced with deciding whether a snake is poisonous, whether a road continues on to our destination beyond the horizon, or whether a storm is going to threaten us, we call on our experience to speculate and make assumptions about how things in the real world behave. We rarely assume that all snakes are the same, that because we can't see a road it ends, or that hail will fall up instead of down. Likewise, we tend to use these same cognitive abilities to create stories to help us understand and explain what is going on in our personal and social lives. These stories, called narratives, often have a theme, which shapes how we interpret events and how we choose to respond. For example, an individual who tends to see him- or herself as a victim based on the ways their family responded to stress or due to early childhood exploitation may cope with adversity by trying to blame others and find people to solve their problems for them.

In contrast, someone who sees her- or himself as a survivor may choose to focus on their strength in the face of adversity and seek solutions for the problem that do not undermine their own sense of control. It is likely that these narrative themes, much like irrational thoughts, evolve over time, are automatic, and even below our conscious awareness and yet strongly influence our lives (Madigan, 2010). Psychologist Jamie Pennebaker (1997) has explored this idea, focusing on the therapeutic benefit of writing about stressful events and on the impact of specific word choices in determining how we view ourselves, what we find stressful, and how others see us.

Learning to persevere in the face of adversity has recently come to be called resilience. This term, which stems from the positive psychology movement (Seligman, 2000), has been applied to military veterans overcoming life-threatening injuries, to athletes performing despite setbacks, and to ordinary people who take action to change their neighborhoods or their communities. The basic idea behind resilience is that we can learn from how others cope in order to achieve our own goals and dreams. The key seems to be developing our awareness of the power of these narratives to shape our lives and of applying our understanding of how thoughts, emotions, and physiological responses to stress interact to make more conscious choices about how to behave in a given situation.

MAKING SENSE OF THE TITLE OF THIS BOOK

On a recent trip to London, I was struck by the recorded message "Mind the Gap," used in the underground tube (subway) stations to remind people to watch for the gap between the platform and the door of the train. The more I thought about it, the more I realized that this was the perfect metaphor for learning to cope with stress effectively by consciously identifying, analyzing, and choosing your responses to the stressful gaps in your life. In short, you can use the acronym to clarify and eventually change your responses to stress by learning to:

> **M**anage your thoughts
> **I**dentify your feelings
> **N**otice physical sensations
> **D**evelop effective coping skills

The next four chapters will delve into each of these topics in order to help you develop the awareness and learn the skills you need to identify and manage your own stress responses. While stress is an inevitable aspect of life, using your mind to consciously choose how you respond to any given event is the key to coping. Whether you are coping with a hassle such as trouble finding a parking space or a major life event such as a serious illness, you can still learn to manage these domains.

PUT YOUR MONEY WHERE YOUR MOUTH IS

Several years ago, I had the opportunity to try out this theory in my own life. It started when I noticed a slight numbness in my right hand, which seemed to center on my index finger. When it got worse over the course of several months I saw my doctor, who suspected that it might be carpal tunnel syndrome, since I use my computer a lot. I then saw a hand specialist, who ran a variety of tests and determined that I had a nerve problem, not carpal tunnel symptoms. It wasn't until my primary doctor sent me to a neurologist, who ordered an MRI, that we realized what was going on.

To make a long story short, I ended up having cervical spinal surgery, twice. It turned out that my spinal cord was both very narrow and slightly curved in my neck, so that when some of the disks slipped a bit with aging, they started to press on the cord. This causes swelling, and also blocked the spinal cord fluid on that side, further irritating the nerves. Left untreated, I would eventually have lost control of my body and even ended up in a wheelchair. Fortunately, in the past decade, advances in the use of lasers and other high-tech tools have enabled surgeons to go into the spinal cord, remove the bulging disks, and replace them with titanium pins and put the whole thing back together again. I eventually had to have five screws placed in my neck to stabilize things. Immediately following the surgery, it wasn't clear how much mobility I would lose or how much better my hands would get.

Fortunately, I am doing well. I will always have some numbness in my hands, which only bothers me when I am trying to put earrings on or to pass out papers in class, and have a full range of motion in my neck. However, I still remember how shocked and scared I was on the day I got the diagnosis and how angry I was that the surgery would disrupt my teaching schedule and my vacation plans. However, after a day of moping, crying, and being angry that this had happened to me, it became clear that I couldn't very well teach the principles of stress management and not at least try to apply them in my own life.

I started by evaluating what made me most scared. Once I started thinking about it, I realized that I trusted my surgeon, our insurance would cover the bulk of my expenses, and work would go on without me. I then spent some time thinking about how easy it was for me to catastrophize about all the things that could go wrong, rather than focusing on how lucky I was that we figured out what was wrong before more damage was done, and that I lived in an era when there was treatment available. I consciously resolved that I would not dwell on "What ifs" and "If onlys," but instead would try to focus on the present as much as I could.

I then went out and read all I could about the surgery and healing and the power of relaxation and positive thought and created a plan for myself. After the surgery, I set exercise and activity goals, and throughout the process I focused on talking and spending time with people I knew would support me rather than making me more anxious, and on accomplishing things I normally did not have time to do, like organizing my recipes and catching up on my reading. The end result was that I came through both surgeries with flying colors, healed well, and now, three years later, am walking, driving, typing, and even skiing, like I never even had the surgery. The point, of course, being that while we can't control many of the things that happen to us, we can control the mind and how we choose to respond to the crisis or threat.

What Do You Think?

Think about your most stressful experience in the past week:

1. What were you thinking? Could you have interpreted the situation differently?
2. What were you feeling at the time? Which emotion was strongest?
3. How do you experience stress physically (rapid breathing, headache, gastrointestinal distress, or other symptoms?
4. How did you try to cope? Was it effective? What else could you have tried?

Repeat this exercise with other stressful experiences and look for the similarities in your responses.

REFERENCES

Beck, J. S. (2011). *Cognitive behavior therapy: Basics and beyond.* 2nd ed. New York: Guilford

Cannon, W. B. (1915). *Bodily Changes in Pain, Hunger, Fear and Rage: An Account of Recent Researches into the Function of Emotional Excitement.* New York: D. Appleton & Co.

Digman, J. M. (1990). "Personality structure: Emergence of the five-factor model." *Annual Review of Psychology,* 41: 417–440.

Ellis, A. (2001). *Overcoming Destructive Beliefs, Feelings, and Behaviors: New Directions for Rational Emotive Behavior Therapy.* New York: Prometheus.

Greenberg, G. (2011). *Comprehensive Stress Management.* New York: McGraw-Hill Humanities/Social Sciences/ Languages.

Holahan, C. J., Moos, R. H., Holahan, C. K., Brennan, P. L., & Schutte, K. K. (2005). Stress generation, avoidance coping, and depressive symptoms: a 10-year model. *J Consult Clin Psychol, 73*(4), 658–666.

Madigan, S. (2010). *Narrative Therapy.* Washington D.C.: APA.

Myers, G. (2001) *William James: His Life and Thought.* Yale University Press.

Mischel, W., & Ayduk, O. (2004). "Willpower in a cognitive-affective processing system: The dynamics of delay of gratification." In R. F. Baumeister & K. D. Vohs (Eds.), *Handbook of Self-Regulation: Research, Theory, and Applications* (pp. 99–129). New York: Guilford.

Mischel, W., Ebbesen, E. B., & Zeiss, A. R. (1972). "Cognitve and attentional mechanisms in delay of gratification." *Journal of Personality and Social Psychology,* 21 (2): 204–218.

Pavlov, I. P. (1927). *Conditioned Reflexes.* London: Oxford University Press.

Pennebaker, J. W. (1997). *Opening Up: The Healing Power of Expressing Emotion.* New York: Guilford Press.

Pervin, L. A., & John, O. P. (2001). *Handbook of Personality: Theory and Research, Second Edition.* New York: Guilford Press.

Seligman, M. E. P. (2006). *Learned Optimism: How to Change Your Mind and Your Life.* New York: Pocket Books, Simon & Schuster.

Seligman, M. E. P. (2000). Positive Psychology. *American Psychologist,* 55, 1, 5–14.

Skinner, B. F. (1953). *Science and Human Behavior.* New York: Macmillan.

Skinner, B. F. (1976). *About Behaviorism.* New York: Vintage Books.

CHAPTER 10

IS IT REALLY ALL IN YOUR HEAD?

KEY POINTS

- The brain often attempts to manage complex input by simplifying impressions and responding in familiar ways.
- Irrational or dysfunctional beliefs are cognitions that predispose us to emotions such as anger, anxiety, and depression.
- Cognitive flexibility is the key to managing stress.

SAY WHAT'S ON YOUR MIND

"Let me think a minute," we say when pausing to decide what to buy for dinner, remember where we put our car keys, or consider whether to marry the person we have been dating for six months. But what does "thinking" really entail? If some thoughts are "deep," does that mean others are shallow? Why do the words of a song or a friend's maiden name evade all your efforts at recall only to come back to you when you are in the shower thinking about something else altogether?

It has often been said that language and the ability to think in verbal, abstract ways are what set humans apart from the rest of the animal kingdom. When babies are born, we coo, lean forward, and immediately start talking to them, even though we know they don't understand what we are saying. Many of us do the same things to our puppies and kittens, despite the fact we are quite sure they will never reply to us in our own language. As noted linguist Noam Chomsky (1998) has written, "Human language appears to be a unique phenomenon, without significant analogue in the animal world." Essentially, any human child with an intact brain and raised by people who communicate verbally will learn to speak simply by listening and participating in the process. In fact, as many parents know, it is extremely hard to get us to stop talking once we start.

Research shows that at birth, an infant will orient or turn his or her head toward the mother's voice rather than that of a stranger. Up until six months of age, infants can tell the difference between any sounds that humans are capable of making. We know this because infants, like adults, get tired of hearing the same thing over and over, so if we introduce a new sound to a child, they turn towards it or suck on a pacifier more than if it is a sound they are familiar with. Interestingly, before six months of age, pretty much any baby can hear the difference between *la* and *ra*. However, since Japanese does not separate these two sounds, Japanese infants lose this ability in the first year of life, while English-speaking babies do not (Garcia-Sierra et al. 2011).

Likewise, all babies start out by babbling a variety of sounds, even those who are deaf and cannot hear. By about a year, children start using words from the language they have been exposed to and then show an unbelievable growth in vocabulary over the next few years. A typical child can speak up to 50 words by 18 months, 200 by 24 months, and 1000 by three years. By five years old, a child knows up to 10,000 words and the basics of grammar, although they may still make errors in tense and structure. Studies of deaf children who are taught sign language indicate that they proceed through these stages of language learning at about the same pace as hearing children. For a good review of language acquisition and development, see Eve Clark's book, *First Language Acquisition* (2009).

In the meantime, our poor dogs and cats often spend 10 to 15 years listening to us babble and never babble back. This is not to say that such animals don't understand at least some of what we are saying. Certainly, pets learn their own names, can fetch objects on demand, and can act out their desires by nudging dog dishes, scratching doors, etc., but they certainly never use language to write poetry, oral histories of their family line, or comparisons of their religious beliefs. So, what is it about humans that makes us so talkative? Early psychologists assumed that dogs and cats were just not smart enough to learn to talk and so decided to see if they could teach language to other primates. Attempts in the 1950s to raise a primate as a baby failed because it turns out that nonhuman primates simply don't have the breath control and vocal cord capacity that we do; thus, they cannot make the sounds that we do. Although we do much of it unconsciously, if you have ever tried to explain to someone how to make a particular sound like *th* or *tr*, it is actually very difficult to break down the process of how to do it. Trying to talk with a numb tongue after a dental visit can also give you a sense of how very complex our ability to produce sounds actually is. It turns out that in our brains, more neurons are tissue devoted to controlling our tongues and our lips than to our entire backs. That's why a paper cut on your lip is likely to seem more painful than a larger scrape on your back.

To get around these vocal limitations of primates, other groups of researchers, including a married couple, Allen and Beatrix Gardner (Hillix & Rumbaugh, 2004), tried teaching apes to use sign language. Working with a female chimpanzee named Washoe, they were able to teach her to use about 160 words by showing her the symbols, manipulating her hands into the shapes, and rewarding her with treats for their use. Subsequent studies have shown that people who know sign language but are not familiar with the trained chimps can easily read the symbols the chimps make. However, there are some significant differences between the language skills of primates and human children. While the apes can learn several hundred words, remember that four-year-old children know thousands. In addition, no matter how long they practice, apes rarely combine more than three or four words at a time, use complex grammar, or get very abstract in their conversations.

Recent studies have demonstrated similar language capabilities in dolphins, sea lions, and parrots, which again seem capable of learning and responding to human words, and in the case of parrots, even saying them, but never exceed the language complexity of young human children (Cambridge University Press).

THE TALKATIVE SIDE OF YOUR BRAIN

So how do our brains generate and produce language? You have undoubtedly heard that the left side of the brain is the language center, while the right side is more spatial or nonverbal. It is, in fact, true that two specific structures have been identified on the left side of the brain, which are crucial for language (Gershwind, 1972). The first, called Broca's area, after the French physician who first realized that damage to this area interfered with people's ability to speak, is located in the left frontal cortex. When it is damaged, people can talk and understand language, but their speech is not normal. They tend to use short phrases which lack grammar and structure, much like small children do. This inability to produce language is called aphasia.

In contrast, a German neurologist named Carl Wernicke identified an area in the left posterior temporal cortex, which, when damaged, results in difficulty understanding language or speaking meaningfully. Such patients produce language and even use words grammatically—for example, they will use the correct past tense of a word, but the overall sentence makes no sense. So, while a Broca's patient might painfully say, "Me water" to indicate they are thirsty, a Wernicke's patient might say something like "I drink pencils very well, please."

Of course, the actual production of speech also involves numerous other brain functions. Broca's and Wernicke's areas are connected by numerous bands of neurons and surrounded by what are known as association areas, which seem to be involved in the coordination and integration of speech production. Of course, to actually speak a word we also have to activate the motor pathways that control our mouths, lips, vocal cords, and tongues, and our brain also instigates complex timing mechanisms to coordinate what we say. However, language is certainly not just a simple matter of sound production. In order to produce meaningful language, we also must integrate sensory, emotional, and memory circuits in our brain.

Assuming that our Broca's and Wernicke's areas are intact, how then do we organize and use language to move beyond simple descriptions of objects and demands for milk or water? It turns out that our brains are also exceedingly good at building what we call categories, or concepts, which we use to organize our thoughts. While we as adults know that beagles and German shepherds are both dogs and that all dogs are mammals, it may take children a while to fully understand the complexity of these concepts—in fact, small children will often mistakenly call all four-legged animals dogs for some time before figuring out the rules about what constitutes a dog. As we get older, we tend to move from learning simple categories to more and more abstract ideas. Hence, we start thinking in terms of Liberals or Conservatives, Christians or Muslims, Caucasians or Hispanics. Each of these categories can, in fact, be described by rules, but the more abstract they become the harder it is for us to identify and agree on those rules. Humans also use language to describe time—for instance, whether you did something in the past or plan to do it in the future—and to talk about ourselves in the abstract.

BUILDING AN ABSTRACT WORLD IN OUR HEADS

This ability to project our actions and to think about ourselves thinking, appears to be uniquely human. It both enables us—and dooms us—to spend much of our time thinking about things that have already happened or may never happen and to worry about things like death and dying. This ability to consciously think about who we are, why we are here, and where we are going allows us to write novels, lose ourselves in movies, debate philosophy and

We will all confront issues and worries surrounding aging and dying.

ethics, and worry incessantly about things we have done or things we are afraid might happen. This means that humans are capable of creating a great deal of stress for themselves regarding things they are not currently experiencing or may never experience. As Robert Sapolsky writes in his book about stress, *Why Zebras Don't Get Ulcers* (2004), a zebra that manages to get away from a lion goes back to eating and doesn't seem to spend much time worrying about what almost happened. Humans, on the other hand, often respond to major stressors by spending a great deal of time talking and thinking about how things could have gone differently. The tendency to do this is actually called counterfactual regret. This has been linked to difficulties getting over such disparate stressors as being in a car accident or losing a child to sudden infant death syndrome.

In one study (Pillow & McNaughton-Cassill, 2001), some colleagues and I looked at how people's tendency to think that the death of Britain's Princess Diana could have been prevented was associated with the amount of time they spent watching media coverage of her death and how upset they were about her dying. Humans are also prone to quite a number of other types of thoughts, or cognitions, which predispose us to interpret events in certain ways and which can contribute to feelings of stress and other negative emotions.

CHANGING YOUR THOUGHTS

As mentioned in earlier chapters, researchers Aaron Beck, Albert Ellis, and Martin Seligman have spent much of their careers characterizing the types of thoughts that contribute to emotional distress. Called alternatively irrational beliefs, dysfunctional beliefs, or faulty attributions, these sorts of thoughts have been reliably linked to distress in the face of stressful events. The commonality among the work of all three theorists is the idea that the way you perceive things that happen in your life automatically determines how you will feel and respond, but that you can choose how you interpret those events.

Ellis, easily the most extreme of the three theorists, argued that much of human unhappiness stems from believing that you have to have the approval of others, that it is awful if things do not go the way you wish, that we should constantly worry about bad things that might happen in order to prevent them, and that the world should always be fair and perfect (Ellis & Harper, 1979; Ellis and MacLaren, 2004). In his writing and his lectures, Ellis was well known for telling people they were creating their own stress by filling their lives full of "musts" and awfulizing, instead of taking responsibility for their own feelings and actions and refusing to continue to view the world in rigid ways.

For his part, Aaron Beck suggested that emotional distress was often the result of negative thoughts about the self, the world and the future, which he labeled the negative cognitive triad. According to this formulation, people who have a tendency to think in terms of things that happen to them being all good or all bad or who easily magnify small problems into large ones, or who see catastrophe in even minor setbacks are likely to have the most trouble coping with stressful events. Beck believed that these sorts of assumptions can be so automatic that people do not even know they are making them. As part of his therapeutic process, Beck often asked patients to keep a log of negative things that happened to them and of what they were thinking and how they felt at that time. Often, patients are surprised by how quickly they jump from their boyfriend not calling them to imagining him dead in a ditch, or from getting a C on a test to failing out of school, never getting a job, and disappointing everyone they know.

Finally, Martin Seligman (1998), a psychologist well known for his work on mental states, studied animals and people who exhibited helplessness or giving up in the face of adversity and those who demonstrate optimism, or the sense that they can manage during a crisis. Seligman concluded that people's attributions about how much control they have over a situation are strongly predictive of how stressed the situation will make them. For example, he suggests that when something happens to us, we tend to make decisions about whose fault it is, how stable the event is, and how much it will affect other areas of our lives. If we decide the event is our own fault, we are making an internal attribution. If we think it is not our fault, we are making an external attribution by blaming the event on chance, fate, a powerful other such as a doctor or a teacher, or a higher religious or spiritual force. When we see an event as stable, we assume that the situation is permanent or long-lasting rather than temporary. When we also generalize from one event to others, we are making global attributions about its meaning. In one study, Seligman showed that Olympic swimmers responded to setbacks like failing to win a race with optimism and the belief that they would succeed the next time they tried. Similarly, successful life insurance salesmen are characterized by an optimistic outlook about their chances of success no matter how many cold calls they have to make to get there. Seligman's work suggests that people who are optimistic are less likely to be depressed, tend to be more successful, and enjoy better health than more pessimistic people. A number of studies have even suggested that the speed of recovery from coronary surgery is related to optimism, with those with a positive outlook showing the fastest recovery.

As a faculty member, I frequently have the opportunity to watch students make such attributions when they get a lower grade than they expected or wanted on a test. Those people who immediately decide that they failed because they are a failure as a person, that the teacher is out to get them, and that they will fail every other test in the class, understandably feel depressed, anxious, and angry. Those less upset are the students who decide that they did poorly because they didn't study enough or did not buy the book, but that the teacher was trying to be fair and that they can perform differently on the next test. Obviously, there are many different ways people can interpret such an event, but what matters is how their choices impact their sense of control and future choices.

IT'S NOT MY FAULT

You may have noticed that many of the irrational beliefs and the attributional errors we have already discussed involve the concept of blame or responsibility. From the very earliest age, human children are concerned about the fairness of events and who is to blame when things go wrong. Parents of toddlers are often surprised by the ferocity with which their children assert that their siblings are at fault and that someone else caused their bad behavior. Conversely, many of us grew up hearing phrases like "you are breaking your mother's heart," "he made me do it," and "I can't help how I feel." Unfortunately, none of these phrases is as clear-cut as it sounds. While other people's behavior certainly impacts us, only we choose how to think, feel, and respond to any event. There is certainly no evidence that disappointment about your child's behavior actually destroys your heart. Few parents would allow a child to justify misbehavior because a friend told them to do it, and we can help and even alter how we feel if we choose to. Taking responsibility for your own actions when you can, in fact, manage or change a situation, and being realistic about your impact on others and their impact on you, are key components of the cognitive behavioral approach to stress management. Blaming yourself for negative things and discounting your successes are surefire ways of becoming depressed. In the meantime, feeling guilty for not meeting the needs of all the people around you can make you feel trapped, stressed, and hopeless. If you then try to cope by overresponding to their needs, you reinforce their false belief that their well-being is dependent on your actions and deprive them of the opportunity to take control of their own situation and emotions.

SOMETIMES THE GLASS IS HALF EMPTY, BUT WHAT CAN YOU DO ABOUT IT?

Of course, arguing that we can control our responses to events by simply thinking differently about them can make people feel that their emotions and responses are being ignored or discounted. However, cognitive approaches to stress management are not designed to convince people that a bad situation isn't bad or that adversity is not stressful. In fact, many bad events cannot be denied. If your spouse is diagnosed with Alzheimer's disease or dies in a car wreck, or your house is destroyed by a hurricane, those are indeed real crises. However, in each of those cases you can make choices about how to respond given the reality of the situation. Wishing that the diagnosis were different will not change the course of your spouse's condition, but educating yourself about the disease, joining a support group, and enlisting caregiving help from other members of the family can make a huge difference to a caregiver's own well-being.

Similarly, grieving the death of a family member may take months or years, but engaging in activities or causes in their honor, letting go of "if only" thoughts about what happened, and seeking social support can significantly impact how we cope. Survivors of even devastating events such as fires and earthquakes are sometimes able to find positive aspects in their situation. For example, they often report being genuinely surprised by how many people go out of their way to help them and describe how the event helped them to reorganize their lives and priorities in ways they might not normally have been able to do.

In fact, there is even a field of research now looking at "posttraumatic growth," or how people find ways to cope with extraordinary stress in ways that enhance their lives or those of the people around them. For example, Candy Lightner, the founder of Mothers Against Drunk Driving, founded the group after her daughter was killed by a drunk driver. While no mother should have to lose a child that way, her efforts helped her to find a meaningful way to respond to a very negative event. Learning to identify your own characteristic responses to stress—for instance, magnifying negative events, personalizing others' actions, or believing that things should be fair—can enable people to generate alternative thoughts that are less likely to contribute to the experience of negative emotions and stress, and to promote responses and behaviors which ameliorate the stressor or facilitate adaptive coping responses.

COGNITIVE BEHAVIORAL THERAPY

Such psychotherapeutic approaches to teaching people to consciously identify and choose their thoughts are often referred to as cognitive behavioral therapy. Although their implementation can vary, such techniques tend to focus on teaching people to recognize dysfunctional thoughts and to generate other possible interpretations of their situations. This enables them to regain a sense of control over these situations or the future. In some cases, this can involve making behavioral changes, such as seeking tutoring or changing your diet. In other instances, it may also involve questioning your assumption that you can't do math or that you write best at the last minute under pressure. Occasionally, people find themselves in stressful situations for which they have no viable behavioral option. However, even people who have been held as a prisoner of war or been tortured have reported they were able to cope and maintain hope by retaining the sense that no matter what happened, they could control their own thoughts.

However, as anyone who has ever lost their temper and said things they didn't mean knows, sometimes thoughts seem to be a poor match for feelings. Strong anger, sadness, and anxiety seem to take us by storm. We feel our bodies tense or sag, our faces flush, and our hands chill, as though we have no control over them at all. Often, we blurt out things that we do not really mean or at least did not want to tell that person in such a way.

WE AREN'T CAVEMEN ANYMORE, ARE WE?

This is actually not an accident. Going back to the way the brain is structured, the parts of the brain that initiate and control emotion are located under the cortex. They are phylogenetically older structures, which have strong survival value. Fighting when you are threatened, running when you are scared, or taking care of offspring you feel attached to, all promote the well-being of the species. In fact, through much of human history, stressors were acute, life threatening, and required immediate responses. If you did not run you were eaten; if you didn't hide your offspring, they were eaten, and so forth. Frequently, this meant that survival was a matter of snap, reflexive decisions, not reflective ruminations. To some degree, this is still true in modern life. If a car swerves into your lane, chances are you will respond almost automatically to avoid a crash, and may later even think that you weren't really aware of making the decision to do so at the time. Similarly, people who survive building collapses, plane crashes, and other catastrophes often report that they operated almost on automatic pilot at the time, following their gut responses, and only later thought about the ramifications of those actions.

How can you better manage your emotions in tense situations?

Unfortunately, however, modern life is filled with stressors which are not life or death or even physical, but which still trigger strong, rapid cognitive and emotional responses. Assuming that the person ahead of you cut in line because they wanted to cheat rather than that they didn't realize you were in line, can rapidly raise your blood pressure; a tendency to say something could result in a fight. Blaming your spouse for wasting money before you realize that they used the cash to buy you a gift may make you say something you wish you hadn't said.

In our quest to make sense of a complicated, rapidly changing world, we often jump to conclusions, filter information through our expectations, and fall back on familiar irrational beliefs. Neurologically, this makes sense. Emotions, controlled by structures deep in the brain, are necessary for survival. Their control varies little between rats, cats, chimps, and humans because they are nonverbal, physiological responses. Thoughts, on the other hand, stem from the cortical areas, which evolved after the emotional system was already firmly in place. In order to allow us to formulate thoughts and convey them verbally, the cortex has to integrate a vast amount of information from the sensory, emotional, and memory centers of our brain.

The language centers in the left frontal and temporal parts of our brain have to form words, produce them in the right sequence, and modulate the tone in which we say them. It turns out, though, that this often happens very quickly, without our conscious awareness. When the ways in which we interpret a situation predispose us to see it as a catastrophe or when the way in which we communicate verbally with others is ineffective, our stress levels are likely to rise quickly.

The good news is that people can learn to consciously choose how they interpret and describe the things that happen to them in ways that enhance their ability to cope effectively. To be clear, this does not mean denying that something bad has happened or pretending that an event was more positive than it was. Instead, it involves learning to recognize the sorts of assumptions you typically make about the world and being far more mindful of those thoughts and their impact on your emotions and actions.

I am sure that some of you are thinking to yourself right now, "this is a crock, I know what I am thinking," so let me give you a little exercise to see if that is the case. Find a pen or pencil somewhere and a watch or clock with a second hand. For a period of 10 seconds, make a tick in the margin of this book every time a thought crosses your mind. (Some of you may also notice that it is hard for you to make yourself write in a book, having been told for years that it is something you should not do!) However, having done this with hundreds of students, I know that the majority of you will report three to five thoughts in that period of time. Some will have fewer, and occasionally someone will manage to squeeze in nine or ten ideas. The thing to notice is how many thoughts you had in such a short period of time and then multiply that by 6 for a minute, then 60 for an hour, etc. In a given day, we have hundreds of thoughts, most of which we neither notice consciously nor need to remember. Those that are repetitive, accompanied by strong emotion or very meaningful to us, may be easier to access, but often we are unaware of even their impact on our functioning.

Typically, in order to identify and start to address the role of cognitions in creating stress, cognitive behavioral approaches suggest that people keep a log or diary for a week or more. Here they will note each time they get stressed or upset, what the external event was, what they were thinking and feeling at the time, and even how they responded behaviorally. Those of us who are prone to dysfunctional or irrational thought patterns are often surprised by how many times we think in terms of what we "must" or "should" do, catastrophize or magnify a problem, personalize the comments or actions of others, think about how "unfair" things are, or engage in "if only" thought patterns. Once you have identified your own pattern of stress-inducing thoughts, the trick is to teach yourself to evaluate those automatic assumptions and come up with alternative ways to think about the problem. Is it true that because you didn't get a job you are a failure, or that you need to revise your résumé? Did the person driving ahead of you cut you off to be aggressive or because they are lost? Are your friends ignoring you or are they waiting for you to follow up on their phone call? The trick in each of these cases is to notice what sorts of situations tend to set you off and what your characteristic thoughts are in response to each one. You also want to avoid negative, polarizing ways of thinking that focus on blame and future disaster, as opposed to realistic acceptance of what has happened and the formulation of a way to manage either the situation or your response to it.

Now obviously, this is something that is easier said than done. Our brain is wired to make decisions fast, to categorize material quickly based on a rapid perusal of a situation, and to respond quickly to threats and stress. In his best-selling book *Blink*, author Malcolm Gladwell (2005) explores how we make snap judgments or decisions, with an emphasis on the fact that we are actually very good at the process. However, human experience is complex, our emotional and cognitive responses are integrated in ways we do not yet fully understand, and the world has changed in ways

Malcolm Gladwell

in the past 100 years that we are just starting to recognize. As a result, most of us must put significant effort into consciously identifying why we respond as we do and to make changes in those patterns.

BANNING THE "IF ONLY" REFRAIN

In a remarkably clear, readable book called *Rapid Relief from Emotional Distress*, authors Gary Emery and James Campbell (1986) describe a number of ways to apply cognitive principles to stress management. One particularly useful technique from this book involves the use of the seemingly innocuous little acronym, ACT. In their formulation, the "A" in the ACT formula stands for Accept Reality. It is the authors' contention that people create a great deal of their stress by spending time wishing that things were different from the way they are. As mentioned earlier, this tendency to ruminate on how things might have been, called counterfactual regret, has been associated with the prolongation of stress in a variety of contexts.

Consequently, Emery and Campbell assert that coming to terms with how things really are is the first step in coping. To do this, you may have to accept that your spouse does not want to stop smoking, your boss isn't fair, you don't make as much money as you wish, your kids are not marrying the people you want them to, etc. The catch is that often, by definition, the stress you are experiencing is occurring because you cannot change the external circumstances or the behavior of others. Once you accept that, your task is to Create a Vision (the "C" in the formula) of how you want to behave given the reality of your circumstances. If your spouse won't quit smoking, how will you minimize the impact of their smoking on you and your children? If you don't like your job, what will you need to do to gain the skills or make the contacts necessary to change jobs? The "T," Take Action, is actually the easiest step if you have figured out the first two.

Ironically, people are usually much better at telling you what is wrong with a situation than telling you how to fix it. When I was doing couples therapy, clients would come in and talk for hours about what their spouse did wrong. However, they were often stymied if I asked them to tell me specifically what the spouse could do that would eliminate the problem. Women who had argued that their spouses never helped with the children were suddenly faced with admitting that it wasn't that the spouse never helped, but that he didn't do things the way she wanted him to do them when he did help. The reality was that she could have his help if she was willing to give up some control or she could choose to retain more control by doing everything herself. Clearly, though, this changes the argument they are having.

I have found that the ACT formula works well for both minor and major stressful events. Because I tend to overbook myself, I frequently find myself racing to find parking, finish errands, or get to class in an impossibly short amount of time. As long as I spend all my energy thinking "if only the light changes, a spot becomes available, the hall isn't crowded, I can still make it," I am not dealing with reality. If I left the house 10 minutes late at rush hour, the reality is that I will be late to my meeting. Once I accept that, I have to take responsibility for my actions, by calling to offer the person I am meeting with the opportunity to decide if they want to wait or not, by eliminating something else out of my schedule to make things fit and sometimes by apologizing for having to reschedule. Simply wishing things were different however, tends to make me feel anxious, mad at myself, and out of control without addressing the particular situation at all.

In the final analysis, recurrent stresses such as being repeatedly late also offer us the opportunity to apply the ACT formula on a larger scale. Since the root of my lateness is my desire to finish one task before starting another, and the tendency to try to do too much to make others happy, in the long run I need to come to terms with the fact that modern life is a series of transitions from one long-running task to another, and that there are far too many people in our lives now for us to please everyone. Basically, I need to accept the fact that I can't get everything done, create a vision of myself scheduling my time more realistically (and saying no), and to then act on those ideals.

However, even scheduling time more realistically is a cognitive task. While bookstores and the Web are filled with books on how to manage, organize, and structure your time more efficiently, the book *Stumbling on Happiness* (2007) by Daniel Gilbert describes how hard it is for us to make decisions and project how things will be in the future, given the ways in which our brain processes information. Gilbert, a Harvard psychologist argues that it is difficult for people to imagine feeling or thinking differently in the future than they do in the present because such projection actually is a relatively new cognitive skill in the first place. Consequently, if you are in Minnesota in the winter, it actually takes effort to think about what to pack for a mid-winter trip to Florida, where it will be 50 degrees warmer.

In addition, according to Gilbert, when thinking about the future, we tend to make decisions based on why we should do something, rather than on how we would actually accomplish it. So, volunteering to serve on a worthy committee at your child's school is commendable and shows that you support your child and community. However, if you are already working too many hours and having trouble accomplishing routine daily tasks, then you really should make the decision based on how you would take on the task, given the reality of your daily life. Clearly prioritizing choices and participating in modern life is not simply a matter of updating your calendar. This requires a complex balance of values, priorities, practical considerations, and conscious cognitive deliberation. Not baking cookies for the band fundraiser does not mean that you are an uncaring parent who is letting your child down. A surprising number of us, however, evaluate such day-to-day events and make decisions in irrational ways that cumulatively contribute to our feeling sad, mad, anxious, inadequate, and stressed.

In another thoughtful book, *The Mindful Way through Depression* (2007), authors Williams, Teasdale, Segal, and Kabat-Zinn raise the idea that paying more attention to the present is a viable means of managing stress. Such focused concentration, called mindfulness, has been thoroughly discussed in Ellen Langer's book *Mindfulness* (1990) and Mihaly Csikszentmihalyi's book *Flow* (2008) as well. The underlying premise of mindfulness approaches is that dwelling on the past and worrying about the future distract us from living in the present. When people are mindful of what they are doing, they can take more joy in their daily activities and avoid worrying about the "if onlys" in their past and "what ifs" in the future. Carrying this further, Williams et al. suggest that when responding to a stressful situation, people evaluate whether they are actually stressed about things as they are or the fact that things are not exactly where they want them to be.

For example, following my spinal cord surgeries, I frequently experienced strange twinges, tingles, and other sensations, both in my neck and my arms and legs. However, even though the surgeon had warned me this would happen, I still worried a lot for the first couple of years. As time went on and my neck healed, the worry receded, but sometimes even now I worry when I have typed for too long and my hands start to feel numb and tingly. When I analyze this rationally, my hands actually feel better now than they did before the surgery, even when they are bothering me. In fact, if my hands stayed exactly as they are for the rest of my life, I would have no problem doing the things I want to do. But what worries me is the insidious idea that maybe they are tingling because something is wrong. Maybe they didn't heal correctly or will get worse and then I won't be able to type or put in my earrings, and what then? Of course, the point is that right now, my situation is bearable, and, in fact, it is only the future worry that is stressful—most of those worries will never come to pass. As Robert Sapolsky points out in his book *Why Zebras Don't Get Ulcers* (2004), other mammals tend to live their lives in the present. It is only our very human, very cognitive approach to the world that tends to predispose us to worry about things that already happened or may never happen, at the expense of our present well-being.

Clearly, becoming accustomed to questioning our thought patterns is not easy, but then again, neither is learning to play the piano, hit a baseball, do algebra, or write a novel, but the human brain can become very good at all of these tasks. The key lies not in pretending that stressful things are not happening, but rather in figuring out how to respond and move forward in ways that minimize their impact. This may mean looking at situations from more than one angle, resisting the tendency to interpret things in the same ways you always have in the past, and being honest about your role and the amount of control you have over a situation. To paraphrase a slogan I saw on a sweatshirt, "life, like gymnastics, is easier if you are flexible."

WHAT DO YOU THINK?

1. Look at the list of irrational beliefs. Which ones are you most likely to think about when you are stressed?
2. Think of a recent stressful event, your thoughts at the time, and alternative interpretations you could have made.
3. For the next week, pay attention to your patterns of irrational beliefs and how you could alter these characteristic thoughts.

REFERENCES

Cambridge University Press. *Can Animals Use Language?* http://www.cambridge.org/resources/0521612357/3215_Ch3AddlTextAnimalLg.pdf

Chomsky, N. (1998). *On Language*: Chomsky's Classic Works *Language and Responsibility* and *Reflections on Language* in one Volume. New Press.

Clark, E. V. (2009). *First Language Acquisition*. Cambridge: Cambridge University Press.

Csikszentmihalyi, M. (2008). *Flow: The Psychology of Optimal Experience*. New York: Harper Perennial Modern Classics.

Ellis, A., & Harper, R. (1979). *A New Guide to Rational Living*. Englewood Cliffs, NJ: Prentice Hall.

Ellis, A., & MacLaren, C. (2004). *Rational Emotive Behavior Therapy: A Therapist's Guide*. Atascadero, CA: Impact Publishers.

Emery, G., & Campbell, J. (1986). *Rapid Relief from Emotional Distress: A New, Clinically Proven Method for Getting over Depression & Other Emotional Problems without Prolonged or Expensive Therapy*. New York: Scribner.

Garcia-Sierra, A., Rivera-Gaxiola, M., Percaccio, C. R., Conboy, B. T., Romo, H., Klarman, L., Ortiz, S., & Kuhl, P. K. (2011). Bilingual language learning: An ERP study relating early brain responses to speech, language input, and later word production. *Journal of Phonetics*, doi: 10.1016/j.wocn.2011.07.002.

Geschwind, N. (1972). Language and the Brain. *Scientific American*, 226 (4), 76–83.

Gilbert, D. (2007). *Stumbling on Happiness*. New York: Vintage Press.

Gladwell, M. (2005). *Blink: The Power of Thinking without Thinking*. New York: Little, Brown and Company.

Hillix, W. A., & Rumbaugh, D. P. (2004). *Animal Bodies, Human Minds: Ape, Dolphin, and Parrot Language Skills*. New York: Springer.

Langer, E. (1990). *Mindfulness*. Reading MA: De Capo Press.

Pillow, D. R., & McNaughton-Cassill, M. E. (2001). Media exposure, perceived similarity, and counterfactual regret: Why did the public grieve when Princess Diana died? *Journal of Applied Social Psychology*, 10, 2072–2094.

Sapolsky, R. (2004). *Why Zebra's Don't Get Ulcers*. Holt Paperbacks.

Schnelle, H. (2010). *Language in the Brain*. Cambridge: Cambridge University Press.

Seligman, M. (1998). *Learned Optimism: How to Change Your Mind and Your Life*. New York: Pocket Books, Simon & Schuster.

Williams, M., Teasdale, J., Segal, Z., & Kabat-Zinn, J. (2007). *The Mindful Way through Depression*. New York: Guilford Press.

CHAPTER 11

FEELING STRESSED: ARE YOU WHAT YOU FEEL?

KEY POINTS

- Emotions are a primal force controlled by parts of the brain that are structured similarly in all mammals.
- Emotions are so important for survival that they can temporarily overwhelm conscious thought and lead to behaviors you regret later.
- Although it is tempting to ignore painful or uncomfortable feelings, they actually provide important clues about the environment, motivate us, help us to respond appropriately to other people, and regulate our well-being.

JUST CAN'T FIGHT THE FEELING

"You hurt my feelings" is a phrase so ubiquitous we rarely even ask what specific feeling is being discussed. Certainly, we all have a subjective sense of what emotions are, although our attempts to describe them verbally are often labored. Nevertheless, most of us would agree that emotions are psychological experiences, including changes in the body ranging from increased breathing and heart rate to gastrointestinal discomfort, to a dry mouth or feelings of faintness. Other changes in our facial expressions, levels of body tension, and even tone of voice are associated with specific emotional responses. So consistent are the physi-

ological aspects of emotional expressions that studies across cultures suggest that we can read the emotions of others, even when we don't speak the same language. In fact, as far as we know, all humans across all cultures smile when they are happy and frown when they are sad.

Learning to identify feelings is the key to understanding why we feel stressed and how best to cope. Although we have hundreds of words to define feelings, they never really seem to capture the experience, which is by definition nonverbal. In fact, it is actually hard to describe a feeling without talking about the way the body feels. "My stomach was upset," "my face was flushed," "I was too scared to breathe," all are the sorts of physical phrases we commonly use to convey our feelings. In our efforts to explain feelings, we may even use colors to try to communicate. "She was green with envy," "he felt sad and blue," and "he was so mad he saw red" are such common phrases we don't even have to think about what they mean. Clearly, emotions are ubiquitous, nonverbal, and visceral experiences that often literally leave us speechless.

I DON'T KNOW HOW I FEEL

To further confound our understanding of emotions, they tend to ebb and flow in ways we are not always consciously aware of. Sometimes, it seems as though our feelings are irrational or inappropriate and other times they seem to be too extreme for our circumstances. In addition, many emotions are uncomfortable and disturbing. The basic emotions commonly are fear, anger, disgust, sadness, surprise, and happiness; all of these have strong survival value. If you are afraid, you hide; if you are scared, you protect yourself or your offspring; if you experience disgust, you avoid behaviors that could be dangerous like eating spoiled fruit. Among social beings like humans, sadness is often a cue that you need to address problems within social relationships which promote survival and well-being. Surprise motivates people to explore, and happiness promotes bonding and caring for others. If such responses are absent, animals and humans may be less likely to survive. In fact, you have probably heard someone complain about a child who "isn't scared of anything" and so takes risks and gets hurt more than other cautious children. While the survival value of maintaining strong social connections may not be immediately apparent to you in the modern world, it is still the case that humans depend on each other in interdependent ways. Having people who will provide us with support, advice, or protection can mean the difference between being homeless, making decisions that harm us, or getting hurt by others.

Dorothea Lange's iconic 1936 photograph, known as "Migrant Mother," depicts Florence Thompson with her children as they contemplate the stresses and uncertainties of The Great Depression.

THE SEAT OF EMOTIONS

In part, the mystery surrounding our own emotions stems from the way in which they are produced deep within our brains. The limbic system, commonly considered the heart of our emotional world, consists of two curving networks of structures (Morgane, Galler, & Mokler, 2005), sometimes described as ram's horns. Essentially, these phylogenetically older parts of the brain are designed to enable us to respond rapidly to life-threatening events and are structurally and functionally very similar in rats, cats, dogs, primates, and humans.

This system, located in the middle of the brain, receives sensory information from the periphery of the body via sensory information relayed through the thalamus and other networks of incoming signals. Although there is some debate about what structures should comprise the limbic system, the amygdala and the hippocampus are typically included.

The amygdala, which actually consists of two small almond-shaped structures located on either side of the brain, is integrally involved in the experience of fear and anger, but not happiness or disgust. When it is damaged, animals fail to avoid threatening things like snakes. Researcher Joseph LeDoux has argued that the amygdala and the thalamus create a rapid-response fear circuit (LeDoux, 2007). It has also been suggested that the amygdala plays a role in determining what we find to be rewarding or reinforcing. In contrast, it has been shown that disgust is generated in a small part of the brain called the insula. If this structure is damaged, the disgust normally generated by disturbing smells and sights does not occur. The key, though, is to remember that much of this processing occurs without our conscious awareness.

The hippocampus, which is involved in the storage of memories, is also an integral part of the limbic system (Bird & Burgess, 2008). The speed with which we respond to events in the environment is, in part, determined by how fast we recognize and identify the threat, which is strongly influenced by our recall of things we have experienced before. But the limbic system does not process emotions in isolation. It is also connected to parts of the frontal and temporal cortex, where much of our thought and language processing occurs. In addition, it is linked to the somatosensory cortex, which is involved in sensory processing, and the cingulate cortex that is associated with the processing of social emotions and pain. It has also been shown that the anterior cingulate cortex helps us to evaluate whether something is rewarding or not, and the orbitofrontal cortex may be involved in our decisions about whether to pursue a small immediate reward or a larger delayed one. LeDoux (1996) has suggested that such pathways integrate emotional and cognitive processing in a more complicated but less rapid manner than our automatic fear responses. This hypothesis is supported in part by the fact that when the frontal lobe is damaged, people often become emotionally and behaviorally impulsive and disinhibited.

It also appears that the two sides of the brain play different roles in our emotional expression. Studies of brain activity suggest that the left hemisphere is associated with positive emotions, while the right hemisphere is involved in negative emotions. For example, people who have left hemisphere damage are typically depressed, while those with right hemisphere damage may actually be quite upbeat. Listening studies suggest that the left hemisphere contributes to our understanding of the meaning of language while the right hemisphere processes the emotional content. However, as with most of the brain, there is a great deal of communication among these structures, so it is unlikely that a particular emotion is coded in only one part of the brain (Damasio, 2000).

Further complicating our experience of emotions is the fact that it is virtually impossible to separate the mental and physical aspects of an emotion when we are experiencing it. So strongly are they linked that our language is peppered with phrases like "keep a stiff upper lip," which imply that we can control our emotions through our body. Interestingly, people who have sustained spinal cord injuries that interfere with the transmission of visceral, gut sensations to the brain do report that their emotions appear to be blunted or less strong than they were prior to their injury.

READING AND (MISREADING) EMOTIONS

In addition to interpreting our own emotions, of course, humans and many animals spend significant amounts of time attempting to read and interpret the emotions of others. In order to do this, we tend to track body position, facial expressions, and even tone of voice. One of the reasons that dogs turn out to be such rewarding companions is that they are extraordinarily good at reading and responding to human expressions and tones of voice, which is probably how they made the long trek from their wild wolf ancestors to becoming our beloved indoor pets. The ability to read others' facial expressions is a key component of human-to-human communication as well (Eckman, 2007; Rilling & Sanfey, 2011).

In order to hide our feelings from others, we often try to manage or control the trembling in our lips, our rate of breathing, flickers of our eyes, and other things that might give others a nonverbal clue as to our responses. The ability to hide feelings this way is probably beneficial during a poker game or if you are trying to pass a lie detector test, but may be less helpful in your interpersonal relationships. When we don't have access to visual cues about a person's emotions and intent, many of us actually find it disconcerting. It turns out the emotional, right side of our brain is most active when we are paying attention to emotional expressions, and people with right temporal lobe damage actually have trouble correctly reading faces.

If you have ever had an argument with someone you care about over the phone or gotten involved in an email or Twitter conversation that went sour because something was misinterpreted, you may well have commented on how hard it is to communicate on a purely verbal level. The fact that so many of us use emoticons like little smiley faces and phrases like LOL in our messages to make sure people understand us suggests that we find it very hard to communicate without the help of our nuanced emotional deliveries. When people have experienced facial paralysis due to injury or diseases like Parkinson's disease, their family members report that they have difficulty adjusting to their lack of expression.

Cultural expressions of emotion vary, too (Elfenbein et al., 2002). In Western cultures, hiding grief, reacting to disappointment and losing with graciousness, and behaving "rationally" are often valued. However, we tend to be fairly demonstrative in terms of touching others, holding hands and showing affection. In contrast, in many non-Western cultures, the degree to which families' outward demonstrations of grief are performed to honor the person who has died—and norms for expressing disagreement, attachment, and respect—vary. The catch is that such expressions work as long as all of those involved agree on the meanings of the emotional expressions. However, conflict between cultures often emerges when people of different backgrounds misinterpret each other's touches, eye contact, or other actions.

INFECTED BY OTHERS' EMOTIONS

Emotions can also be contagious (Barsade, 2002). A number of studies suggest that feelings such as fear, aggression, and even happiness seem to spread. When experimental subjects are put into waiting rooms with actors demonstrating strong emotion, it tends to impact their own emotional state. Other studies suggest that on occasion, we actually seek to use this social influence to manipulate our emotions. People who are feeling sad or lonely may actually choose to go to a social event with other people to "cheer up," and people who are angry may choose to associate with others who share their views and "shore up" their anger. Preliminary research on mirror neurons suggests it is likely that they play a role in this process; by responding when we see others' emotional expressions, they may trigger similar emotions in us.

Even putting on an emotional expression, such as smiling when you aren't happy or frowning when you aren't sad, has been shown to generate the emotion that was mimicked. It may well be that the people we consider to be great actors because of their ability to convey emotions so clearly, can do so because their mirror neurons enable them to be particularly attuned to the nuances of facial expressions. In contrast, people with autism have great difficulty reading and responding to emotions, and there is some evidence that people with autism do indeed have a dysfunctional mirror neuron system.

MEMORIES AND EMOTIONS

Clearly, memory plays a strong role in our experiences of emotion as well (McGaugh, 2006). The sights of places we have been, the sounds of familiar activities and smells, can all trigger emotional responses, sometimes regarding things we thought we had long forgotten. While most of the time we are able to recognize that these triggered emotions are related to something in our past, there are cases where the system goes awry. In the case of posttraumatic stress disorder (PTSD), people who have experienced extremely stressful situations such as rape, torture, combat, serious car accidents or disasters, may be plagued by nightmares and sudden memories or flashbacks of the event years later (Gilbertson, Rauch, Orr, & Pitman, 2008). One Vietnam veteran I worked with had trouble smelling wet grass because it reminded him of being in the jungle, and many Iraqi and Afghani vets report that even though they know they are back in the United States, they have trouble not jumping and hiding when they hear loud noises such as fireworks or thunder. This

A soldier calls for air support, Vietnam, 1969.

jumpiness, called hypervigilance, is often seen as an aspect of the fight-or-flight response that, once activated, fails to turn off once the threat is over. It is believed that under extreme emotional stress, our bodies produce a great deal of a hormone called cortisol as part of the fight-or-flight response (Roozendaal, McEwen, & Chattarji, 2009).

This hormone, involved in both metabolism and immune function, also seems to have a strong effect on the hippocampus. In short, people who develop PTSD symptoms in response to extraordinary stress also show a reduction in the volume of their hippocampus, the very structure necessary to consolidate and form memories. Whether this cell loss in the hippocampus is reversible depends on a number of factors, including the age of the victim, the amount of time the stress lasts, etc., but it clearly indicates that in the presence of major stress, our body's and brain's attempts to cope generate strong emotional responses, which can affect coping even after the stress has abated. Studies of children growing up in abusive homes, or disrupted settings such as refugee camps, suggest that such prolonged childhood stress may actually predispose them to increased stress responses and higher rates of depression in later life.

Paradoxically, because of their nonverbal nature, it can be tempting to ignore feelings that are uncomfortable or disturbing. In addition, those around us often urge us to forget about things, to deny our feelings, or at least to keep our feelings quiet enough that others don't have to deal with them! Even when people seek psychological help, they often open sessions by saying "I know I shouldn't feel this way, but ..." Ignoring how you feel, though, is about as logical as ignoring pain in an injured ankle. After all, you would never go to the doctor and say that you know your ankle shouldn't hurt. When you have a physical injury, you ask why it hurts, and the same should be true of emotional pain. Fictional characters like Mr. Spock notwithstanding, research shows that, rather than clouding our judgment, emotions provide crucial information about the environment, which we ignore at our own peril.

FEELINGS DON'T LIE—OR DO THEY?

Conversely, assuming that the way we feel always defines reality is also problematic. As just about any woman could tell you, feeling fat, which in our appearance-centered culture is typically a reflection of feeling bad about yourself, is more about your emotional state then your actual weight on a given day. Since emotions by their very nature are strong and nonverbal, it can be hard to view them objectively. This is particularly true if our thought patterns predispose us to interpret situations in ways that contribute to negative, disturbing feelings. The key, then, is to find ways to notice and pay attention to the signals your emotions are giving you while balancing those signals against the feedback you are getting from the environment and avoiding the sorts of negative attributions and irrational thoughts that in themselves obscure our interpretations of the world. Of course, this is far easier said than done, but being aware of how emotions work and of how they are related to our thoughts can give us a whole new way to cope when stressors arise.

Thus, the key to managing the emotional aspects of stress is to strike a balance between ignoring and focusing on emotions. If we ignore feelings, we tend to miss valuable information about our environments and the ways in which we are being treated. However, if we focus only on the pure emotion, we may also misinterpret situations and fail to communicate effectively. Clearly, in order to negotiate these two sides of the equation, we may have to adopt a number of new approaches to coping.

IT MAKES ME FEEL SICK

The first step lies in paying attention to the physical sensations underlying your emotional state. Most of us respond to stress in certain characteristic ways. We may experience muscle tension, headaches, stomach and gastrointestinal distress, changes in our body temperature, dryness in our mouths, or jitteriness. Often when we are in the grip of a strong emotion we have the urge to laugh or cry, sometimes in ways that feel inappropriate. The point of all of these signals, however, is that they are physical expressions of the emotions we are experiencing and are often an outgrowth of our body's physiological fight-or-flight arousal mechanisms. When we deny such sensations they don't conveniently disappear, but instead become chronic aspects of our lives which can, in fact, contribute to a number of long-term conditions and illnesses. This will be discussed in the next chapter.

The practice of mindfulness or paying attention to your experience in the present rather than focusing on the past or worrying about the future is associated with increased feelings of relaxation and well-being. Although slowing down and focusing on how it feels to grip the steering wheel or wash the dish or brush your hair may seem inefficient, it actually allows people to experience their lives more fully and to become more aware of their genuine responses. Consequently, mindfulness techniques are increasingly being introduced in clinical situations (Baer, 2003).

Noticing and acknowledging the physical manifestations of our emotions is the first step to bringing them into conscious awareness, which, in turn, lets us begin to deal with them effectively. Just for a second, pay attention to how tightly you are gripping this book, whether your neck is comfortable or how your feet feel, and you will immediately see how much information we tend to simply ignore in our daily lives. If I now ask you to identify what you can smell right now or what you hear, you may be surprised to realize how little you were paying attention to the sounds of the lights or a fan in your room, to the smell of the print in the book, or other sensations in your immediate situation.

Once you start noticing your physical emotional sensations, you will probably be much more aware of how often you experience certain emotions during your daily life. As creatures of habit, we often repeat behaviors and responses without even being aware that we are doing so. When I ask my students to keep a list of the thoughts and emotions they have for a week, they are often surprised by how frequently they return to a particular feeling such as hopelessness, anger, irritation, shame, or disappointment. Noticing how often we encounter such feelings and how and when they occur can be the next step in taking greater control of our emotional experiences (Greenberg, 2010).

RULING EMOTIONS INSTEAD OF BEING RULED BY THEM

Because emotions are nonverbal, it is easy to assume that we have little control over them or that we can change them consciously. Nothing could be further from the truth, however. As we have discussed, the emotional centers of our brain, including the amygdala and hippocampus, are closely linked with the forebrain areas that control thought, language, and abstract reasoning. The ways in which we interpret the world mentally shape our emotions and vice versa. Consequently, it shouldn't be surprising that changing our thoughts can change our emotions. As discussed in the previous chapter, certain thoughts tend to be associated with certain emotions. If you assume that anything bad that happens to you is your fault, will last forever, and may taint other areas of your life, we would expect you to feel sad and depressed. If, on the other hand, you assume that every time someone gets in your way, slows you down, or fails to do what you want they are being hostile and aggressive, we could very well expect you to experience anger and hostility. Recognizing how such thoughts shape your thinking is important, but of course we often have a long history of telling ourselves about how the world works and may not be able to easily change such scenarios (Emery and Campbell, 1986).

But research into how we formulate our life stories indicates that we can actually learn alternative ways to tell the tale. The work of Jamie Pennebaker (1997) at the University of Texas–Austin indicates that keeping a journal—online or on paper—actually helps people cope with past trauma and stress and improves physical health as well. In his book *The Neuropsychology of Psychotherapy*, Louis Cozolino (2006) argues that we have long relied on stories to record our personal experiences, but that because of the ways in which our memories work, such stories are constantly subject to change. In Cozolino's review of how memory works, he notes that our memories of childhood and early life are actually an amalgamation of things we actually did, and the stories, pictures, media images and other things we incorporated into the memories over the years.

Research on long-term memory by Elizabeth Loftus (1997) actually suggests that people will alter their personal stories if questions are asked in leading ways and that some people can be convinced they remember events that, in fact, never happened to them, but were only suggested or insinuated. In my learning class, I often tell students about my "memory" of watching President John F. Kennedy's funeral on television. In my mind's eye, I see myself sitting on the rug in the family room in my parents' home, watching the funeral with my mother who was visibly upset by

The funeral of President John F. Kennedy.

the death. The problem is that in 1963, when Kennedy was killed, our house did not have that family room—it was added on several years later. I suspect what happened is that somewhere along the way I did see video clips of the funeral on the television in that room, and somehow incorporated them into my story of the event.

If you doubt that people's recall of events can differ over time, perhaps you might want to see if you can remember your own response to some seminal event such as the death of John Lennon, the Oklahoma City bombings, or 9/11. Then see if your recall makes sense given what other people who were with you remember of the event. Researchers Neisser and Harsch (1982) asked students to record what they were doing and thinking when the space shuttle *Challenger* exploded. They then compared the responses they got just after the crash to their version of the event several years later, and they found significant discrepancies in many people's reports. But rather than see this as a depressing sign that our memories are fallible, it can be argued that having the ability to reframe or reassess the things that happen to us actually means that we are not doomed to live our lives at the mercy of our past.

Revisiting old assumptions about how things happened in the past, reevaluating the blame we assigned ourselves or others in our narratives, and refocusing on aspects of prior events and our behaviors may all give us new insight into how we feel about those events and how they shape our future choices. If, in fact, a failure to achieve a goal was all our fault, then perhaps it is reasonable to assume that we should just give up on trying to pursue new goals in the future. If a divorce really was all our partner's fault, then feeling hopeless and deciding never to trust anyone again is understandable. However, if we can rethink the event in terms of how our behaviors interacted with our partner's in the context of our lives at that time, we are in a much better place to think about learning from the experience and risking another relationship, in which we avoid some of the pitfalls we fell into the first time.

Even people coping with extremely difficult situations such as the loss of a child through potentially preventable events such as sudden infant death syndrome or a car accident can pay attention to how they are thinking and feeling about the event. They can determine whether the narrative they have repeated to themselves about who is to blame and how things might have gone is the only way to think about—and respond to—the situation. While many events are truly tragic and our negative emotional responses to them are inevitable, we nevertheless have the capacity to deal with those events by finding ways to use the knowledge, empathy, faith, and strengths we develop while coping to help ourselves and others.

Managing our emotions, however, is not a simple skill, and some of us may find it easier than others to do. Mayer, Salovey, and Caruso (2000) argue that people who vary in terms of their emotional intelligence or ability to perceive, understand, and express emotions in ways that meet the demands of their environment, are at an advantage in coping with the world. In his popular books on emotional intelligence, author Daniel Goleman (2005) in the book *Emotional Intelligence* argues that people can, in fact, be taught such skills, even if those skills do not come naturally to them. According to his formulation, emotional IQ consists of having the ability to recognize and express your own emotions, to read and empathize with other people's emotions, and to manage your feelings in ways that allow you to persist in the face of setbacks, and to delay short-term gratification in order to pursue long-term goals that may be more desirable, but are less accessible or immediately rewarding. In support of these assertions, he refers readers to the work of Walter Mischel at Stanford University, who offered four-year-old children the chance to eat a marshmallow immediately or to receive more marshmallows if they were able to wait 15–20 minutes. It was later found that the children who were able to wait showed significantly better emotional academic and social adjustment than the children who could not wait. They continued to excel throughout their high school years.

Clearly, emotional adjustment is not simply a matter of avoiding bad feelings. The bottom line seems to be that trying to ignore our feelings is about as efficient as trying to function while totally ignoring one half of our bodies. By acknowledging and validating our feelings, we gain access to a world of information and insight, which we can then integrate with our memories of past experiences and expectations about a current situation, to respond in ways that meet our needs and those of the people around us.

WHAT DO YOU THINK?

1. What is your most common emotional response when you are stressed?
2. Are there emotional states you actively try to avoid because you don't want to deal with their implications (anger, depression, anxiety, etc.)?
3. What people, activities, and situations increase your sense of calm?

REFERENCES

Baer R.A. (2003). Mindfulness training as clinical intervention: A conceptual and empirical review. *Clinical Psychology: Science and Practice*, 10, 125–143.

Barsade, S. G. (2002). The ripple effect: Emotional contagion and its influence on group behavior. *Administrative Science Quarterly*, 47 (4), 644–667.

Bird, C. M., & Burgess, N. (2008). The hippocampus and memory: Insights from spatial processing. *Nature Reviews Neuroscience*, 9, 182–194.

Cozolino, L. (2006). *The Neuroscience of Human Relationships: Attachment and the Developing Social Brain*. New York: W. W. Norton & Company.

Damasio, A. R. (2000). *The Feeling of What Happens: Body and Emotion in the Making of Consciousness*. New York: Harcourt Brace.

Eckman, (2007). *Emotions Revealed, Second Edition: Recognizing Faces and Feelings to Improve Communication and Emotional Life*. New York: Holt Paperbacks.

Elfenbein, H. A., Mandal, M. K., Ambady, N., Harizzuka, S., & Kumar, S. (2002). Cross-cultural patterns in emotion recognition: Highlighting design and analytical techniques. *Emotion*, 2 (1), 75–84.

Emery, G., & Campbell, J. (1986). *Rapid Relief from Emotional Distress: A New, Clinically Proven Method for Getting over Depression & Other Emotional Problems without Prolonged or Expensive Therapy.* New York: Scribner.

Gilbertson, M. W., Orr, S. P., Rauch, S. L., & Pitman, R. K. (2008). Trauma and posttraumatic stress disorder. In: Stern, T. A., Rosenbaum, J. F., Fava, M., Biederman, J., Rauch, S. L., eds. *Massachusetts General Hospital Comprehensive Clinical Psychiatry.* 1st ed. Philadelphia: Mosby Elsevier.

Goleman, D. (2005). *Emotional Intelligence: Why It Can Matter Even More than Intelligence.* 10th Anniversary Edition, New York: Bantam Books.

Greenberg, G. (2011). *Comprehensive Stress Management.* New York: McGraw-Hill Humanities/Social Sciences/ Languages.

LeDoux, J. (1996). *The Emotional Brain: The Mysterious Underpinnings of Emotional Life.* London: Simon & Schuster.

LeDoux, J. (2007). The Amygdala. *Current Biology*, 17, 20, 868–874.

Loftus, E. F. (1997). "Creating False Memories." *Scientific American*, 277, 3, 70–75.

Mayer, J. D., Salovey, P., & Caruso, D. (2000). Models of emotional intelligence. In Sternberg, R. *Handbook of Intelligence.* Cambridge, UK; Cambridge University Press, 396–420.

McGaugh, J. L. (2006). *Memory and Emotion: The Making of Lasting Memories (Maps of the Mind).* Columbia University Press.

Morgane, P. J., Galler, J. R., & Mokler, D. J. (2005). A review of systems and networks of the limbic forebrain/limbic midbrain. *Prog Neurobiol*, 5(2): 143–60.

Neisser, U. (1982). Snapshots or benchmarks? In U. Neisser (Ed.), *Memory observed: Remembering in natural contexts.* New York: Freeman.

Pennebaker, J. W. (1997). Writing about emotional experiences as a therapeutic process. *Psychological Science*, 8(3), 162-166.

Rilling, J. K., & Sanfey, A. G. (2011). The Neuroscience of Social Decision Making. *Annual Review of Psychology*, 62, 23–48.

Roozendaal, B. , McEwen, B. A., & Chattarji, S. (2009). Stress, memory and the amygdala. *Nature Reviews Neuroscience*, 10, 423–433.

CHAPTER 12
THE PHYSIOLOGY OF STRESS: DOES STRESS REALLY MAKE YOU SICK?

KEY POINTS

+ The body's sympathetic responses involve the complex interaction of transmitters, hormones, metabolic processes, and immune reactions designed to increase energy and strength and to decrease pain in response to acute stress.
+ During chronic stress, the fight-or-flight response can harm the body by suppressing immune function, increasing the risk of cardiovascular disease, and contributing to headaches, gastrointestinal distress, and other health problems.
+ The counterpoint to the sympathetic system, the parasympathetic system, promotes homeostasis and repair and recovery of the body. These functions can be enhanced through the use of relaxation, meditation, and exercise.

IS IT ALL IN YOUR HEAD?

When I first started studying psychology in 1977, there was still a tendency to think of the brain and body as separate entities. In fact, we used to talk about "real illness," which meant there was something actually wrong with the body, and psychosomatic illnesses, which were "all in the mind." However, over the last 30 years, that distinction has all but disappeared. Now we know that the mind and the body are in constant communication and that perturbations in either system necessarily affect the other. When people are stressed or anxious, there are physiological changes in their body which can influence illness. Likewise, people who are sick or in pain may experience depression and anxiety as a function of both their physiological state and the psychological ramifications of their condition.

In the late 1970s and early 1980s when people first started studying these interactions, we often had to rely on simple correlations between observations. When people lost a spouse, they were at increased risk for depression and poor health themselves. Some people do have a heart attack after experiencing a stressful event, and pain feels worse when we are under stress. Similarly, when subjects in a laboratory were stressed, they were more likely to get sick when exposed to a virus, and when rats were raised in crowded cages, they were less able to fight off implanted tumors. Researchers have since made tremendous gains in understanding the biology of these links (Lovallo, 2004).

SYMPATHETIC RESPONSES TO STRESS

The process begins with the body's fight-or-flight response, a system evolved over thousands of years of life on the savanna when most threats were acute and physical. In order to avoid predators while finding food and protecting offspring, humans developed the ability to mobilize physical energy for short periods of time. This sympathetic response—initiated in a structure in the brain called the hypothalamus—triggers a series of hormonal responses that ultimately increase our heart rate and blood pressure, increase our breathing rate, release metabolic energy such as glucose into the bloodstream, enhance alertness and focus, and diminish pain sensations. In the face of an acute physical stress, these changes allow us to run fast or to fight or flee. Such actions, in turn, burn the energy our body has generated (Sapolsky, 2004).

However, many modern stressors are not acute, but instead are chronic and psychological, meaning that there is no quick physical way to escape the stress. Over time, repeated physiological responses to stress can have an adverse impact on cardiovascular health, diminish immune response capabilities predisposing people to illness, and contribute to painful conditions such as headaches, ulcers, and rashes. The counterpoint to the sympathetic system, the parasympathetic system, typically promotes homeostasis, or the ongoing maintenance of the body. The parasympathetic nervous system controls such functions as hunger, satiety, and digestion, energy storage, temperature regulation, and healing and restoration of the body. If, however, you are operating largely in a sympathetic state, such responses may become disregulated, leading to poor health and increased stress. The impact of chronic sympathetic nervous system activation on cardiovascular health (Dimsdale, 2008) and the immune system (Ader, 2006) have been of particular interest to researchers.

STRESS AND THE HEART

Cardiovascular disease is the leading cause of death in the United States today (Nabel, 2003). While most of us know someone who has had a heart attack or stroke, it is often a disease we fail to think much about. Perhaps because they are so dramatic, many people fear cancer or AIDS more than heart problems, even though heart issues are more common. So, what does cause cardiovascular problems? In a nutshell, cardiovascular problems are caused by the blockage of arteries which carry blood throughout the body. When blocked or ruptured arteries supply the heart, heart tissue dies and a heart attack ensues. When the arteries supplying the brain are involved, people have a stroke. When the blockage occurs in the periphery of the body, often the feet, it is called peripheral artery disease. This can result in infection, tissue death, and even the need to amputate all or part of the foot. The website How Stuff Works has an excellent section on the heart and cardiovascular system.

In young people, the arteries tend to be wide and smooth, allowing blood to travel easily. However, over time, they often become clogged with a substance called plaque. This sticky substance—made up of cholesterol, fats, and tissue, which build up and harden over time—essentially blocks blood flow, just like a clogged pipe. Depending on where the clog occurs, the result could be brain damage, heart disease, or peripheral artery disease because these organs and arteries are deprived of nutrients and oxygen. There are a number of factors that contribute to this buildup, including aging, genetics, gender, diet, and lack of exercise. As people age, this build-up reduces the elasticity of the arteries, which are then more prone to rupture as well. This clogging of the arteries is more common in men until women go through menopause; it tends to run in families.

Diet is a key factor too. Saturated fats, including red meat, dairy products, and a number of vegetable oils, contribute to the build-up of unhealthy cholesterol, called low-density lipoproteins. Nicotine and the use of birth control pills also contribute to this. Blood cholesterol levels have also been shown to rise in response to stressors ranging from workplace and exam stress to psychological worries. However, cholesterol is not all bad. Your body needs it for normal function, and extremely low levels have been associated with increased violence, suicide, and accidental death.

Another factor contributing to heart disease is hypertension, or high blood pressure. This pressure reflects how hard the heart is working. When the pressure is high, the heart has to work harder, and the arteries are more likely to rupture. Conditions like kidney disease or obesity can also exacerbate the problem, but 90 percent of the time there is no specific cause; this is called essential hypertension. In some cases, pressure increases with salt intake, but reducing the amount of salt in the diet only reduces hypertension in about one third of patients. Smoking also exacerbates blood pressure. On the other hand, increased dietary calcium and potassium reduce blood pressure, as does exercise.

Exercise is particularly important to the management of heart disease. Not only does it lead to weight loss, which reduces blood pressure, but it seems to increase levels of high-density lipoproteins, which reduce artery build up, and to decrease levels of low-density lipoproteins, which contribute to build-up.

In recent years, research has suggested that infectious agents may also contribute to arterial disease. For example, it has long been known that people who were experiencing periodontal disease had an increased risk of cardiovascular disease. Following up on this observation, researchers suggest that the bacteria responsible for gum disease (gingivitis) is also found in the arteries, where it causes inflammation and irritation, which then leads to increased plaque build-up (Morrison, Ellison, & Taylor, 1999). The fact that the use of aspirin, an anti-inflammatory medication, reduces heart disease risk is consistent with this finding.

Psychological factors such as stress and hostility are also associated with high blood pressure, increased cholesterol, artery disease, and mortality (Friedman & Rosenman, 1959; Shekelle, Gale, Ostfeld, & Paul, 1983). If you think back to how the fight-or-flight response works, this isn't so surprising. When people experience stress, their hypothalamus triggers the release of chemicals which increase heart rate and blood pressure and provide glucose and nutrients through the blood. The magnitude of this response, though, varies across individuals. Studies suggest that some people—typically men—respond to stress with greater increases in blood pressure and cholesterol than others. Such folks have been labeled "hot reactors" because they get a bigger bang for their adrenalin buck than the rest of us. (Eliot, 1989). Sapolsky has done a number of studies which indicate that primates forced into stressful social settings where they must fight for dominance, also exhibit exaggerated fight-or-flight responses and poor health.

Studies of personality types suggest that anger and hostility often contribute to the size of this response as well. The concept of Type A behavior was originally coined by cardiologists Meyer Friedman and Ray

Rosenman (1959), who noticed that many of the men they were treating for heart problems also had a tendency to be competitive, to feel pressed for time, and to show higher levels of hostility and cynicism (Barefoot, Dahlstrom & Williams, 1985). Later research has suggested that it is really the emotional components of these responses that matter the most. Suppressed anger may also be a factor, as it often results in rumination, depression, and other negative feelings. In short, feelings that are likely to trigger fight-or-flight responses may well contribute to heart disease by aggravating a cardiovascular system that is already stressed. And, of course, stressed people often make lifestyle choices that are not good for their health, either. In order to manage stress, people often smoke, overeat, cut back on sleep, and quit exercising, all of which increase the strain on their heart. There is even a link between sudden catastrophic loss and heart attacks (Bhattacharyya & Steptoe, 2007). The work of Engel (1971) and others indicates that the death of a close relative, sudden danger such as a tornado or physical attack, and the loss of possessions or self-esteem may contribute to so-called "sudden death" episodes, where people who already have heart disease experience a heart attack following a sudden fight-or-flight surge. Fortunately relaxation can mitigate some of the adverse effects of stress on the heart (Benson & Klipper, 2000).

STRESS, STOMACH ACHES, AND PAIN

Of course, the effects of stress are not limited solely to the cardiovascular system. When stressed, many people report problems with their gastrointestinal system, musculoskeletal system, and skin. In fact, stomach ulcers (sores in the lining of the stomach) used to be considered the classic stress-related illness, since they often emerged in stressed people, got worse when people were under stress, and were less symptomatic when people were calmer. It turns out, though, that most ulcers of the GI tract are actually caused by a bacteria called *H. pylori*, and the ulcers respond to specific regimens of antibiotics. Stress, however, can disrupt stomach function and exacerbate the symptoms of the ulcers, so managing stress can provide some relief but on its own is not enough to eliminate the irritation. Interestingly, physician Barry Marshall, who won a Nobel Prize in 2005 for his work on *H. pylori*, first had to spend years trying to get the medical community to take his research seriously because the stress/ulcer link was so well established. (Nobel Prize Press Release).

The gastrointestinal system is also sensitive to stress (Levy et al., 2006). For years, people believed that symptoms such as an upset stomach, nausea, or irritable bowel (alternating bouts of constipation and diarrhea) were caused by failure to manage stress mentally. However, it turns out that there are more receptors for serotonin in the gut than in the brain and that very low doses of drugs such as Prozac that promote serotonin activity actually mitigate the symptoms of irritable bowel syndrome at levels that are not effective for depression (Clouse, 2003).

Most of us would also acknowledge that stress has the capacity to cause or aggravate pain, in the back and shoulder, or in the form of headaches and joint discomfort. In terms of muscular pain, the tension inherent in chronic stress and fight-or-flight responses is a factor, although emerging research suggests that inflammation, pain thresholds, and even exercise levels can have an influence. It is also the case that stress and its attendant negative emotions can contribute to how much pain bothers us. Think, perhaps, of a time when you had an injury. Do you recall feeling less upset about the discomfort if your day was going well and more frustrated if things weren't going your way?

Stress may also play a role in other less understood disorders, including migraine headaches, which appear to be caused by the constriction and dilation of blood vessels, although we don't know as yet what triggers these variations or why such problems occur only in certain people (Loder, Rizzoli, & Neporent, 2012).

Disorders such as chronic fatigue syndrome and fibromyalgia also appear to be influenced by tension and stress, perhaps through immunological and inflammatory processes (Van Houdenhove, Ulrich, & Luyten, 2005). Interestingly, in the case of many pain disorders, continuing to exercise actually mitigates symptoms, although convincing people who hurt that they should push themselves physically can be difficult.

Equally confusing is the link between stress and skin (Koo & Lebwohl, 2001). We know that sympathetic nervous system responses cause changes in sweat gland activity and temperature and so can impact the skin. People who flush easily, young adults with acne, and individuals with sensitive skin can all provide stories of times when stress appeared to trigger or exacerbate these problems. The fact that the skin itself is an incredibly complex system doesn't help. The emphasis in many cultures on unblemished, unwrinkled skin as a mark of attractiveness, youth, and health also comes into play, since skin disorders are often themselves a source of stress.

STRESS AND THE IMMUNE SYSTEM

In the past 30 years, a great deal of research has been devoted to the relationship between stress and infectious diseases. Prior to that time, it was assumed that the cells of the immune system functioned autonomously to detect and combat invaders (called antigens) to the body, including bacteria, viruses, parasites, and rogue cancer cells. However, with the 1981 publication of the first edition of the book *Psychoneuroimmunology*, edited by Robert Ader (2006), it became clear that immunity is a complex process involving the coordination of numerous types of cells, transmitters, and brain functions. In order to understand how stress impacts this system, it is necessary to present a brief overview of this process.

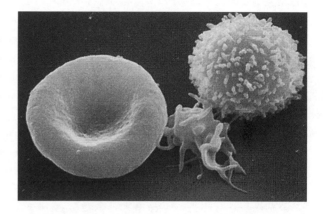

Red and white blood cells.

Basically, the immune system is made up of a series of specialized cells, which we are still trying to understand (see Sompayrac, 2012 for a comprehensive review of how the immune system works). These cells, called white cells, circulate in the blood, are found in the tissues of the body, and are particularly concentrated in the body's lymph glands and lymphatic system. These glands, including the tonsils, thymus, and appendix, serve as incubators for immune cells, as does the bone marrow. From the body's point of view, invaders that can cause danger are called antigens, and they come in many versions. For example, bacteria are independent organisms and fortunately can be destroyed by antibiotics. Parasites are also organisms that invade and disrupt normal function. Viruses, on the other hand, carry their own DNA/RNA but can only exist by taking over other cells and co-opting their mechanisms to produce more virus. In order to damage a virus, it is often necessary to damage the cells they have inhabited. Cancer, basically cells that have mutated and are spreading in the body, is also very difficult to destroy without damaging the rest of the body. So how does the immune system recognize and eliminate these threats?

If you cast your mind back to your high school biology class, you may remember videos (or film strips as the case may be!) of animated cells running around the blood vessels, responding to emergencies. The front runners belong to a class of cells called phagocytes. They tend to be dispatched to sites of injury or invasion because they have the ability to engulf, digest, and destroy antigens using a complex series of enzymes. They also signal the rest of the immune system, indicating that they are responding to a threat but could use help, by displaying bits of the antigens they have destroyed so other cells can recognize them. Recent research suggests that another type of cell, called the dendritic cell, also captures antigens and helps to trigger immune responses.

T-cells, which originate in the thymus, respond to macrophage signals by releasing chemical signals of their own to amplify immune responses. There are two types of T-cells. The first, T Helper cells, coordinate immune responses by activating other white cells. The second, T Killer/Suppressor Cells, have the ability to kill cells that are infected with a virus as well as some tumor cells and parasites. In response to signals from macrophages and T-cells, B-cells, which originate in the bone marrow in humans, proliferate and produce proteins called antibodies that have the ability to recognize and bind to antigens, thereby enabling other cells to destroy the antigen. The first time your body encounters an invader, it has to recognize and produce a specific antibody, which takes time and metabolic energy. However, the next time you encounter that specific invader, B-cells that carry the memory for that antigen can rapidly begin to produce the necessary antibody.

Consequently, people don't get the same virus or infection more than once, assuming their immune system is functioning. For example, the first time a person comes into contact with chicken pox, their body has to generate an antibody. During the time it is ramping up production, the infected person experiences symptoms such as a sore throat, fever, and an itchy rash. However, most people don't get chicken pox again, although they are undoubtedly exposed to it on subsequent occasions. Instead, when they encounter the virus again, their body is able to disable it, often before they even feel sick. Now, chicken pox caused by the varicella-zoster virus is a bit trickier. After you have been infected, the virus can lie dormant in your nervous system for years, only to become active again later as shingles, a painful disease characterized by a rash on one side of the body and pain. Although we do not know what specifically causes a shingles outbreak, it often occurs when people are stressed, older, or in poor health, all of which can compromise immune function.

It is the memory capacity of B-cells that enables us to vaccinate people against illness. A typical vaccination is composed of a synthetic, or deactivated portion, of an antigen, which has the capacity to trigger immune recognition without actually causing illness. When you later encounter the actual virus or trigger, the immune system is able to respond as though it had already encountered the actual virus. While some modern vaccines can cause adverse responses in some individuals, be glad that you live in the 21st century. The first known vaccine, developed by physician Edward Jenner to treat smallpox, actually consisted of an injection of the virus that causes cowpox. Jenner realized that women who worked as milkmaids, and so usually had had cowpox, often survived smallpox. It turns out that the virus that causes cowpox is very similar to the one that causes smallpox, although fortunately not as deadly (Riedel, 2005).

Luckily, the technology has improved, although the principle remains the same. At this point, though, you may be wondering why we all seem to get more than one head cold (Drescher, Dumitru, Adams, & Gulbins, 2007). The catch is that there are actually hundreds of rhinoviruses or the type of virus that most often cause the symptoms of a head cold. So, although the symptoms you experience—sore throat, fever, runny nose, headache, cough—seem similar, this is largely because there are only so many responses the body can make. As far as your immune system is concerned, each rhinovirus is a new invader, requiring a new response.

B-cells also make more than one kind of antibody. Some types circulate in the blood and tissues, others are found in your saliva, and some are even thought to be responsible in part for allergies, or the tendency of the body to overrespond to invaders like pollen or dust mites that are not actually dangerous to the body. Ironically, allergies seem to be more prevalent in hygienic cultures, suggesting that the immune system is primed to be on the alert for invaders at all times. So if there isn't anything particularly dangerous around, it may go to work on other environmental components, even if they are not problematic. In the most extreme cases, a potentially fatal immune response called anaphylaxis can occur. This response is often triggered by food, insect stings, or snake bites. Anaphylaxis occurs when specialized immune cells, called basophils and mast cells, respond to an antigen. Symptoms can include rashes and flushing, vomiting and diarrhea, wheezing and coughing; and cardiovascular complications such as low blood pressure and tachycardia.

Specific antibodies can be used to determine whether you have ever had a particular illness before because you will only have that antibody present in your blood if your immune system has been exposed to the antigen. For example, tests for the human immunodeficiency virus (HIV), responsible for AIDS, are typically based on detecting the antibody to HIV, not the HIV itself. Incidentally, the HIV virus is so deadly precisely be-

cause it targets a specific component of the immune system—T-cells. Essentially, HIV is able to enter T-cells and co-opt their functions so that they begin to produce more HIV and eventually die. As a result, the immune systems of people with HIV are unable to combat infection, so they often suffer and die from infections and tumors. The treatments typically used to treat AIDS today are designed to destroy the HIV virus, allowing the immune system to stabilize and continue to work efficiently.

Other diseases, called autoimmune diseases, are the result of an overactive immune system. These include rheumatoid arthritis, Type 1 diabetes, and multiple sclerosis. In these cases, the immune system, often for as yet undetermined reasons, begins to attack elements of the person's own body. In rheu-

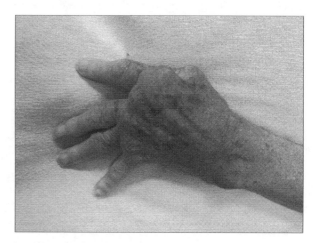

Rheumatoid arthritis.

matoid arthritis, the immune system attacks the lining of joints, causing crippling, swelling, and damage. The insulin-producing cells in the pancreas are destroyed in Type 1 diabetes, and in multiple sclerosis, the myelin-insulating neurons are degraded, leading to a host of neurological deficits. Unfortunately, efforts to treat such diseases using drugs that suppress immune function cause other problems, including increased susceptibility to viral infection. Yet another component of the immune system, natural killer cells have the ability to respond to foreign invaders without being dependent on signals from other immune cells, providing another layer of protection for the body. The complement system, made up of at least 25 proteins, help or complement antibody responses. In the process, they are responsible for many of the symptoms we recognize as an infection, including redness, warmth, swelling, and pain.

Clearly, protecting your body from invaders is a multilayered process (Linnemayer, 2008). A bacteria or virus first has to cross the barrier presented by intact skin, either through a cut in the skin, or through natural openings such as the mouth, eyes, and ears. These openings, however, are protected by mucous, saliva, tears, and other fluids that can also repel or destroy invaders. If they manage to survive these barriers, they are attacked by macrophages, complement, and T-cells that in turn call in B-cells so they can multiply and produce the relevant antibodies. This process can take several days, which accounts for the common comment that people are often contagious before they even know they are sick. In fact, the symptoms we associate with being ill—fever, swelling, pain, etc.,—are actually the result of the immune system's assault on the invader.

By now, you are probably wondering why this book on managing stress has wandered off into a discussion about immunity. It turns out that the immune system and the brain are in constant communication. Studies suggest that when the hypothalamus is damaged, immune function is disrupted, and that when the immune system is activated there is increased activity in parts of the hypothalamus. Furthermore, there is a constant flow of chemical signals between the brain and immune cells. Chemicals called lymphokines carry information to the brain about immune responses. For example, a chemical called interleukin-1 instigates fevers. At the same time, research suggests that there are receptors on immune cells, including B- and T-cells, for a variety of chemical transmitters such as serotonin, norepinephrine, adrenalin, and cortisol. Such findings provide the biological basis for something we have all known for a long time: namely, that stress can cause illness.

Haven't we all been told that if we don't sleep, rest, calm down, eat better, or quit burning the candle at both ends we are going to get sick? We have often had the experience of working really hard or studying for finals, only to get sick as soon as we went on vacation. By now, you have probably figured out that this is not simply a coincidence. Animal studies indicate that physical stress such as crowding and psychological stress such as exposure to the scent of a predator can suppress immune function and lead to illness. Stressed rats are more likely to develop tumors and less able to fight off infections. Primates exposed to stress are also prone to illness, but of course it is difficult to ask animals how they feel about their circumstances. When it comes to humans, we can explore their thoughts as well as their biology. Stressors as varied as a spouse dying, divorce, caring for an ill family member, a high-pressure job, and academic pressure have all been related to diminished immune function and subsequent illness. Psychological stress is even associated with cold susceptibility (Cohen, Tyrell, & Smith, 1991).

Psychologist Janice Kiecolt-Glaser and her husband Ronald Glaser (Glaser & Kiecolt-Glaser, 2005; Kiecolt-Glaser, McGuire, Robles, & Glaser, 2002), an immunologist, have been front-runners in the study of stress and immune function in humans. Their studies indicate that caring for a family member with Alzheimer's disease is associated with depression, exhaustion, decreased immune responsivity, and increased illness. Marital conflict impedes wound healing, as does the stress of being a medical student. As you might expect, these adverse outcomes are the result of the interaction of stress hormones with B-cells, T-cells, natural killer cells, etc. Other researchers have demonstrated that bereavement has a negative impact on lymphocyte function (Schleifer et al., 1983). However, you may also be wondering why the physiological responses that enable us to fight or flee from stress would decrease our ability to fight off illness (Yazdanbakhsh, Kremsner, & van Ree, 2002).

SO WHY DOES STRESS SUPPRESS OUR IMMUNE SYSTEM?

The answer comes down to the energy it takes to mount each of these responses and their conflicting missions (APA, 2006). The increased heart rate, respiration, and metabolic demands of a sympathetic nervous system response are energy intensive. At the same time, pain sensations are suppressed and vigilance is increased. In contrast, a great deal of energy is required to produce the cells, antibody, and chemical signals necessary to protect the body. When people are ill, pain signals are amplified to protect the injured area, and they tend to be tired and sleepy as well. Clearly, these two responses are competitive rather than complementary. Given that both systems evolved when most stressors were physical, the fight-or-flight system takes precedence. While you are trying to run away from the tiger you need all your energy to do so. At that point, it doesn't matter whether you fight off an infection or not. If you don't escape, the issue will be moot. If you do get away, you can then expend energy healing. To ensure this staging, the hormones that facilitate the sympathetic response actually inhibit immune responses. For example, cortisol increases metabolic energy, but also causes the redistribution of B- and T-cells to the bone marrow. If you think about it, this is an elegant adaptation. Assuming you are running from a tiger or some other physical stress, it is likely that you will experience injuries that result in blood loss and the potential loss of B- and T-cells, antibody, and other components of immunity. If instead you sequester immune cells in the bone marrow closet, you are more likely to avoid infection later. You probably didn't know it, but if you have ever had a cortisone shot to decrease swelling from an injury or used a cortisone cream on a rash, you have seen this phenomenon for yourself. In the short run, you probably felt better. The problem occurs if the stress is chronic rather than acute, and so results in long-term immune suppression.

THE LINK BETWEEN STRESS AND CANCER

Of particular interest to many people is the link between stress and cancer. However, studying this potential

relationship has proved difficult. First off, cancer—the uncontrolled growth of cells in the body—is really not a single disease (National Cancer Institute, 2006). Differences in where the cells develop, what sorts of cells they are, how fast they spread, and how strong the immune system is to begin with—all influence the progression of the disease. Over the course of a lifetime, it is likely that the immune system detects and destroys numerous mutated cells, but scientists are still not sure about why the system sometimes breaks down. Age-related changes in immune function, environmental exposure to toxins or carcinogens, and temperamental and psychological responses may all play a role. But it is difficult to know who will eventually develop cancer, so studies of such factors must either involve huge numbers of people over long periods of time in order to predict who will develop a particular form of the disease, or retrospective studies, in which people who are already

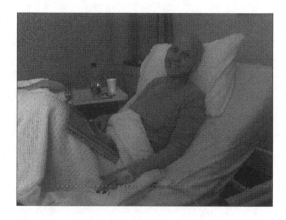

It has taken decades for people to become more comfortable talking about cancer and its treatment.

sick are asked to recall the risk factors they may have experienced before getting sick. Given the faulty nature of memory and the human desire to make sense of bad events, this is not always an unbiased process. Furthermore, when people are dealing with a potentially fatal disease and experiencing pain and discomfort, either from the cancer or from attempts to treat it with surgery or radiation, it is difficult to assess how they might have functioned prior to the diagnosis.

It is somewhat easier to study whether interventions designed to boost mental or physical health slow or halt the progression of cancer, but again, such studies are complicated, given the variable symptoms and progression of cancer and the complexity of psychological responses to intervention. For example, studies conducted in the 1980s (Spiegel, Bloom, & Gottheil, 1989) of women with advanced breast cancer suggested that women who participated in support groups were statistically likely to live longer than women who did not join the groups. However, later studies failed to find significant differences. Of course, in the intervening years, the ways in which we treat cancer and cancer patients have changed. In the early part of the last century, a diagnosis of cancer was virtually a death sentence. Physicians often opted to not even tell patients they had the disease, for fear it would cause them to give up hope. When former first lady Betty Ford announced in

1974 that she was being treated for breast cancer, it was seen as an unprecedented act of honesty and courage on the part of a celebrity. Even so, it still took decades for people to become more comfortable talking about the disease. As a result, it is likely that the effects found in the early social support studies reflected the fact that at that time, women found it a relief to have a place to talk honestly about their feelings, while in later decades people were much more likely to have such outlets in their personal lives.

Further complicating things is the fact that the experience of stress in general varies among different people. There is even evidence that in some circumstances, low levels of stress can be protective by strengthening subsequent stress responses. However, the fact remains that chronic stress—particularly stressors that result in adverse emotional responses such as depression and hostility—are especially likely to result in poor health.

Boosting Immune Function

Fortunately, there is also emerging evidence that relaxation techniques, social support, and even exercise may enhance immune function, and so have a protective effect against stress-induced illness or be used to enhance healing. Humor may also bolster immune function (Bennet, Zeller, Rosenberg, & McCann, 2003; Christie & Moore, 2005). Studies with patients in nursing homes, individuals with HIV, and even medical students indicate that learning to relax boosts actual immune function, prevents infectious illness, and in some cases, speeds up healing (Harvard Health Publications, 2010).

Finally, it should be said that, exciting as these findings are about the links between stress and the immune system, it is easy to overstate them. A quick walk down the self-help aisle of any bookstore will reveal numerous books claiming that perfect health and longevity are ours for the taking. While understanding how psychological stress diminishes immune function certainly has the potential to improve our attempts to prevent and treat illness, it is easy to overstate the links.

Regardless of how well we learn to manage stress, we live in a world where gravity is a constant, bacteria and viruses multiply and mutate, and our bodies will eventually wear out. Taken to the extreme, the principles of psychoimmunology can imply that only people who cope poorly get sick and that the failure to recover from illness reflects a personal failing. Not only is this inaccurate, but it also has the potential to cause anxiety and depression on the part of the ill person, ultimately decreasing the effectiveness of their immune system. Furthermore, the complexity of the immune system and the variety of types of viruses, bacteria, parasites, tumor cells, and other threats to our health suggest that we are still far from a clear understanding of how stress in a particular person might impact a particular disease process. However, as I tell my students, managing stress may not make you live forever, but it will certainly help you to enjoy the time you are alive.

What Do You Think?

1. What is your characteristic physiological response to stress? (Headaches, skin disruption, breathing problems, stomach problems, etc.)
2. Do you pay attention to the onset of these physical symptoms or do you ignore them until they are extreme?
3. Have you tried to diminish such symptoms through exercise or relaxation techniques? What would you be willing to try for a month?

REFERENCES

Ader, R. (2006). *Psychoneuroimmunology, Two-Volume Set, Fourth Edition*. Burlington MA: Academic Press.

American Psychological Association (2006). *Stress Weakens the Immune System*. Review: http://www.apa.org/research/action/immune.aspx

Barefoot, J. C., Dahlstrom, W. G., & Williams, W. B. (1985). Hostility, CHD incidence, and total mortality: A 25-year follow-up study of 255 physicians. *Psychosomatic Medicine, 45*, 59–64.

Bennet, M. P., Zeller, J. M., Rosenberg, L., & McCann, J. (2003). The effect of mirthful laughter on stress and natural killer cell activity. *Alternative Therapeutic Health Medicine, 9*, 38–45.

Benson, H., & Klipper, M. Z. (2000). *The Relaxation Response*. New York: HarperCollins.

Bhattacharyya, M. R., & Steptoe, A. (2007). Emotional triggers of acute coronary syndromes: Strength of evidence, biological processes, and clinical implications. *Progress in Cardiovascular Diseases, 49*, 353–365.

Christie, W., & Moore, C. (2005). The impact of humor on patients with cancer. *Clinical Journal of Oncological Nursing, 9*, 211–218.

Clouse, R. E. (2003). Antidepressants for irritable bowel syndrome. *Gut, 52*: 598–599 doi:10.1136/gut.52.4.598.

Cohen, S., Tyrell, D. A., & Smith, A. P. (1991). Psychological stress and susceptibility to the common cold. *New England Journal of Medicine, 325*, 606–612.

Dimsdale, J. E. (2008). Psychological Stress and Cardiovascular Disease. *J Am Coll Cardiol, 51*: 1237–1246.

Dreschers, S., Dumitru, C. A., Adams, C., & Gulbins, E. (2007). The cold case: Are rhinoviruses perfectly adapted pathogens? *Cellular and Molecular Life Science, 64* (2): 181–91.

Eliot, R. S. (1989). *Is It Worth Dying For?: How To Make Stress Work For You—Not Against You*. New York: Random House Digital, Inc.

Engel, G. L. (1971). Sudden and Rapid Death during Psychological Stress: Folklore or Folk Wisdom? *Annals of Internal Medicine, 74* (5): 771–783.

Friedman, M., & Rosenman, R. (1959). "Association of specific overt behaviour pattern with blood and cardiovascular findings." *Journal of the American Medical Association* (169): 1286–1296.

Glaser, R., & Kiecolt-Glaser, J. K. (2005). Stress-induced immune dysfunction: Implications for health. *Nature Review/Immunology, 5*, 243.

Harvard Health Publications. (2010). *The Truth about Your Immune System*. http://www.health.harvard.edu/special_health_reports/the-truth-about-your-immune-system

Kiecolt-Glaser, J. K., McGuire, L., Robles, T., & Glaser, R. (2002). Psychoneuroimmunology: Psychological influences on immune function and health. *Journal of Consulting and Clinical Psychology, 70*, 537–547.

Koo, J., & Lebwohl, A. (2001). Psychodermatology: The mind and skin connection. *American Family Physician, 1*: 64(1), 1873–1879.

Linnemeyer, P.A. (2008). *The Immune System-An Overview*. http://www.thebody.com/content/art1788.html

Loder, E., Rizzoli, P., & Neporent, L. (2012). *The Migraine Solution*. Oakland, CA: St. Martin's Paperbacks.

Lovallo, W. R. (2004). *Stress and Health: Biological and Psychological Interactions Behavioral Medicine and Health Psychology*. Sage Publications, Inc.

Levy, R. L., Olden, K. W., Baliboff, B. D., Bradley, L. A., Francisconi, C., Drossman, D. A., & Creed, F. (2006). Psychosocial Aspects of the Functional Gastrointestinal Disorders. *Gastroenterology, 130*, 1447–1458.

Morrison, H. I., Ellison, L. F., & Taylor, G. W. (1999). Periodontal disease and risk of fatal coronary heart and cerebrovascular diseases. *J Cardiovasc Risk. 6*, 7–11.

Nabel, E. G. (2003). Cardiovascular Disease. *N Engl J Med, 349*, 60–72.

National Cancer Institute. (2006). *Understanding Cancer Series: The Immune System.* http://www.cancer.gov/cancertopics/understandingcancer/immunesystem

"Press Release: The 2005 Nobel Prize in Physiology or Medicine." Nobelprize.org, 17 Jun 2012. http://www.nobelprize.org/nobel_prizes/medicine/laureates/2005/press.html

Riedel, S. (2005). Edward Jenner and the history of smallpox and vaccination. *Proceedings of the Baylor University Medical Center*, 18(1).

Sapolsky, R. (2004). *Why Zebras Don't Get Ulcers.* New York: Holt Paperbacks.

Schleifer, S. J., Keller, S. E., Camerino, M., Thornton, J. C., & Stein, M. (1983). Suppression of lymphocyte stimulation following bereavement. *JAMA*, 250 (3), 374–377.

Shekelle, R. B., Gale, M., Ostfeld, A. M., & Paul, O. (1983). Hostility, risk of coronary heart disease, and mortality. *Psychosom Med*, May, 45.

Sompayrac, L. M. (2012). *How the Immune System Works (Blackwell's How It Works).* Malden, MA: Wiley-Blackwell.

Spiegel, D., Bloom, J. R., & Gottheil, E. (1989). Effects of Psychosocial Treatment on Survival of Patients with Metastatic Breast Cancer. *Lancet*, 2, 891.

Yazdanbakhsh, M., Kremsner, P. G., & van Ree, R. (2002). Allergy, parasites, and the hygiene hypothesis. *Science*, 19, 296, 5567, 490–494.

Van Houdenhove, B., Ulrich, E., & Luyten, P. (2005). The Role of Life Stress in Fibromyalgia. *Current Rheumatology Reports*, 7: 365–370.

CHAPTER 13

STRESS RESPONSES: DOES YOUR COPING STYLE HELP OR HURT YOU?

KEY POINTS

- In order to manage stress efficiently, you need to evaluate which of your behavioral responses to stress are actually helping you and which are making things worse.
- Often, people need to learn new skills to make changes in their lives. You would not expect to get good at a sport without practicing, and the same is true of learning to relax, to communicate better, to manage anger, or to parent effectively.
- Behavioral change is a process, not an end. You will occasionally fail. The key to coping is learning to recover from such failures so you can move on.

WHY WE DO WHAT WE DO

In response to the perceived intangibility of mental processes, American psychologists, dubbed behaviorists, developed an independent branch of research devoted to figuring out how to reliably measure and explain behavior. The father of this movement, B. F. Skinner (1976), argued that traditional psychological theories were too dependent on assumptions about the internal workings of the brain. It was his contention that focusing on past experiences, underlying motivations, and subconscious processes was not necessary to understand why people do what they do. Skinner called the brain a "black box"; measuring the components of this black box such as intelligence, emotion, and motives was merely speculative. Skinner hypothesized that you could measure only behavior—therefore, only behavior could be studied. According to Skinner, though behaviors are consistently associated with their antecedents, they are ultimately controlled by their consequences. If we like the results of a behavior, we

B. F. Skinner

will do it again. If we find the outcome aversive, on the other hand, we will not. When consequences increase our tendency to produce a response, we call them reinforcing. Conversely, when consequences inhibit a response, they are labeled punishment.

Giving people something they like or taking away things they don't like can both increase behavior; and giving something negative or taking away something positive can both decrease behavior. In practice, we often apply combinations of these techniques. For example, an exhausted parent whose child won't fall asleep may: (1) offer them a cookie if they will lie down; (2) swat them if they try to get up; (3) give them a drink of water if they say they are thirsty; and (4) leave the room if they cry. Can you label each of these responses? Giving a cookie to increase a behavior is reinforcing, as is giving the child water to reduce thirst. In both cases, the parent is trying to increase the child's tendency to fall asleep. Swatting the child is an example of using punishment to decrease the behavior of getting up, and leaving the room is designed to decrease the child's whining by removing the parental attention they crave.

Skinner went on to explore other influencing factors, including the schedules on which consequences of the behavior are delivered. It turns out that if we are reinforced every time we behave in a certain way, we come to expect that level of reward. If the reward is not forthcoming, we will stop relatively rapidly. However, if we are intermittently reinforced for a behavior, we will continue to perform it for a while even after the reward has been removed.

If this is confusing, think about the difference between a soda machine and a slot machine. In both cases, you put coins in, push a button, and wait to see what you will receive. When you expect a soda and it doesn't arrive, you are likely to be angry. You may even try kicking or shaking the machine, but you rarely add more money just to see what will happen. On the other hand, people will spend large amounts of money on a slot machine, hoping that the next push of the button will make them a winner. Although Skinner didn't like to talk about the workings of the brain, it is strongly believed that our expectations about behaviors influence our subsequent behaviors.

However, it turns out that understanding how behaviors are reinforced and punished does not always allow people to engage in positive, helpful behaviors. As anyone who has tried to change a habit knows, change is not easy. Brain research suggests that our brain creates routines that enable it to expend as little energy as possible on specific activities, thereby saving resources for more complex or novel actions. Revamping, reversing, or eliminating those neurological routines can be challenging and time consuming. In addition, complex patterns of reinforcement and motivation determine whether we are satisfied with the outcome of a behavior or driven to achieve something different. For example, why are some people content with a B in a class while others view an A- as a failure? Or why do some people find playing a contact sport like football deeply satisfying, while others would see the same sport as terrifying and intimidating?

A MATTER OF HABIT

When we wish to change a behavior, doing so in the long run can be surprisingly difficult. In my Learning class, I always challenge students to explore the strength of their daily habits by asking them to think about how they brush their teeth. Are they a person who puts the water on the brush first and then the toothpaste, or the other way around? Chances are this is something you have been doing once or twice a day for decades. It is a simple task which doesn't require a lot of concentration, and there aren't notable differences between people who wet first and those who don't. However, as you will find if you try this experiment, it is very hard to change the pattern and do the reverse. The more automatic a habit is, the harder it can be to change. If the behavior itself is gratifying or rewarding, then changing it might even be construed as punishing, making it that much more difficult. This style of behaviorism is supported by the theory of classical conditioning (Pavlov, 1927). Classical conditioning is a form of learning or conditioning in which one stimulus comes to signal the occurrence of a second stimulus. The paired stimuli can summon feelings and desires to behave in ways that range from highly desirable to highly undesirable.

For example, many people eat out of habit when they are watching television, experiencing stress, socializing, working, or driving. If they decide to try to change their eating behavior, they may find that in the early stages of change, it is difficult not to fall back into old patterns. However, even if they do manage to change their actions, dieting can lead to aversive sensations like hunger or feeling light-headed. Eating is also rewarding and consequently influences behavioral choices. Unfortunately for dieters, the best way to combat hunger is to go back to their prior eating habits, with the result that they either don't lose weight or can't maintain the loss they have achieved. To avoid this pattern, dieters may need to expand their eating behavior skill set as well as change their attitudes about food. Learning how to compare calories, cook healthy foods, or manage stress in ways that don't involve food can help people substitute new behaviors for old ones.

However, dieters may also need to learn to focus on the difference between short- and long-term gratification, such that they learn to tolerate short-term discomfort or distress for long-term gain. If the dieter is not yet ready to accept that trade-off, they may not be ready to make a real attempt to change their eating behaviors. University of Rhode Island researcher James Prochaska studied smokers and determined that people vary in their readiness to change a particular behavior. He went on to empirically investigate his hypothesis and distilled five distinct levels of readiness to change (Prochaska, DiClemente, & Norcross, 1992). According to Prochaskas's theory, people who don't see any need to change are categorized as precontemplators. Thus, smokers who claim that they know lots of people who smoke and don't have cancer are examples of people in this category. On the other hand, contemplators are people who suspect that they may need to change a behavior, but are not yet actively trying. In this stage, people may be gathering information, learning specific skills, or talking about changing, but have yet to put their intentions into action. The preparation stage is when people have had some experience with change and plan to do so within the next month. They are "testing the waters." When people actually start to try to quit smoking, they enter into the active stage. The final stage, labeled the maintenance stage, is when smokers are trying to maintain or make their new behavior consistent.

Cigarette advertisement, 1915.

Of course, smoking, like eating, is not simply a matter of education and willpower. In both cases, there are complex brain mechanisms at work. Through their ability to activate brain reinforcement pathways, food and nicotine are immediately satisfying. Thus, impactful short-term reward effects tend to counter potential positive long-term effects. According to Prochaska, psychologists must first determine what stage of change a person is in and then develop a plan that will move them to the next stage. Perhaps precontemplating smokers need exposure to more accurate facts about the health problems caused by smoking, while contemplators and preparers need to be made aware of available smoking cessation services and techniques. Changers may need significant support and even tangible help in the form of antismoking medications. Whereas, people trying to maintain smoking cessation may need to identify the situations and triggers that are likely to cause them to want to revert to their old behavior patterns.

FALLING OFF THE WAGON AND REFUSING TO CLIMB BACK ON

People who have initially changed a behavior may have trouble maintaining the change. This phenomenon, sometimes called the Abstinence Violation Effect (AVE), occurs when people feel so bad about a lapse that they decide they have ruined their efforts and might as well give up (Curry, Marlatt, & Gordon, 1987). First identified in alcoholics who "fell off the wagon" and then went on a bender, it has since been observed in a variety of behavioral contexts. In order to avoid this negative spiral, people can learn to anticipate the circumstances or situations that are likely to cause them to return to a previous behavior and create a plan to get back on schedule as quickly as possible. For example, if a dieter knows that they are going to be tempted by the variety of food at their mother's house on Thanksgiving Day, they may decide to give themselves permission to eat on that day and then be extra vigilant with their caloric intake and exercise the rest of the weekend.

Sometimes people have valid reasons for not changing or maintaining their behaviors. For example, a college student who wants to eat a more healthy diet may struggle to find the time to shop and cook and may not have the money to buy more expensive fresh or organic food. These very real problems, or barriers, may make it difficult for people to change or maintain behaviors even if they wish to. In the health literature, a number of theories have been formulated to explain why behavior change can be difficult. While these theories evolved to explain behaviors that impact health or illness, their components can also be applied to other behavioral changes.

BELIEFS AND BEHAVIOR

The Health Beliefs Model (Rosenstock, Strecher, & Becker, 1988) postulates that in order to get people to change a health-related behavior, you have to find a way to convince them that: (1) They are susceptible to a particular health threat; (2) the health threat is a serious concern; (3) there is a behavioral change they can make which would be beneficial to them; and (4) there are not too many valid barriers to the change. This theory can be used to assess behavioral responses to specific concerns (Harrison, Mullen, & Green, 1992; Janz & Becker, 1984).

For example, a very serious and high-rated fatality disease called AIDS (acquired immune deficiency syndrome) first emerged in the United States among homosexual males on the West Coast. This led many heterosexual individuals to assume that they were not at risk of developing the disease. Even though heterosexuals knew it was a serious health threat, they did not view themselves as being susceptible, and many did not change their sexual behaviors. On the other hand, most people know they could get a cold or the flu but do not view these illnesses as particularly serious, despite the fact that they can be life threatening under certain circumstances. Thus, due to their belief that flu viruses are generally not a serious health threat, many people will not change behaviors that can lead to contracting such viruses. Even when people do decide that there is a serious health threat, they still need to determine whether there is a behavioral action they could take that would help them avoid or manage the illness and if there are barriers that would prevent them from taking action. If people do not believe that condoms prevent AIDS, they are unlikely to use them. In addition, if people don't have access to condoms, it won't matter whether they believe their use would be helpful or not, so lack of availability can be a barrier to change.

An example of beliefs and behaviors involving a non-health situation is that college freshmen are notorious for underestimating the difficulty of college course work. If they were successful in high school without working particularly hard, they may assume that they are not susceptible to academic failure and may not realize the serious impact that bad grades might have on their future career options. Likewise, these first-year students may not believe that behavioral changes such as studying in the library, having papers proofread, and using established study techniques will improve their performance. They may also struggle with barriers such as time constraints. They may feel they don't have the time necessary to attend all of their classes or to study adequately. Often they will not change this pattern until a tough semester convinces them that they are at risk of failure. Soon thereafter, they find that failing to pass a class may affect their financial aid and prevent them from getting into the graduate school of their choice. As a result, they realize that a behavioral change such as learning systematic study skills is worth the time and effort.

REASON AND ACTION

However, the Health Beliefs Model does not explore how people's attitudes about health, illness, and behavior change develop in the first place. The Theory of Reasoned Action attempts to fill this conceptual gap. This theory, originated by Ajzen and Fishbein (1980), suggests that people in general are goal oriented and tend to use information from a variety of sources when trying to decide whether to take an action or not. The decision of whether or not to act is a function of their intentions, which reflect their own beliefs and subsequent attitudes about the behavior. In addition to their own beliefs and attitudes, people will consider subjective norms which are constituted by their assumptions about the ways in which they believe their social group sees the action. Clearly, intentions are shaped by our personal experiences and thoughts, as well as by our culture and social world. When these factors are considered together, they are not only predictive of health behaviors in particular, but can also help us understand other choices as well.

For example, despite major advances in the ability to detect specific cancers in the early stages, many women still don't get annual mammograms to detect breast cancer and men don't talk to their doctors about prostate cancer. Using the Theory of Reasoned Action, we can hypothesize that, for many people the fear of cancer and concerns about the costs of preventive care result in their adopting the attitude that early tests do not make that much difference. Or perhaps people believe they are not at risk for the disease and therefore don't need to go through the stress of the test. If their friends reinforce this attitude, they are even more likely to avoid treatment. On the other hand, if they have a friend who had personal experience with the benefits of early detection, they might be persuaded to change their mind.

Similar processes may be in play as people approach other decisions. For instance, if you were raised in a family that put a high premium on academic performance, hard work, and not procrastinating, you may experience very high stress if you get sick, fail to prepare adequately for a test, and get a lower grade than you usually do. Your assessment of your failure may be exacerbated if your roommates also worry a great deal about test scores. Students who are excessively worried about academic success tend to blame themselves when they don't do well and tend to spend significant amounts of time thinking about the test. Often, they will choose to exclude themselves from activities such as exercise, socializing, or relaxation, feeling that their poor performance does not deserve a reward. In the meantime, people who see tests as less crucial and less indicative of their intrinsic worth may choose not to worry about one poor performance, and so decide to carry on with their weekend plans. If they believe that their friends see grades the way they do, it is even easier for them to forget about the exam and turn to other activities.

BUT CAN YOU DO IT?

As mentioned earlier, in order to perform an action, it is likely that you have to possess the necessary skills to do so. In addition to skill sets, in many cases you also have to believe in your ability to take the action as well. The sense that you personally have the ability to do something was defined by Albert Bandura as self-efficacy (Bandura, 1977). According to his research, there are multiple ways we can develop self-efficacy. One way is by performing the behavior successfully and another is in watching someone else do so. A third stems from the verbal encouragement or persuasion of someone else. And the last is reaching the necessary physiological arousal to perform without becoming overwhelmed by stress or anxiety, which, in turn, can hurt performance. Although you may not have thought about behavior in quite these ways before, it is likely that you can think of instances from your own life in which self-efficacy had a strong impact on your behavioral choices.

For example, if you have ever attempted a difficult or scary feat, whether on your own or as part of a sporting or performing event, you may well have struggled to develop and maintain self-efficacy. If you have previously done the cartwheel on the balance beam or given a speech, it may not be difficult for you to believe that you can do it again. Likewise, if you have seen your friend try the zip line or are listening to someone from your neighborhood who got into the college you would like to attend, you are likely to believe that you can do the same. In addition, if someone you trust, like your parents, coach, or teacher provide encouragement, you might try something new, thus increasing your sense of self-efficacy about that task.

It turns out that self-efficacy is situation specific, and just as it can be systematically fostered, it can also be systematically eroded. For example, critical and mean coaching or commentary can convince someone that they can't do something when they are actually capable of accomplishing the task. Because self-efficacy can vary with situations, you also have to consider a person's expectations about the probable outcome of a behavior, as well as their sense of whether they can perform it or not. While I might be perfectly willing to concede that getting a gold medal in figure skating at the Olympics will bring fame, endorsements, and satisfaction, I also know that I do not have the physical prowess necessary to achieve that goal no matter how hard I work. In contrast, even though I might have full confidence that I have the ability to be the fastest runner in my class, if I don't have an interest in being recognized for running, I may not feel that seeking such a reward is worth the effort.

COPING WITH THE PAST

As if understanding stress management wasn't already difficult, we now know that coping varies, depending on its temporal relations to a stressful event. When we are trying to deal with a negative event that has already occurred, it is called reactive coping. This type of response has traditionally been conceptualized as either problem-focused or emotion-focused coping. In the early research in this area, it was assumed that problem-focused coping—essentially finding ways to eliminate or solve a problem—was the best approach. So, if you don't like your job, a problem-based solution would be to quit or request a transfer. It turns out that people are typically good at trying to find problem-based solutions to problems. However, not all stressors can be easily resolved. When this is the case, people may turn to emotion-focused coping, which essentially refers to trying to manage their emotions about the event. Unfortunately, much of the early coping literature lumped responses ranging from avoidance to prayer to seeking social support under emotion-focused coping and argued that these reflected ineffective coping techniques.

Consider elderly individuals who are starting to have trouble remembering names, dates, and where they put things. Initially, they may assume that they are just busy or tired and may try to organize better or to use lists that trigger memories. However, if these techniques don't help, they may decide to see their doctor. If it turns out that they have an infection (e.g., urinary tract infections in the elderly sometimes cause confusion), are low on something like vitamin B-12, which can affect thought and memory, or are taking a medication that is affecting them adversely, they may be able to easily fix the problem with antibiotics, supplements or a change in medications.

HOWEVER, IF THE DIAGNOSIS IS ALZHEIMER'S DISEASE, THERE IS NO EASY SOLUTION

Recent advances in therapy and medication suggest that we can slow the process of the disease, but we cannot stop or cure it. Most people with Alzheimer's disease live for eight to 11 years after the diagnosis, but their memory problems become progressively worse. In these cases, problem-focused coping may help the patient or their family find ways to cope with daily life, but dealing with the emotional response to the event is a necessary and unavoidable piece of the equation.

When I was in graduate school, I actually worked on a research project looking at stress among Alzheimer caregivers. I remember one couple in particular because of the loving way they interacted. The husband had Alzheimer's disease and had been losing his cognitive

President Ronald Reagan was diagnosed with Alzheimer's disease after his time in office.

abilities over several years. Prior to his illness, he had loved working on his car and always kept it in top condition. However, his wife was afraid to let him drive anymore and eventually had to take away his car keys. Not being able to get in the car to clean or putter made him angry and agitated. Then his wife hit on the idea of having a set of keys made that opened the car door, but wouldn't start it. From that point on, the husband was quite content to wash and clean the car, check the oil, and putter for hours on end. When he would decide to try to drive the key wouldn't work, so he would come into the house complaining. His wife told me that at that point she would distract him by offering him a snack or asking him a question until he forgot he had wanted to drive. While this was an ingenious example of problem solving, she teared up when she told me the story, suggesting that despite finding a practical approach to managing his behavior, she still felt quite bad about the fact that she was losing the husband she had married. More recent research supports that people tend to use both problem- and emotion-based approaches to coping with bad events and that either can be appropriate depending on the circumstance.

COPING WITH THE FUTURE

While dealing with negative events that have already happened is one aspect of coping, people often find themselves engaging in anticipatory coping as well. Most of us don't simply wait for bad things to happen, but put significant time and energy into figuring out how to avoid possible future threats. When people are faced with dealing with a future negative event, they may demonstrate preventive coping. This technique is characterized by efforts to avoid the stressful event or to build up resources with which to manage it were it to occur. In some cases, people find themselves preparing to deal with a threat by trying to use the situation to help themselves or others. In these cases, efforts to anticipate a future stressor focus on meeting the event as a challenge and on managing future goals. According to Greenglass, Schwarzer, Jakubiec, Fiksenbaum, and Taubert (1999), proactive coping involves the integration of planning and preventive strategies with social support to achieve goals. In some instances, people may even try to find the positive or silver lining in an upcoming threat. A student who thinks they might lose their job could spend time thinking about how nice it will be not having to see their boss and how they will have more time to study.

Despite the behaviorists' view that behavior offered a clean, easily measured record of people's motives and intentions, the processes underlying behavioral choices are far from simple. Attitudes, social norms, your belief in yourself, and whether you are trying to cope with something that has already happened—or that might happen—all come into play. Sometimes, the same behavior can be adaptive in one setting and problematic in another. Take, for example, the stress-coping technique of distraction. If you found a lump under your arm and are afraid it is cancer, deciding to go to a movie so you can ignore it and hope it will go away may make the problem worse. However, if you are waiting to get the results from a biopsy, distraction in the form of a movie may actually allow you to avoid anxiety and cope more effectively.

MODIFYING BEHAVIOR

A useful rubric to apply to thinking about possible behavioral approaches to any stressful event is to decide whether the situation calls for action, distraction, or interaction with others. As we saw in the chapter on social support, we are human creatures and often find that associating with other people helps us both to change problems and to manage our emotions.

Another practical approach to coping involves applying behavioral principles to changing specific behaviors in practical ways. Most behavior modification plans are based on a series of steps which can be applied either to your own behavior or that of someone else. The first step of a behavior modification plan is establishing a baseline. It is important to know what the behavior looks like before you try to modify it. Sometimes baselines are simple logs of when and where you did a behavior (e.g., how often you exercise or study), whereas at other times they can take the form of detailed charts, graphs, or visual representations. If you have ever been asked to record everything you ate for a day or a week, you have collected a baseline measure of the behavior of eating. Interestingly, simply paying attention to a behavior can change it. For example, think about how likely you would be to snack on a handful of chips if you had to record every single bite on a tracking sheet.

Once you have an idea of what you are doing in regard to the behavior, the next step is to formulate your goals. The more clear, specific, and comprehensive you are, the better. For instance, many people make the general resolution to exercise more and find they are unable to do so. A better resolution would be to decide that you are going to exercise on Mondays, Wednesdays, and Fridays from 7:00 to 8:00 in the morning at your gym. During that workout you are going to spend 30 minutes on the bike or treadmill, 20 minutes using

the machines, and 10 minutes stretching. In describing exactly when, where, and what you are going to do, you have the opportunity to set up a plan that actually works with your lifestyle. For example, if you are a night owl and rarely get to work on time, you are not likely to stick with an exercise plan that has you getting up even earlier to exercise. Similarly, if you don't have the money to join a gym and don't get home in time to run safely in your neighborhood, you might consider getting a workout DVD so you can exercise in your apartment. Adjusting your plan to accommodate the real barriers in your life is key.

Making sure that the goal is reasonable is also important. Fundamental irrational beliefs include putting emphasis on what you "should" do and thinking in all-or-nothing terms. If you simply don't have time to work out for hours every day, you might consider trying to increase the amount of routine exercise you are getting. Research suggests that as little as three 10-minute episodes of exercise (e.g., walking, gardening, using the stairs) is associated with increased cardiovascular health. Setting goals that are too ambitious or are incompatible with your lifestyle is a surefire way to fail to change.

Situational factors also matter. Typical behavior logs require you not only to record instances of a behavior, but also to look at when and where it does or does not occur. People who are trying to quit smoking or overeating often find that they engage in the behavior at certain times during the day. Smokers often use their breaks to smoke and socialize, whereas overeaters often eat when they are driving, studying, watching television, or experiencing stress. During these routine activities and times, people may not even be paying attention to how much they are smoking or what they are ingesting. Learning to control these factors can improve the efficacy of your behavioral plan. Finding alternative things to do during your break can reduce smoking, and structuring things so you only eat at a certain place at the table with certain plates can help you to appreciate what you eat and eliminate thoughtless snacking. Likewise, by stocking the house with healthy foods instead of unhealthy snacks and by learning ways to manage stress instead of smoking or eating are all examples of managing the environment to promote your desired behavior change.

Since changing behaviors is so difficult to do, you may have to build specific incentives into your behavioral plan. Chances are the behavior you want to change is there for a reason. Eating reduces anxiety and chewing your nails helps you calm down. While you hope that changing the behavior will in itself become rewarding over time, in practice you may need to set up rewards for your initial changes which, in the early stages of change, address the problem of short-term satisfaction and delayed gratification. Since rewards generally work better than punishment, especially if the plan requires you to punish yourself, it is usually a good idea to set up a reward structure. This could be as simple as a checklist or a star chart or as complex as rewarding your efforts with shopping, travel, or other tangible short-term incentives that won't undermine the behavioral change. These incentives could include medals, trophies, food, recognition, money, and attention. They may in some cases even be things you were planning to do anyway. If you like to watch a certain show or talk to someone specifically in the evening, you might consider setting up your schedule so you study first, and then use the call or the show as your reward. The rewards can be basically anything that humans consider desirable.

In conclusion, behavioral responses to stress have the potential to either ameliorate or exacerbate stressful situations. For example, the gratification and solace provided by food, alcohol, or spending money can themselves become stressful when people are faced with obesity, alcoholism, and mounting debts. On the other hand, efforts to change stressful situations by altering the circumstances or changing one's expectations can improve the situation. A parent faced with a mentally challenged child may have to learn new parenting skills and adjust their expectations for their child, but in turn may also find unexpected joy in the process.

Though at times it is unclear why we do what we do or how to modify and maintain desirable behaviors, what is crystal clear is that how people cope in accord to their behaviors and behavior modifications is relevant and vital in the well-being and success of humankind. Clearly, learning to cope effectively benefits us both physiologically and psychologically. Because our behaviors affect those around us too, it behooves us to develop stress management strategies that avoid stress when possible, and to minimize the adverse impact of stressors that can't be avoided.

WHAT DO YOU THINK?

1. What are your characteristic behavioral responses to stress?
2. Which of your behaviors actively helps you to manage stress? Which makes it worse?
3. What alternative techniques would you like to learn or adopt?

REFERENCES

Ajzen, I., & Fishbein, M. (1980). *Understanding attitudes and predicting social behavior*. Englewood Cliffs, NJ: Prentice-Hall.

Bandura, A. (1977). Self-efficacy: toward a unifying theory of behavioral change. *Psychological Review*, 84 (2), 191–215.

Curry, S., Marlatt, G. A., & Gordon, J. R. (1987). Abstinence violation effect: Validation of an attributional construct with smoking cessation. *Journal of Consulting and Clinical Psychology*, 55(2), 145–149.

Greenglass, E., Schwarzer, R., Jakubiec, S. D., Fiksenbaum, L., & Taubert, S. *The Proactive Coping Inventory (PCI): A multidimensional research instrument*. Paper presented at the 20th International Conference of the STAR (Stress and Anxiety Research Society) Cracow, Poland, July 12–14, 1999.

Harrison, J. A., Mullen, P. D., & Green, L. W. (1992). A meta-analysis of studies of the health belief model with adults. *Health Education Research*, 7 (1), 107–116.

Janz, N. K., & Becker, M. H. (1984). The Health Beliefs Model: A Decade Later. *Health Education Quarterly*, (Spring 1984).

Pavlov, I. P. (1927). *Conditioned Reflexes: An Investigation of the Physiological Activity of the Cerebral Cortex*. Translated and Edited by G. V. Anrep. London: Oxford University Press.

Prochaska, J., DiClemente, C. C., & Norcross, J. D. (1992). In search of how people change: applications to addictive behaviors. *American Psychologist*, 47, 1102–1114.

Rosenstock, I. M., Strecher, V. J., & Becker, M. H. (1984). Social Learning Theory and the Health Belief Model. *Health Education Quarterly*, (Spring 1988).

Skinner, B. F. (1976). *About Behaviorism*. New York: Vintage.

CHAPTER 14

MINDING THE GAP—DO YOU REALLY LIVE IN YOUR OWN MIND?

KEY POINTS

- ✦ Stress can be conceptualized as the gap between what we have and what we need or want.
- ✦ Since many stressors cannot be changed, effective coping often depends on our ability to manage our cognitive and emotional responses to the event or situation.
- ✦ In the end, our life experiences truly are all in our head.

Clearly, stress is an enduring component of human life. Whether people are struggling to feed their children, get good grades in a class, or deal with a difficult boss, the brain and body respond in much the same way. Certainly, mobilizing energy through the fight-or-flight system is an adaptive response when the stress is environmental and requires an active response. In fact, if people are able to change the situation actively, there may be no further need for coping. However, many of the stressors of modern life reflect gaps between what we have and what we want and are not amenable to quick solutions that eliminate the problem. Instead, people find themselves trying to manage discrepancies between their reality and their goals or expectations.

Whether the gap is a function of the loss of material resources, the disruption or lack of social connection, or a failure to attain a physical or psychological goal, we are faced with finding a way to bypass, minimize or bridge the divide. On the whole, humans are very good at finding practical solutions for physical problems. We have developed more than one way to light fires, build houses, and travel. We grow and harvest a variety of foods in order to reduce our dependence on any one nutritional source. We are constantly developing new tools and repurposing those we already have. In the short run, we fight, we run, and we hide with purpose and tenacity. Throughout much of human history, this ingenuity was devoted to staying alive. Although the process was never easy, the required tasks were typically practical and physical.

However, as modern life has grown more technological and complex, the problems we face have often become more interdependent and complex. Where once a farmer was at the mercy of the weather to grow his crops, it was his battle, and possible solutions such as growing other vegetables, hunting or foraging for food, or moving somewhere else were largely under his control. In our interdependent, industrialized urban world, many of us do not have the land, resources, or knowledge to grow or raise our own food. When a natural disaster such as a hurricane, flood, or earthquake causes widespread damage in an area, people have no choice but to depend on others for sustenance. Without electricity, telephones, cash registers, and ATMs no longer function. Even if resources are available, the normal standards of commerce break down and bartering becomes the only option.

Furthermore, since most cities only have enough food to sustain their population for a few days, disaster victims often find themselves depending on government and aid groups for shelters, meals, water, ice, and transportation. If these response efforts break down, as they did during Hurricane Katrina, people rapidly become anxious, depressed, or angry. In the meantime, people around the world not directly affected by the disaster find themselves watching news coverage of the event and feeling powerless to help in meaningful ways.

A Texas Army National Guard Blackhawk helicopter deposits a 6,000 pound-plus bag of sand and gravel on-target, Sunday, September 4, 2005 as work progressed to close the breach in the 17th Street Canal, New Orleans.

Their frustration can, in turn, lead to compassion fatigue or frustration with the victims of the disaster. Fortunately, most of us don't face such drastic sources of stress on a daily basis, but in an uncertain world, political, economic, and environmental stressors can strike without warning and threaten or destroy the resources people have struggled to stockpile. Even though such losses are rare and unpredictable, simply thinking about the possibility of such a calamity can activate sympathetic nervous system responses, without an actual physical need to respond. The fact that the news media records, replays, and amplifies the negative impact of the event and the possibility that its ill effects will spread does not help people to cope, either.

Of course, the physical loss of resources is only one type of stress. Humans, like most mammals, are warm-blooded, sociable creatures. Our young must be fed and nurtured for extended periods of time before they can survive on their own, and we live in social groups which provide sustenance, security, and emotional closeness over long periods of time. It is ironic, but not surprising, then, that disruptions in our social network are perceived as extremely stressful. The death of someone we care about can take humans months to accept and years to really come to terms with. If a separation is due to interpersonal conflict such as a break-up or a divorce, the anger and acrimony brought about by the separation often extends far beyond the original disagreement. Losing a job, being rejected for a club or team we aspire to or simply being excluded from a social activity is enough to cause significant distress in many people. The fact such losses don't have the same immediate disastrous consequences as being ostracized by your herd and subsequently eaten by a predator, doesn't mean that they are not stressful. Because of our mental ability to magnify the meaning of a given event, many of us can catastrophize one lost or broken relationship into a lifetime of loneliness at the drop of a hat.

Even if we have an intact circle of friends, our need to belong—probably a crucial element of social survival in the past—is being severely tried in our electronic present. Comparing yourself to the real people around you, whose resources, lifestyle, and appearance reflect reasonable effort and resource allocation, is far less threatening than comparing yourself and your lifestyle to people who have enough material resources to outsource much of their daily household and self-care. The fact that media depictions of wealthy people's homes, cars, hairstyles, tans, clothes, and partners are often selective, photoshopped, or even staged also does not help. And yet, knowing that even the people who appear perfect in glossy pictures aren't in real life does not always eliminate our longing to bridge the gap between the lifestyle we lead and the one we think celebrities are party to. In actuality, lottery winners, reality show stars, celebrities, politicians, and even people born into real royal families (the Windsors) or dynasties such as the Kennedys and the Bushes are often even more unhappy than we are. Still, even knowing this doesn't always keep us from feeling that we are falling behind.

Multitasking in our technology-filled modern world.

Even when we aren't facing major gaps in our resource accumulation or social connections, daily modern life has its challenges. Deadlines, time pressure, noise, lack of sleep, lack of exercise, artificial environments, electronic sensory overload, and multitasking all take their toll. All too often, we find ourselves trying to achieve impossible to-do lists, both at home and in our professional or academic lives, with little opportunity to rejuvenate our bodies or our minds. As I sit here typing at 12:43 a.m., when I know I have an important meeting in the morning, I am struck by just how ingrained the pressures of modern life really are. Over the course of the evening, I have carried on several phone and text conversations, checked my email twice and Facebook once, and half watched several television shows, all the while trying to work on this chapter. And now that everyone else has gone to bed, the sounds of the refrigerator, the fish tank, and the air conditioner simply become more prominent. Clearly, our daily (and nightly lives) are far removed from the nature-based, circadian-driven cycles of our ancestors. Learning to listen more to our bodies and less to the electronic chatter around us, bridging the gap between our insidious adoption of technology, and our need to stay connected with the natural world is yet another task of modern life. While the odds of rolling back or eliminating technology in our lives is probably as unrealistic as aiming for a stress-free life, the option we do have is to eliminate stressful situations when we can and mind the way we deal with unavoidable circumstances.

When we can solve a problem by getting more information about our options, enlisting social support, or changing a situation, the impact of the stressor can be fleeting. For example, finding out that you can change positions in your company, garner support from those around you, or even go to work somewhere else can all minimize the stress of having a bad boss. However, if there is not an easy solution to a problem, your only option may be to focus on your inner life and choose how you wish to cope with the situation. Whether the gap is real or actual, learning to use your mind to bridge it becomes the difference between tripping and falling and successfully moving on in your life. To do so, it is essential to understand the interaction of your thoughts, feelings, and physical sensations with each other and their influence on your behavioral choices, as well as how those behaviors alter subsequent responses.

Certainly, people have long struggled to understand how thoughts and feelings interact. While we still don't fully understand the anatomical and structural basis of these brain processes, in practice, most of us simply want to find ways to analyze and respond to stress effectively. Of course, this is easier said than done.

Paradoxically, as humans, our language and cognitive abilities enable us to anticipate and even prevent future threats, but can also trick us into worrying incessantly about things that never come to pass, or spending a great deal of time regretting things that have already happened. Rather than living in the moment, we often spend a great deal of time and emotion thinking about things that we cannot change or necessarily control. The incessant media drumbeat regarding potential threats and negative events does not help.

Fortunately, psychological techniques such as cognitive behavioral therapy can allow us to learn to recognize and challenge patterns of thought which perpetuate this cycle. Using the theories of Albert Ellis and Aaron Beck regarding irrational or dysfunctional thoughts, we can begin to recognize our own tendencies. Many of us become focused on maintaining the approval of others, even if we don't really need it. Trying to please a critical parent, worrying about the one customer who complains about our service, or spending inordinate amounts of time trying to keep up appearances are all indicative of this obsession. Certainly, if you believe that you are only a good person if you please all of the people around you all the time, you are doomed to failure.

If the need for approval is paired with perfectionism, the pattern of thoughts can become even more deadly. Almost all teachers have had the student in their class who scores the highest grade, but still wants to argue about the one or two points they missed or the boss or family member who never thinks things are done well enough. The problem, however, is that standards of perfection vary across situations, cultures, and individuals. In addition, not all tasks need to be done perfectly. In fact, worrying too much about never making errors can result in paralyzing procrastination, constant feelings of inadequacy, and wasted time. If the quest for perfectionism is also a function of media-driven ideals, the seeker may even find themselves chasing a truly impossible dream. Even the celebrities featured in the photo shoots and movie trailers don't look like that in real life. With enough stylists, makeup artists, photographers, and Photoshop tools, anyone can look beautiful for a fleeting moment in a picture—but expecting yourself to meet those standards in daily life is truly irrational!

Another cognitive pitfall lies in magnifying or exaggerating threats; or in believing that because you feel something, it must be true. Feeling fat, stupid, or victimized does not necessarily mean you are any of those things. Focusing on negative rather than positive events and filtering or responding only to aspects of a situation can also skew your reality. A friend's comment that you look especially nice on a certain day doesn't have to mean that they think you usually look terrible. Sometimes, too, your friend's irritability or distraction is a consequence of their personal problems and has little or nothing to do with you. Recognizing these cognitive traps is the key to successfully changing your thought patterns.

Of course, if any of these thoughts were true, feeling depressed, anxious, or angry would make sense. In evolutionary terms, responding rapidly to threats with a take-no-prisoners approach can promote survival. If a lion is threatening, you must respond very quickly to avoid disaster. However, determining whether abstract economic factors, distant environmental disasters, or someone's random comment about you on Facebook is a real threat isn't always easy. But if we can learn to view emotions as an early warning system rather than reality, they can provide invaluable information. Picking up on the nonverbal nuances of communication, seeing problems in new creative ways, and using feelings to motivate us to tackle desired life changes can all be effective coping techniques.

Of course, feelings also have a physiological component. It is no accident that we use phrases like "trust your gut feelings," "she had a broken heart," and "brace yourself for some bad news" to describe how we feel. Just as we fall into characteristic thought and emotional feelings, our temperament, physiology, and life experience also put us at risk of repetitive physical response to stress. Clenching your jaw, grinding your teeth, hunching your shoulders, experiencing acid reflux or other gastrointestinal distress, developing headaches or skin problems can all be physiological expressions of tension. In addition to routing irrational thoughts and managing emotions, physical approaches to stress management, including breathing techniques, laughing, crying, meditation, prayer, and exercise can all release physical tension and arousal. As this sympathetic activation diminishes, it becomes easier to think clearly and to choose behavioral responses more consciously.

However, just as with any skill, from playing a sport or an instrument to writing or studying effectively, it can take practice to become proficient. In his book *Outliers*, Malcolm Gladwell argues that it takes 10,000 hours to become an expert in a field. Although we rarely think of it this way, by early adulthood many of us have had 10,000 hours of practice responding

Practice makes perfect.

to stress with irrational thoughts, exaggerated emotions, and physical discomfort. Learning to change such patterns cannot happen overnight, but as with any skill, our abilities increase with practice, feedback, and encouragement. Simply expecting someone to stop coping in a familiar way without helping them to develop an alternative plan is doomed to fail. Smokers who wish to stop and overeaters who want to diet successfully have to actively identify noncompatible alternative responses. It is hard to smoke while chewing gum, and if the gum itself contains nicotine, you may be addressing two problems with one action. Similarly, it is asking a lot of someone who self-medicates with alcohol or drugs to stop doing so without providing them with a less destructive way to manage their emotions.

Sometimes, too, we are afraid to let go of a behavior, even if we know consciously that it is not helpful. Many students and athletes have developed superstitious behaviors that they feel foster positive performance. Even when they know that their grades or success on the field isn't really likely to be the result of their lucky necklace, pre-game breakfast, or ritual claps, chants, or dances, the very act of performing the action makes them feel like they have some control. When the preferred behavior itself is part of a problem, though, changing it may be essential. For example, for many students, procrastinating by cleaning, checking email or Facebook, or working on material that is not due immediately, provides short-term relief from the anxiety of tackling whatever task you are truly anxious about. In the long run though, putting off the pressing task simply means that when you do tackle it, you have even less time, which in turn becomes overwhelming. Teaching people how to study effectively, to break tasks down into manageable chunks and to create a study environment that is comfortable and not distracting can make a huge difference in their performance. Often, when people fail to change behaviors, it is not because they don't want to or haven't tried, but rather because they don't have the skills necessary to do so.

In the end, we cannot choose to live a stress-free life. Danger, loss, threats, time pressure, and interpersonal conflicts are part of the human condition. We can, however, choose how we respond when faced with adversity. The way we appraise and interpret the event determines our response choices and whether the event becomes an enduring source of stress in our lives or an opportunity for mastery or growth. I will never forget the afternoon my daughter qualified to play in the junior varsity doubles tennis finals for her school district. After a long day of tennis, the last match literally went on for hours. The two well-matched teams played out every point and eventually ended up in a tiebreaker. When my daughter and her teammate finally lost the last point, they came off the court with tears in their eyes.

While I watched helplessly, their young, enthusiastic coach came up and put an arm around each of them. As they walked off, I heard him tell them that he understood how hard it was to come that close to winning and then to fail, so he would give them a few minutes to think about what might have happened. Then he wanted them to think about the fact that they had come in second in a tournament in one of the largest school districts in the state, and about how many other students hadn't even qualified, never mind made it into the finals. The beauty of his comment was that he did not deny or minimize the disappointment they felt. He simply offered them the opportunity to think about the situation a little bit differently and in so doing reframed their sense of loss and focused on what they had accomplished. Although we often give lip service to the value of sports for building character and promoting teamwork, watching those who manage to lose gracefully cope can be far more educational than watching winners celebrate—or worse yet, gloat.

Perhaps it is the human tendency to constantly strive for success and to move the bar further and further out that accounts for our remarkable success as a species. However, having developed the technology to micromanage our environments, combat illness and disease, feed millions of people, and entertain ourselves at unprecedented rates has not been without personal cost. Just as we as a society still grapple with the ethical issues posed by our medical, communication, and defense breakthroughs, we as individuals need to focus on managing the impact of our ever expanding technology and expectations in our own lives. There will always be gaps between what we have and what we can imagine. The trick is to imagine ways to Mind that Gap effectively.

WHAT DO YOU THINK?

1. Do you find yourself coping with stress in negative ways that you learned from your family or other influential people around you? Do you think it would be helpful to start teaching children about stress management and coping as an integral part of their early education?

2. Which aspect of the four elements of stress and stress management (thoughts, feelings, sensations, and behavior) is the hardest for you to manage? What do you think you will need to do to make effective changes in that area?

3. Can you compare and contrast a specific stressful incident which you think you handled well and another you think you handled poorly? What were the similarities or differences between the two circumstances? What skills or techniques do you use to cope well? What were the factors that prevented you from coping as effectively in the second situation? How could you overcome such barriers in the future?

4. What is the single most important thing about stress management that you would like to share with other people?

5. Can you work on applying the principles of stress management discussed in this book without being excessively hard on yourself? It may take a while to find the process that works best for you, but can you practice the skills and techniques you need to cope?

6. Remember, there is nothing more ironic than generating more stress in your life by setting irrational goals for managing the unavoidable stress of modern life!

REFERENCE

Gladwell, M. (2008). *Outliers: The Story of Success*. New York: Little, Brown and Company.